MASTERING THE OLD TESTAMENT

MASTERING THE OLD TESTAMENT

ISAIAH 40–66

DAVID McKENNA

LLOYD J. OGILVIE, GENERAL EDITOR

WORD PUBLISHING
Dallas•London•Vancouver•Melbourne

[Formerly, *The Communicator's Commentary Series, Old Testament*]

Library of Congress Cataloging-in-Publication Data
Main entry under title:

Mastering the Old Testament
[The Communicator's Commentary]
  Bibliography: p.
  Contents: OT16b. Isaiah 40–66/by David L. McKenna
  1. Bible. O.T.—Commentaries. I. Ogilvie, Lloyd
David L. McKenna,
[(BS1151.2.C66 1993 221.7′7 93-39330)]
ISBN 0–8499–1139–7 (v. OT16b) [hd]
ISBN 0–8499–3563–6 (v. OT16b) [pbk]

Printed in the United States of America
    456789AGF987654321

Contents

Editor's Preface

God has called all of His people to be communicators. Everyone who is in Christ is called into ministry. As ministers of "the manifold grace of God," all of us—clergy and laity—are commissioned with challenge to communicate our faith to individuals and groups, classes and congregations.

The Bible, God's Word , is the objective basis of the truth of His love and power that we seek to communicate. In response to urgent, unexpressed needs of pastors, teachers, Bible study leaders, church school teachers, small group enablers, and individual Christians, the Communicator's Commentary is offered as a penetrating search of the Scriptures of the Old and New Testament to enable vital personal and practical communication of the abundant life.

Many current commentaries and Bible study guides provide only some aspects of a communicator's needs. Some offer in-depth scholarship but no application to daily life. Others are so popular in approach that biblical roots are left unexplained. Few offer impelling illustrations that open windows for the reader to see the exciting application for today's struggles. And most of all, seldom have the expositors given the valuable outlines of passages so needed to help the preacher or teacher in his or her busy life to prepare for communicating the Word to congregations or classes.

This Communicator's Commentary series brings all of these elements together. The authors are scholar-preachers and teachers outstanding in their ability to make the Scriptures come alive for individuals and groups. They are noted for bringing together excellence in biblical scholarship, knowledge of the original Hebrew and Greek, sensitivity to people's needs, vivid illustrative material from biblical, classical, and contemporary sources, and lucid communication by the use of clear outlines of thought. Each has been selected to contribute to this series because of his Spirit-empowered ability to help people live in the skins of biblical characters and provide a "you-are-there" intensity to the drama of events of the Bible which have so much to say about our relationships and responsibilities today.

The design for the communicator's Commentary gives the reader an overall outline of each book of the Bible. Following the introduction, which reveals the author's approach and salient background on the book, each chapter of the commentary provides the Scripture to be exposited. The New King James Bible has been chosen for the Communicator's Commentary because it combines with integrity the beauty of language, underlying Hebrew and Greek textual basis, and thought-flow of the 1611 King James Version, while replacing obsolete verb forms and other archaisms with their everyday contemporary counterparts for greater readability. Reverence for God is preserved in the capitalization of all pronouns referring to the Father, Son, or Holy Spirit. Readers who are more comfortable with another translation can readily find the parallel passage by means of the chapter and verse reference at the end of each passage being exposited. The paragraphs of exposition combine fresh insights to the Scripture, application, rich illustrative material, and innovative ways of utilizing the vibrant truth for his or her own life and for the challenge of communicating it with vigor and vitality.

It has been gratifying to me as editor of this series to receive enthusiastic progress reports from each contributor. As they worked, all were gripped with new truths from Scripture—God-given insights into passages, previously not written in the literature of biblical explanation. A prime objective of this series is for each user to find the same awareness: that God speaks with newness through the Scriptures when we approach them with a ready mind and a willingness to communicate what He has given; that God delights to give communicators of His Word "I-never-saw-that-in-that-verse-before" intellectual insights so that our listeners and readers can have "I-never-realized-all-that-was-in-that-verse" spiritual experiences.

The thrust of the commentary series unequivocally affirms that God speaks through the Scriptures today to engender faith, enable adventuresome living of the abundant life, and establish the basis of obedient discipleship. The Bible, the unique Word of God, is unlimited as a resource for Christians in communicating our hope to others. It is our weapon in the battle for truth, the guide for ministry, and the irresistible force for introducing others to God.

A biblically rooted communication of the Gospel holds in unity and oneness what divergent movements have wrought asunder. This commentary series courageously presents personal faith, caring for individuals, and social responsibility as essential, inseparable dimensions of biblical Christianity. It seeks to present the quadrilateral Gospel in its fullness which calls us to unreserved commitment to Christ, unrestricted self-esteem in His grace, unqualified love for others in personal evangelism, and undying efforts to work for justice and righteousness in a sick and suffering world.

A growing renaissance in the church today is being led by clergy and laity who are biblically rooted, Christ-centered, and Holy Spirit-empowered. They have dared to listen to people's most urgent questions and deepest needs and then to God as He speaks throughout the Bible. Biblical preaching is the secret of growing churches. Bible study classes and small groups are equipping the laity for ministry in the world. Dynamic Christians are finding that daily study of God's Word allows the Spirit to do in them what He wishes to communicate through them to others. These days are the most exciting time since Pentecost. The Communicator's Commentary is offered to be a primary resource of new life for this renaissance.

It has been very encouraging to receive the enthusiastic responses of pastors and teachers to the twelve New Testament volumes of the Communicator's Commentary series. The letters from communicators on the firing line in pulpits, classes, study groups, and Bible fellowship clusters across the nation, as well as the reviews of scholars and publication analysts, have indicated that we have been on target meeting a need for a distinctly different kind of commentary on the Scriptures, a commentary that is primarily aimed at helping interpreters of the Bible to equip the laity for ministry.

This positive response has led the publisher to press on with an additional twenty-one volumes covering the books of the Old Testament. These new volumes rest upon the same goals and guidelines that undergird the New Testament volumes. Scholar-preachers with facility in Hebrew as well as vivid contemporary exposition have been selected as authors. The purpose throughout is to aid the preacher and teacher in the challenge and adventure of Old Testament exposition in communication. In each volume you will meet Yahweh, the "I AM" Lord who is Creator, Sustainer, and Redeemer in the unfolding drama of His call and care of Israel. He is the Lord who acts, intervenes, judges, and presses His people into the immense challenges and privileges of being a chosen people, a holy nation. And in the descriptive exposition of each passage, the implications of the ultimate revelation of Yahweh in Jesus Christ, His Son, our Lord, are carefully spelled out to maintain unity and oneness in the preaching and teaching of the Gospel.

Once again, it is my privilege to introduce the author of this volume, Dr. David McKenna. He is already familiar to many readers of the Communicator's Commentary because of his previous work on Mark and Job. These volumes, highly praised for their interpretive insight and practical wisdom, create an expectation that Dr. McKenna's study will be equally outstanding. Indeed, he has fulfilled this deservedly high expectation with this marvelous commentary on Isaiah.

Dr. McKenna approaches the text of Isaiah in full view of its theological, linguistic, and historical challenges. Though he has mastered the analytic discussions of the book, this commentary does far more than examine the prophecies of Isaiah in microscopic, analytic detail. Rather, it attempts to grasp the wholistic vision of God revealed to Isaiah the prophet. What Dr. McKenna undertakes as a commentator transcends the narrowly defined task of critical scholarship. If we are to see Isaiah's vision afresh, "we need to do more than just read the book of Isaiah," Dr. McKenna urges. We must prepare ourselves for an experience of the living, holy, righteous God. That is exactly what this commentary helps us to do.

Readers familiar with Dr. McKenna's work will once again appreciate his very thorough scholarship and clear exposition of the biblical text. New readers will be delighted to find him to be a very trustworthy interpreter of Scripture. As in his previous commentaries, Dr. McKenna illustrates the text of Isaiah with a wide range of materials, including personal stories, literary quotations, and trenchant applications to our contemporary culture. This commentary reflects not only careful scholarship and wise reflection but also Dr. McKenna's personal engagement with the biblical text. As he explains in the Author's Preface, Dr. McKenna' heard God's voice through Isaiah at a crucial juncture in his professional life. He writes, therefore, as one who has been deeply impacted by the prophet's vision.

Since completing this commentary, David McKenna has been called by God into a new focus of ministry. After 12 years as President of Asbury Theological Seminary, he will retire in July, 1994 in order to devote more time to writing and consulting. During his tenure as president, Dr. McKenna has led Asbury onto the cutting edge of theological education. In the process, he has been recognized as a great statesman for God's Kingdom. His leadership touches not only Asbury Seminary and theological education in general but the church throughout the world. Dr. McKenna has exercised this leadership through an international speaking ministry, through more than a dozen books, and through his service to many Christian and educational organizations.

I am privileged to count David McKenna as a covenant brother and a close friend. My experience of his personal faith and integrity increases my respect for this man of God and under girds my endorsement of his commentary. I a especially grateful to David for his outstanding contributions to the Communicator's Commentary series, including this volume on Isaiah. He had helped the series to reach the highest standards for excellence and usefulness to the modern communicator of God's word.

LLOYD J. OGILVIE

Author's Preface

Stepping off the top of an escalator in a department store, I came upon a crowd of people witnessing a demonstration of "virtual reality." One by one, venturesome volunteers donned space-age gloves and goggles, and grasped a computerized control panel that put them virtually into the driver's dear of a speeding race car with all of the sensations of reality, including a variation of driving situations they could create and control. Although still high-tech toys today, the space-age goggles and hand-held computer are serious symbols of a sobering future. As the age of information moves from dawn to daylight, we will be able to predict and control the future with uncanny accuracy and awesome power. Experts in the fast-growing field of virtual reality are already utilizing information systems by which the commercial markets of the world are seen, analyzed, and projected as a tool of strategic planning. Virtual reality is another instance in which humans will play God with all of the oral implications for the exercise of good and evil. And, like the exit of Adam and Eve from the Garden of innocence, "there is no turning back." For good or evil, virtual reality awaits us.

Think of Isaiah as an eighth century B.C. pioneer in the experience of virtual reality. Through the eyes of the Spirit, he saw God's vision for the future, and under the control of the Spirit, he watched world history being revealed from the human perspective of God's viewpoint. Salvation is the ever–present theme of Isaiah in chapters 40–66 but like a touch on a computerized control panel, we see its meaning projected on the prophetic scene from every angle. One moment our eyes are fixed on the words of comfort for Judah in exile, then in a flash we see the counter-reality of judgment upon Babylon. Or one moment the focus of virtual reality is upon the restoration of Jerusalem, then just as quickly the four corners of the earth come into view as the light of the world shines into every corner. Or again, the destiny of the Jews as God's Servant Nation is seen in detail, but only as a figure in the background for the larger image of a spiritual Zion, which includes salvation for foreigners, strangers, eunuchs, and Gentiles—all people of all nations. And then, the virtual reality of God's ultimate redemptive purpose bursts upon us with the glorious vision of the new heaven and the new earth along with the *Shalom* of the redeemed and a literal hell for the lost.

When virtual reality becomes a common experience for us in the future, our understanding of Isaiah in chapters 40–66 will deepen and our appreciation for his perspective will rise. But even before the space-age goggles and hand-held computers are available to us, we can enter into the experience of virtual reality as we read and study chapters 40–66 of Isaiah by fixing our eyes upon the dominate theme of salvation, seeing redemptive history unfold in many dimensions through the eyes of the Spirit, and praying for the meaning of the "big picture" through the mind of God. We will then become identified with Isaiah as visionary realists with unswerving trust in God's redemptive purpose.

Assume that we are already in the fantastic future of virtual reality. With just the touch of a button on our hand-held computer we are vaulted backward through time to the second century before Christ. The visage of a Jewish scholar named Ben Sira comes into view and his words of tribute to the prophet Isaiah are portrayed on the screen. Ben Sira wrote:

> . . . a great man trustworthy in his vision.
> In his days the sun went backward;
> he lengthened the life of the king.
> By the power of the Spirit he saw the last things.
> Then he comforted the mourners in Zion,
> he revealed what was to occur in the end of time
> and hidden things long before they happened.

As we read this tribute, we realize that virtual reality is a new term for old truth. By divine inspiration, God revealed His vision of the future to a prophet named Isaiah who faithfully reported what he saw—whether in past history, present events, or future reality. Only the timing of history and the theme of emphasis distinguish chapters 40–66 from 1–39 in the prophecy of Isaiah. The virtual reality of God's redemptive purpose remains the same. Whether punishing sin or promising the Savior, we see the goal of God to "gather all nations and tongues; and they shall come to see My glory" (66:18).

* *

Max DePree writes that a leader's first responsibility is to define reality, the leader's last responsibility is to say "Thank you," and in between the leader is to become a servant and a debtor.

In the author's preface to volume one I said "thank you" to those who were partners in my writing—the Board of Trustees of Asbury Theological Seminary, chaired by Dr. Maxie Dunnam, M. Robert Mulholland, who served as acting president during by writing sabbatical, Executive Assistant Sheila Lovell, who edited the manuscript, Presidential Secretary Carolyn Dock, who typed the copy on computer disk, covenant brothers Lloyd Ogilvie and Floyd Thatcher who urged me to write, and my wife, Janet, and youngest son, Rob, who sacrificed space and time for an author under the compelling inspiration of the publisher's deadline. To each and all of them I am their debtor in order that I might be your servant.

DAVID L. MCKENNA

An Outline of Isaiah 40:1–66:24

Part VII—The Vision Tested 40:1–41:29
XVIII. The Comfort of God (40)
    A. The Good News of God (40:1–11)
        1. The Tone of Love (40:1)
        2. The Theme of Salvation (40:2)
        3. The Text of Promise (40:3–11)
           a. Deliverance from Babylon (40:3–5)
           b. Return to Judah (40:6–8)
           c. The Restoration of Jerusalem (40:9–11)
    B. The Transcendence of God (40:12–31)
        1. His Transcendence Over Nations (40:12–17)
        2. His Transcendence Over Graven Images (40:18–20)
        3. His Transcendence Over Rulers (40:21–24)
        4. His Transcendence Over Gods (40:25–26)
        5. His Transcendence Over All Powers (40:27–31)
XIX. The Character of God (41:1–29)
    A. The Trial of Heathen Nations (41:1–7)
        1. God's Summons (41:1)
        2. God's Case (41:2–5)
        3. The Heathen's Response (41:6)
        4. The Verdict of History (41:7)
    B. The Call to Servanthood (41:8–20)
        1. Chosen by Love (41:8–9)
        2. Empowered by Grace (41:10–20)
    C. The Trial of the Gods (41:21–29)
        1. God's Summons (41:21)
        2. God's Test (41:22–24)
        3. God's Proof (41:25–28)
        4. God's Verdict (41:29)
Part VIII—The Vision Verified 42:1–48:22
XX. The New Order (42:1–43:28)
    A. Introducing the New Servant (42:1–4)
        1. Affirming His Relationship (42:1)
        2. Distinguishing His Character (42:2–4)
    B. Empowering the New Servant (42:5–13)
        1. A New Energy (42:5)
        2. A New Righteousness (42:6a)
        3. A New Covenant (42:6b)

PART SEVEN

The Vision Tested

Isaiah 40:1–41:29

CHAPTER EIGHTEEN

The Comfort of God

Isaiah 40

Isaiah's vision shifts forward a hundred years into the land of Babylon where the children of Judah have languished so long in exile that they have given up hope of returning to their homeland. Despair has overtaken them with the thought that God has canceled His covenant with them and abandoned them because of their sins. In response to their need, God speaks directly through His prophet Isaiah to reveal the other side of His character. They had seen His holiness, which exposed their sin, and His justice, which required their punishment. Now, He will show them His creative power and His redemptive love. In the theology of God as Creator and Redeemer, the children of Judah will be assured of the power of God to take them home to Jerusalem and the grace of God to restore their covenant relationship with Him.

THE GOOD NEWS OF GOD (40:1–11)

1 "Comfort, yes, comfort My people!"
  Says your God.
2 "Speak comfort to Jerusalem, and cry out to her,
  That her warfare is ended,
  That her iniquity is pardoned;
  For she has received from the LORD's hand
  Double for all her sins."
3 The voice of one crying in the wilderness:
  "Prepare the way of the LORD;
  Make straight in the desert
  A highway for our God.
4 Every valley shall be exalted,

And every mountain and hill
  shall be made low;
The crooked places
  shall be made straight,
And the rough places smooth;
5 The glory of the LORD
  shall be revealed,
And all flesh shall see it together;
For the mouth of the Lord has spoken."
6 The voice said, "Cry out!"
And he said, "What shall I cry?"
"All flesh is grass,
And all its loveliness is like the flower of the field.
7 The grass withers, the flower fades,
Because the breath of the LORD blows upon it;
Surely the people are grass.
8 The grass withers, the flower fades,
But the word of our God stands forever."
9 O Zion,
You who bring good tidings,
Get up into the high mountain;
O Jerusalem,
You who bring good tidings,
Lift up your voice with strength,
Lift it up, be not afraid;
Say to the cities of Judah,
  "Behold your God!"
10 Behold, the Lord GOD shall come
  with a strong hand,
And His arm shall rule for Him;
Behold, His reward is with Him,
And His work before Him.
11 He will feed His flock like a shepherd;
He will gather the lambs with His arm,
And carry them in His bosom,
And gently lead those who are with young.

Isaiah 40:1–11

Consistent with his style of writing, Isaiah opens the second section of his prophecy with a prologue. As a communicator, he asks the same questions that he asked in the opening verses of his prophecy:

what, where, when, and *how* (1:1). In the first case he left the question *why* to be answered by the oracles that followed. Now, he answers that question immediately but leaves the question *who* unanswered, either because the author is obvious, the message is more important, or the prophet will not be alive when the prophecy is fulfilled. The answer is most likely a combination of all three.

Another parallel between the prologues in chapter 1 and chapter 40 is the clear statement of the major themes to which Isaiah will speak on behalf of God through chapters 40–66. As we noted in the Introduction to Volume I, Isaiah has a genius for stating a theme and staying with it as his writing expands. Nothing he writes, then, is extraneous; everything he writes has meaning. His original declaration of intent to write of "Judah and Jerusalem" is an example. Scholars who disagree on the authorship of Isaiah still agree that the prophet never varies from the central focus upon Judah and Jerusalem, in both their historical setting and theological symbolism.

As in chapter 1, the purpose of the prologue is to (1) set the tone, (2) state the theme, and (3) cite the text for the oracles to come. In the same way that Isaiah's first prologue (1:1–9) fulfilled this purpose for chapters 1–39, so the prologue to the second section fulfills this threefold purpose for chapters 40–66.

THE TONE OF LOVE (40:1)

For the third time, Isaiah takes us into the courts of heaven where God speaks and angels sing. On the first occasion, God called the cosmic court into session to bring His charge against His rebellious children of Judah and Jerusalem. A severe tone of judgment resounded in His voice as the heavens and earth were called as witnesses to hear Him say, "I have nourished and brought up children, and they have rebelled against Me" (1:2). On the second occasion, Isaiah took us into a setting of worship in heaven where He saw the Lord in His holiness as the angels sang, "Holy, Holy, Holy, is the LORD of Hosts; the whole earth is full of His glory!" (6:3). Out of that awesome setting, Isaiah received the call of God to his prophetic ministry.

Isaiah's third vision of the Lord in His heavenly court results in a report that is all sound and no sight. Without identifying the voices, the prophet hears the heralds of heaven speak the Word of God that will become his message. George Adam Smith outlines the prologue through the voices of four heralds who speak: (1) Voice of Grace (vv. 1–2); (2) Voice of Providence (vv. 3–5); (3) Voice of Truth (vv. 6–8); and (4) Voice of Love (vv. 9–11).[1] Although the content of the message of the four voices may differ, the tone is the same. Rather than crying out judgment against His rebellious children, God is speaking words of comfort for His wounded children in exile.

The double use of the word *comfort* reinforces the depth of feeling in the heart of God. From the deepest reaches of His being, He sets the new tone for His people. In their present distress they will be comforted, and in their future history they will be restored. Quite in contrast with the first prologue when God spoke as a wounded father whose children had rebelled against His love, He now speaks as a lover wooing a bride. With the tenderness of a lover, God addresses the children of Judah as *"My people"* and acknowledges His relationship to them as *"Your God."* All questions about God forgetting or abandoning His people are answered. The covenant that He established with their father Abraham and continued through David is still intact. The tone of covenant love will pervade chapters 40–66 as the contrast to the pervasive tone of judgment in chapters 1–39.

THE THEME OF SALVATION (40:2)

Out of the tone of love, God has good news for His people. Grace takes over judgment as He announces that their *"warfare is ended."* His choice of military terms to signal the end of exile gives us the contemporary image of prisoners of war released from Vietnamese concentration camps or diplomatic hostages freed from their dungeons in Iran. We can imagine the joy of the good news to Jews who felt as if God had forgotten them. When a reporter asked a hostage who had been freed from Iranian captivity what he would do to celebrate his freedom, he answered, "Eat a good meal, read a good book, and talk with good friends." Bondage has a way of taking us back to the fundamentals of life that we take for granted when we are free. Like the liberated hostage, in their bondage the children of Judah had learned the basics of trust in God, and the good news of freedom would be cause for celebration. Deliverance is on the way.

Grace expands with God's second word of comfort. He informs His people that their *"iniquity is pardoned."* It is one thing to serve a sentence for a crime and another to be pardoned. After serving a sentence, probation follows and the record remains. But with a pardon, full freedom is given and the record is erased. God's relationship with His people takes a quantum leap with this promise. While they had to serve the term of their exile, only an act of grace or "unmerited favor" could pardon their iniquities. Forgiveness is introduced as a theological concept and an accomplished fact. The means of forgiveness are yet to be revealed, but Isaiah has laid the groundwork for the coming of the Messiah as the Suffering Servant through whom the children of Israel will be redeemed.

Grace takes yet another step with God's third word of comfort for His people. He announces to them that, like a cup that is more than full, the purpose of His punishment has been fulfilled, and the time has come for them to receive His blessing. As they received their punishment for sin from the Lord's hand, so they will now receive the overflowing fullness of blessing from His hand. John, the Gospel writer, gives us the meaning of this third promise when he writes of the coming of Christ, "And of His fullness we have all received, and grace for grace" (John 1:16). Like the waves of the sea rolling incessantly one after another, the fullness of His grace comes to us wave after wave.

The Text of Promise (40:3–11)

Isaiah's theme of salvation, then, has three promises that form the text for his writing in chapters 40–66. Historically, the children of Israel are promised deliverance from Babylon, return to Judah, and the restoration of Jerusalem. But more important, they are given the spiritual promises of the grace of God, who will set them free, forgive them of their sins, and bless them with His fullness. As we found in the study of chapters 1–39, Isaiah stated his theme in the prologue to his prophecy and never deviated from his purpose. We can anticipate the same consistency between prologue and text in chapters 40–66. As a good communicator, Isaiah followed the advice given to public speakers today: "Say what you are going to say, say it, and then say what you have said." Although we encounter many complexities in

Isaiah's prophecy, the integrity of his message cannot be questioned. In chapters 40–66, the threefold theme of salvation—deliverance, pardon, and blessing—absorbs the text, and every part contributes to the whole.

Deliverance From Babylon (40:3–5)

After setting the tone of comfort, the theme of salvation, and the text of God's good news to the children of Judah, Isaiah hears another voice in heaven heralding the promise of God's initiative for their return to Jerusalem (vv. 3–5). The metaphor of a highway, originally promised in 35:8–10, is expanded in the image of a royal caravan traversing a smooth and speedy road through the wilderness. When a royal party traveled through rugged country, "sappers" went before the caravan to remove obstacles, straighten crooked paths, and smooth out the hills and valleys. To back up the word of comfort that the children of Judah will be freed from Babylonian bondage, the voice of the herald announces that God is the "sapper" who is preparing the way for their return to Jerusalem and the coming of the Messiah. As unmistakable evidence of grace, God is taking the initiative of going before His people and preparing the way for their redemption.

It is often said that the Old Testament is the story of sinful humanity seeking God while the New Testament is the story of God seeking sinful humanity. If so, the New Testament is foreseen in this passage of Scripture. The voice crying in the wilderness, *"Prepare the way of the LORD"* is a turning point in revelation. Despite the fact that His children ran away from Him, God is like the prodigal's father who ran out to meet his son when he came to his senses and started home. Even before we repent, God has made the first move.

Whenever and wherever the transcendent God touches down in human history, His glory is revealed (v. 5a). With this insight, Isaiah pulls the thread of another major theological theme that he first introduced in chapters 1–39. When God becomes immanent in human history and takes the initiative to seek and save sinful humanity, the revelation of His glory will be seen by *"all flesh,"* not just by His chosen children. Earlier, we were told of the day when Judah would "Sing to the LORD, for He has done excellent things; this is known in all the earth" (12:5). We were also told of the time when Judah would fulfill its chosen purpose so that "The inhabitants of the world will learn righteousness" (9b). This idealized vision takes on reality in chapters 40–66 when Isaiah specifically sees Gentiles, who because of their faith, will walk with the ransomed on the highway of holiness. The prophet is treading on holy ground.

Return to Judah (40:6–8)

Still another herald voice is heard echoing across the court of heaven with the command to the prophet, *"Cry out!"* Isaiah had heard the command before. In his encounter with God in the temple, when God gave him the word "Go and tell this people" a message of judgment that they would not hear, Isaiah asked woefully, "Lord, how long?" (6:9–11). Timing is no longer his first interest in this second call to prophecy. Here he asks *"What shall I cry?"* rather than "Lord, how long?"

Having been assured of God's initiative in bringing them home from exile, the children of Israel are now assured that *"the Word of our God stands forever"* (v. 8b). God's grace is backed up by God's truth in His word of comfort. To set the message in sharp relief, the prophet must remind the people of their mortality. Adapting the analogy of the grass and flowers in the desert, which wither and fade when the hot winds blow, so the children of Israel have learned that their trust in the flesh and their assurance of prosperity are short-lived. Isaiah would dig deeply into their guilt by reminding them that they had been unfaithful to God. Yet, He had never been unfaithful to them. By His grace, they knew that they could count upon His Word, which stands forever. He had promised to "pardon their iniquities" and on the surety of His Word, it would be so.

The Restoration of Jerusalem (40:9–11)

A final herald voice is heard with the resounding call from the highest mountain to Zion and Jerusalem, *"Behold your God!"* Isaiah lived for this moment. After a lifetime of pronouncing "woes" upon Judah and Jerusalem, he becomes the herald of joy with *"good tidings"* that are the best news of all. Just when the children of Judah felt as if

God might have abandoned them because of their sin, He comes back to them *"like a shepherd."* All sheep need the shepherd's strong arm for their protection and the shepherd's open hand for their feeding. Lambs, in particular, need the shepherd's bosom for their security, and pregnant ewes need the gentle guidance of the shepherd's staff to keep from falling. According to Isaiah, God will be all of these things as the shepherd for the flock of Judah. They can trust Him implicitly because He cares for them with the love of a faithful shepherd.

What a contrast in Isaiah's message. In chapters 1–39, God carried the image of a raging lion taking out his wrath upon an enemy. A shepherd is just the opposite. Rather than being a lion, the shepherd will give his life to protect his sheep from a lion. As one more word of comfort, the children of Judah would hear again the voice of their greatest king singing the psalm, "The LORD is my shepherd, I shall not want" (Psalm 23:1).

With the tone, theme, and text of the prologue in mind, we foresee the rest of Isaiah's prophecy. Chapters 40 to 48 will unfold the story of God's initiative in delivering Judah from the judgment of sin; chapters 49 to 57 will assure us that God's Word stands forever in His promise of salvation from sin through the Suffering Servant; and Chapters 58 to 66 will see Him shepherding His people through to the abundant blessings of His salvation as seen in the restoration of Jerusalem. Isaiah's prologue will live up to its promises.

THE TRANSCENDENCE OF GOD (40:12–31)

12 Who has measured the waters
    in the hollow of his hand,
   Measured heaven with a span
   And calculated the dust of the earth in a measure?
   Weighed the mountains in scales
   And the hills in a balance?
13 Who has directed the Spirit of the LORD,
   Or as His counselor has taught Him?
14 With whom did He take counsel,
    and who instructed Him,
   And taught Him in the path of justice?
   Who taught Him knowledge,

And showed Him the way of understanding?

15 Behold, the nations are as a drop
    in a bucket,
    And are counted as the small dust
        on the balance;
    Look, He lifts up the isles as a very little thing.

16 And Lebanon is not sufficient to burn,
    Nor its beasts sufficient for a burnt offering.

17 All nations before Him are as nothing,
    And they are counted by Him less than nothing
        and worthless.

18 To whom then will you liken God?
    Or what likeness will you compare to Him?

19 The workman molds a graven image,
    The goldsmith overspreads it with gold,
    And the silversmith casts silver chains.

20 Whoever is too impoverished for such a contribution
    Chooses a tree that will not rot;
    He seeks for himself a skillful workman
    To prepare a carved image that will not totter.

21 Have you not known?
    Have you not heard?
    Has it not been told you
        from the beginning?
    Have you not understood
        from the foundations of the earth?

22 It is He who sits above the circle
        of the earth,
    And its inhabitants are like grasshoppers,
    Who stretches out the heavens
        like a curtain,
    And spreads them out like a tent
        to dwell in.

23 He brings the princes to nothing;
    He makes the judges of the earth useless.

24 Scarcely shall they be planted,
    Scarcely shall they be sown,
    Scarcely shall their stock take root in the earth,
    When He will also blow on them,
    And they will wither,
    And the whirlwind will take them away like stubble.

25 "To whom then will you liken Me,

Or to whom shall I be equal?"
　　says the Holy One.
26 Lift up your eyes on high,
　　And see who has created these things,
　　Who brings out their host by number;
　　He calls them all by name,
　　By the greatness of His might
　　And the strength of His power;
　　Not one is missing.
27 Why do you say, O Jacob,
　　And speak, O Israel:
　　"My way is hidden from the LORD,
　　And my just claim is passed over
　　　　by my God"?
28 Have you not known?
　　Have you not heard?
　　The everlasting God, the LORD,
　　The Creator of the ends of the earth,
　　Neither faints nor is weary.
　　There is no searching of His understanding.
29 He gives power to the weak,
　　And to those who have no might
　　　　He increases strength.
30 Even the youths shall faint
　　　　and be weary,
　　And the young men shall utterly fall,
31 But those who wait on the LORD
　　Shall renew their strength;
　　They shall mount up with wings like eagles,
　　They shall run and not be weary,
　　They shall walk and not faint.

Isaiah 40:12–31

Put yourself in the place of the children of Israel in Babylonian exile. The generation of people who remembered the homeland of Judah and the city of Jerusalem had died. Without the vision of Zion, a second generation of deportees had only the prophet's word of God's promise upon which to depend. Countering this unfulfilled promise, each day they awakened to see the grandeur and the power of Babylon. Moreover, many of the exiles had exercised an entrepreneurial genius in the commercial world to become wealthy and secure merchants. To think of leaving Babylon on a seven-hundred-mile march through treacherous terrain and taking only the possessions that could be carried on their back or pulled in a cart—all on the basis of an unfulfilled promise from God—was a risk that provoked second thoughts.

Underneath the temptation to remain in Babylon lurked fears that had to be overcome before faith in the promise of God could take hold. The exiles needed comfort for their fears as much as for their doubts. Therefore, after promising to be the shepherd with a strong arm and a tender touch who knows just what his flock needs, God speaks first to their fears. In a best-selling book entitled *Yes or No* by Spencer Johnson, one of the key questions leading to effective decision-making is to ask, "What would I decide if I weren't afraid?"[2] God asks the same thing of His people in exile. But before asking that question, He gives them four reasons for freedom from fear based upon His transcendence as the Creator, Controller, and Caretaker of all the earth.

HIS TRANSCENDENCE OVER NATIONS (40:12–17)

Fear must have gripped the hearts of the exiles as they thought about the power of Babylon to control their destiny. To declare their intention to return home might be interpreted as rebellion against their captors. Or, after they had made their declaration and prepared to leave, public opinion might shift from passive permission to active persecution. Knowing the reputation of the Babylonians for being people of vicious nature and arbitrary action gave the children of Israel good reason to fear the power of the Empire.

God addresses their fear of Babylon by a question rather than a declaration. Showing His respect for human intelligence, God might well have said again, "Come now, and let us reason together" (1:18). This time, however, He wants to pose rhetorical questions about His character rather than their sins. First, to deal with the fear of Babylonian power, He asks questions that demonstrate His omnipotence. Showing His sense of humor by playing with the ludicrous and taking it to an extreme, God asks: (a) Who has measured the waters of the seas in the hollow of the hand? (b) Who has measured the heavens by the span of the hand stretched from the tip of the thumb to the tip of the little finger? (c) Who has calculated the dust of the earth in a measuring cup? (d) Who has weighed the mountains on a balancing scale? Job heard the same questions from God. The answer is obvious. "For since the creation of the world His invisible attributes are clearly seen, being understood by the things that are made, even His eternal power and Godhead" (Romans 1:20). With Job, we have one of two choices: either shut our mouth or confess our sins. He and He alone has the eternal power of creation.

Another set of rhetorical questions is asked of the children of Israel in exile who fear Babylon. Kings are only as wise as their counsel. Good kings, in particular, seek direction for decision-making, counsel for doing justice, instruction for knowledge, and guidance for understanding. The courts of kings are always filled with wise men, scribes, priests, and even sorcerers. Against the best of human wisdom, then, God asks the questions: (a) Who directs the Spirit of the Lord? (b) Who is His counselor? (c) Who instructs Him? (d) Who has taught Him justice, knowledge, and understanding? By reference to the Spirit of God, the earlier promise of the Messiah echoes again through these words, "The Spirit of the LORD shall rest upon Him, the Spirit of wisdom and understanding, the Spirit of counsel and might, the Spirit of knowledge, and of the fear of the LORD" (11:2). In this case, however, the transcendence rather than the immanence of God is being declared. He is omniscient in knowledge and understanding as well as omnipotent in power and might. No one directs, counsels, or teaches God. He, and He alone, is all-just, all-knowing, and all-understanding. In sum, He is all-wise.

With the givens of His omnipotence and omniscience, God draws the comparison between Himself and the nations of the world, specifically the Babylonian Empire that His children fear. Isaiah's choice word for lifting the veil on revelation to reveal eternal truth is "Behold." Who can mistake the simple, common language of the Lord when He declares, *"Behold, the nations are as a drop in a bucket, and are counted as the small dust on the balance; look, He lifts up the isles as a very little thing"* (v. 15)? He further declares that all of the wood and animals in the forests of Lebanon are not sufficient for a burning sacrifice in His holy presence to atone for the sins of humanity (v. 16). Weighing the power of all nations on the scale against His omnipotence, they become less than a drop in the bucket or a speck on the balance. They are *as nothing . . . less than nothing . . . worthless"* (v. 17).

God's case is made. Because He is transcendent over all nations in omnipotence, His children need not fear the power of Babylon, which is "less than nothing" in His sight. Compared to God, Babylon is "a cipher with the rim knocked off."

His Transcendence Over Graven Images (40:18–20)

Wherever the Israelites looked around the magnificent city of Babylon, they saw the exquisite handiwork of statues to the heroes and gods of the Empire. Even though they remembered the second commandment of the Law of Moses, which forbade the making of graven images as representative of God, they still nursed the fear of trusting in the God whom they could not see. Like the little girl in her darkened bedroom whose mother told her that God was present with her, she answered, "But Mommy, I want a God with a face." Honesty requires that we all confess the same need, so we cannot be too hard on the children of Israel in Babylonian exile. Yahweh had not spoken to them for a full generation. At least the graven images of the Babylonian gods had faces!

In response to this natural fear, God asks a question and cites the facts. Still working within the framework of His transcendent power and wisdom, God asks, *"To whom then will you liken God? Or what likeness will you compare to Him?"* (v. 18). A comparison is then drawn between the invisible Spirit of God and the graven image of human craftsmen. All of the skills of the most gifted artisan go into the quality of the hard wood, the gold overlay, and the silver chains, with the hope of producing a precious and permanent representation of the Babylonian gods. Even the poorest of the poor who cannot afford gold or silver scout for the best of hardwoods that will not rot. But when the exquisite work is finished, the idol must be chained to the wall to keep it from falling over. God's sense of humor has turned to sarcasm. What a laughable sight to see the labor of Babylon's best craftsmen and the investment of Babylon's wealth in a statue of a god that totters and falls unless silver chains hold it upright! The scene has the making of a classic comedy.

No answer is needed for God's question. The statues of the Babylonian gods are products of the raw materials created by God and are subject to all of the laws that He instituted, including the law of gravity. Within themselves, they are lifeless, powerless, and dumb. No comparison can be drawn between earthbound graven images and the eternal, living, and transcendent God of all creation. The fear of trusting God, whose face they cannot see, is dispelled in the cartoon of tottering statues. A caption for the cartoon might show one of the artisans saying to another, "It's perfect, but how do you keep it from falling over?"

HIS TRANSCENDENCE OVER RULERS (40:21–24)

In concert with their fear of the power of Babylon, the children of Israel must have dreaded the dictatorial style of the Babylonian rulers. Their reputation for ruthless slaughter and whimsical decrees, rising from drunken orgies like the one held by Belshazzar in Daniel 5, lays an air of uncertainty over the prospect of a return to Jerusalem. Perhaps they thought, "What if the king of Babylon uses the exodus to justify a holocaust as the final resolution of the Jewish question?" An Eastern despot enjoyed absolute power without moral compunction.

God addresses this fear with His third set of questions. A bit impatient now, He asks in rapid fire:

> Have you not known?
> Have you not heard?
> Has it not been told you
>   from the beginning?
> Have you not understood
>   from the foundations of the earth?

Isaiah 40:21

These are open questions of recall for the children of Judah. In His transcendence, God sits on a throne high above the circle of the earth and sees its inhabitants as *"grasshoppers."* God would appreciate children giggling over the pun, "God is up so high that to Him our uncles look like ants!"

From His exalted position, God controls, as well as sees, human affairs. The princes and rulers whom the children of Judah fear can be brought down to nothing or rendered useless by the power of His will (v. 23). At best, their reign is as temporary as vegetation whose lifespan is limited to the season between planting, sowing, growing, and reaping, after which they wither and become the stubble blown away by a whirlwind (v. 24). The exiles, then, are asked to remember what they have known, heard, and understood. All rulers are under God's control; He will determine how long they rule and when they die. Because the rulers' powers are limited and transitory, the children of Judah are assured that if God blows on them, *"they will wither, and the whirlwind will take them away"* (v. 24).

HIS TRANSCENDENCE OVER GODS (40:25–26)

Statues of gods are objects made of raw materials created by the hand of God. If God is accepted as Creator, the fear of those objects fades. But what about the gods of the Babylonians that are part of the natural creation, such as the astrological gods of the stars? They, too, pose a threat to the Jews because the stars are part of God's creation, and the reading of the stars is occasionally right—after all, God used a star to signal the birth of the Savior and lead the wise men into His presence.

Using the same questions that He asked about the graven images, God again invites comparison, *"To whom then will you liken Me, or to whom shall I be equal?"* (v. 25). The same argument is used to dispel the children of Israel's fear of graven images. God asks them to look up at the stars and realize that by His power He created them, named them, and perfected them in a system where none is missing.

Astrology is still an attractive substitute for the Lord of the universe. Nancy Reagan caused a stir when it was reported that she consulted an astrologer for advice on world events when her husband was President of the United States. New Age adherents mix astrology with the ingredients of world religions, and everyone is curious to read their horoscope and share the sayings of fortune cookies. Fascination with the stars is a natural impulse, but if the creation is worshiped rather than the Creator, astrology is idolatry. Perhaps the Jews in exile had read the stars and received negative vibrations on the return to Jerusalem. God lets them know that He is the transcendent and *"Holy One"* who created, controls, and cares for the stars.

HIS TRANSCENDENCE OVER ALL POWERS (40:27–31)

Marshaling the facts of His transcendence over nations, graven images, rulers, and gods, the Lord asks one more question of the exiles: *"Why do you say, O Jacob, and speak, O Israel, My way is hidden from the LORD, and my just claim is passed over by my God?"* (v. 27). Once again, He asks them to remember what they have heard and what they have known. He, the Lord of Jacob and the Holy One of Israel, is also *"The everlasting God, The LORD, The Creator of the ends of the earth"* (v. 28b). His power never weakens or grows weary, and His understanding is perfect. With that declaration of His omnipotence and omniscience, God offers to the exiles the final resolution of their fears about the return to Jerusalem. He will exchange His power for their weakness and His strength for their weariness (v. 29). When He does, their energy will exceed the vigor of youth. If they are willing to trust God for the timing and the strength to fulfill His promise, *"they shall mount up with wings like eagles, they shall run and not be weary, they shall walk and not faint"* (v. 31).

By God's great exchange, their weakness will be renewed by His omnipotent strength and their fears will be relieved by His omniscient understanding. They were now ready for the seven-hundred-mile walk home.

On the peak of His promise, which is still good for God's weak and weary children, we understand why J. Gresham Machen wrote of this chapter, "It is quite impossible, the wondering reader will say, for prose style ever to attain greater heights than these."[3]

NOTES

1. G. A. Smith, *The Expositor's Bible. Volume II (Isaiah XL-LXVI)* (New York: A. C. Armstrong and Son, 1890), 74–75.

2. S. Johnson, *Yes or No: The Guide to Better Decisions* (New York: Harper Busn., 1992).

3. J. G. Machen, *God Transcendent and Other Selected Sermons*, ed. N. B. Stonehouse (Grand Rapids: Eerdmans, 1949), 17.

CHAPTER NINETEEN

The Character of God

Isaiah 41:1–29

Words of comfort for the children of Israel continue in the expansion of God's challenge, "To whom then will you liken Me, or to whom shall I be equal?" (40:25). The answer has already been given as the word of comfort for the weak and weary Jews in exile. God's omnipotence is their strength, and His omniscience is their assurance. Now the case for their comfort is taken into the context of world history. Summoning to the bar of the cosmic court the nations that worship false gods, God makes the case for His omnipotence and omniscience, and then challenges the heathen nations to do the same. After pronouncing the verdict of His sovereignty, God takes the opportunity to draw the contrast between the heathen nations and Israel, whom He has chosen to be His Servant Nation. With a new set of promises that comfort His people and lift their spirits, God returns to the setting of the cosmic court and calls a second session in which the false gods themselves are put on trial. In the same sequence as the first trial, God issues the summons to the false gods, makes His case against them, and pronounces the verdict as another word of comfort.

THE TRIAL OF HEATHEN NATIONS (41:1–7)

1 "Keep silence before Me,
   O coastlands,
 And let the people renew their strength!
 Let them come near,
     then let them speak;
 Let us come near together for judgment.

2 "Who raised up one from the east?
Who in righteousness called him to His feet?
Who gave the nations before him,
And made him rule over kings?
Who gave them as the dust to his sword,
As driven stubble to his bow?
3 Who pursued them, and passed safely
By the way that he had not gone with his feet?
4 Who has performed and done it,
Calling the generations from the beginning?
'I, the LORD, am the first;
And with the last I am He.'"
5 The coastlands saw it and feared,
The ends of the earth were afraid;
They drew near and came.
6 Everyone helped his neighbor,
And said to his brother,
"Be of good courage!"
7 So the craftsman encouraged the goldsmith,
And he who smooths with the hammer
    inspired him who strikes the anvil,
Saying, "It is ready for the soldering";
Then he fastened it with pegs,
That it might not totter.

Isaiah 41:1–7

GOD'S SUMMONS (41:1)

The summons to trial goes out to the *"coastlands"* or nations along the Mediterranean Sea who are firsthand witnesses of world events taking place at the time of Israel's exile. God asks for silence as He speaks, and then invites the gathered nations to interrogate Him. After they have spoken, judgment will be pronounced. Following the pattern for past and future sessions of the cosmic court, God (a) summons the court; (b) makes His case; (c) invites interrogation; and (d) declares the verdict.

GOD'S CASE (41:2–5)

When God presented His case in chapter 40 for the comfort of His children in exile, He affirmed the omnipotence of His power and the omniscience of His purpose. The same attributes of His character are central to the case He presents before the nations who worship false gods. In a series of questions beginning with the word *who*, God establishes His omnipotence and omniscience before the cosmic court.

To frame the history for His case, God introduces Cyrus as the one whom He raised up from the east (v. 2). A Persian by birth, Cyrus became king of Anshan in 559 B.C. From this minor state in the Median Empire, he began a series of conquests that took him to prominence within ten years. After capturing Echatana, the Median capital, he led his troops over the mountains of present-day Turkey to Lydia where he surprised King Croesus and took his capital with its world reputation for gold. Turning back south, Cyrus took dead aim upon Babylon. Of course, word of his conquests rippled through the Middle East and particularly to the coastlands and islands of the Mediterranean Seas, which usually became ready targets for kings with ambitions to conquer the world. Isaiah 41 is a prophecy related to this period of time. Cyrus is marching toward Babylon where the children of Israel are in exile, and the word of his reputation is spreading through the nations along the seacoast that must be conquered to create a world empire with control of land and sea.

To make the case for His omnipotence and omniscience, God asks, "who" seven times in the short passage of verses 2–4. Who raised up Cyrus? Who put him on his feet? Who put the nations before him? Who gave him power to conquer? Who kept him safe and gave him speed? Who gave him his victories? Who has done it from the beginning? God wastes no time in answering these questions. Reaching back to his self-introduction to Moses through the burning bush, He answers, "*I, the* LORD, *am the first; and with the last I am He*" (v. 4b). At the same time, He reaches forward to Revelation 1:8 when He declares at the end time, "I am the Alpha and the Omega, the Beginning and the End . . . who is and who was and who is to come, the Almighty."

The meaning of *"I am He"* is more than a declaration of omnipotence and omniscience as theological attributes of God. He is also the Lord of history, at one and the same time above, beyond, and within world events such as the conquests of Cyrus. He does not explain why He chose a pagan as the instrument for His judgment or a servant of His grace. "I am He" sums up God's case for His challenge to the nations who fashion statues of their gods. Are they uncreated and eternal? Do

423

they claim to be omnipotent and omniscient? Are they the Lord of history? What word of comfort do they have for weak and weary people?

THE HEATHEN'S RESPONSE (41:6)

Satire bordering on sarcasm is used to describe the response of the heathen nations. Trembling in fear at the news of Cyrus' conquests, they leaned upon each other and offered the word, *"Be of good courage!"* (v. 6). Rather than bowing before the statues of old gods that they created, they saw the need for a new god to address the current crisis. Craftsmen, goldsmiths, carpenters, and blacksmiths all work together to create a new god that cannot stand by itself. Pegs as well as chains are used to tie it down and keep it from tottering. Isaiah's picture is crystal clear. The false gods of heathen nations are lifeless, temporary, and tottering. Since these gods are unable to speak a word of comfort backed up by strength and wisdom, their creators must rely upon mutual encouragement for help.

Humanitarian efforts in response to crisis are often built upon the same principles as statues of heathen gods. When a crisis comes to a community or a region, urgent action creates a new program of response to the need. Professionals and volunteers work together and encourage each other. But more often than not, disaster relief does not deal with the cause of the crisis or provide a long-term solution. Only the eternal values and redemptive resources of God can ultimately address the human condition and bring a word of hope beyond mutual encouragement.

THE VERDICT OF HISTORY (41:7)

Thus, the verdict of history thunders down upon the heathen nations. Their gods do not live, speak, create, control, care, or stand. They are powerless and dumb. As George Adam Smith writes, "The imagemakers have been laughed out of court."[1] God is the author and finisher of human history.

THE CALL TO SERVANTHOOD (41:8–20)

> 8 "But you, Israel, are My servant,
> Jacob, whom I have chosen,

The descendants of Abraham My friend.
9 You whom I have taken from the ends of the earth,
And called from its farthest regions,
And said to You,
'You are My servant,
I have chosen you
    and have not cast you away:
10 Fear not, for I am with you;
Be not dismayed, for I am your God.
I will strengthen you,
Yes, I will help you,
I will uphold you with My righteous right hand.'
11 "Behold, all those who were incensed against you
Shall be ashamed and disgraced;
They shall be as nothing,
And those who strive with you shall perish.
12 You shall seek them
    and not find them—
Those who contended with you.
Those who war against you
Shall be as nothing,
As a nonexistent thing.
13 For I, the LORD your God,
    will hold your right hand,
Saying to you, 'Fear not,
    I will help you.'
14 "Fear not, you worm Jacob,
You men of Israel!
I will help you," says the LORD
And your Redeemer,
    The Holy One of Israel.
15 "Behold, I will make you into a new threshing sledge
    with sharp teeth;
You shall thresh the mountains
    and beat them small,
And make the hills like chaff.
16 You shall winnow them,
    the wind shall carry them away,
And the whirlwind shall scatter them;
You shall rejoice in the LORD,
And glory in the Holy One of Israel.

17 "When the poor and needy seek water,
      and there is none,
   And their tongues fail for thirst,
   I, the LORD, will hear them;
   I, the God of Israel,
      will not forsake them.
18 I will open rivers in desolate heights,
   And fountains in the midst of the valleys;
   I will make the wilderness a pool of water,
   And the dry land springs of water.
19 I will plant in the wilderness the cedar
      and the acacia tree,
   The myrtle and the oil tree;
   I will set in the desert the cypress tree and the pine
   And the box tree together,
20 That they may see and know,
   And consider and understand together,
   That the hand of the LORD has done this,
   And the Holy One of Israel
      has created it.

Isaiah 41:8–20

CHOSEN BY LOVE (41:8–9)

Striking contrast is one of Isaiah's most effective means of communicating his message. With the introductory words, *"But you, Israel"* he prepares us for the contrast between God's relationship with the heathen nations and His beloved children. Rather than calling Israel to court as He did the heathen nations, God seals His covenant with His people by the salutation, *"My servant, Jacob, whom I have chosen."*

Servanthood will now become a major theme of Isaiah's prophecy and an unending theme for the future of Christian history. Scholars debate the specific application of the term *servant* as it is used repeatedly in Isaiah. Some contend that its meaning is limited to the nation of Israel in its historic setting. They are also willing to apply the term to Cyrus, whom the Lord identified as "My servant." Reluctance comes when the term is applied to the Messiah, or Christ. To make that confession opens the door to the miraculous meaning of the incarnation, the crucifixion, and the resurrection. For us who believe that Jesus Christ is the Son of God, there should be no problem. *Servant* is a term that may apply to the servant role to which God calls Israel, to Cyrus, to Christ, and to us. As servants who do the bidding of the Master, our purpose is to glorify His name so that all the world may know that He is God.

Israel, a collective term for the chosen people of God, desperately needs to hear the Lord say, *"But you, Israel, are My servant."* After enduring long years in exile and wallowing in self-doubt, God's words must have sounded like His promise of extended life to the dying Hezekiah. To be called "Israel" once again restored their identity as a people; to hear God say "You" and "My" assured them that the love relationship of the Covenant was still intact; and the title of "servant" reassured them of their role in His redemptive plan.

EMPOWERED BY GRACE (41:10–20)

To back up His call, God illustrates the contrast between the heathen nations and Israel with four promises to His people. First, God gives them the **Promise of His Providence** (vv. 8–10). He says that He has chosen them as descendants of His friend Abraham, gathered them from the corners of the earth, called them from its farthest regions, followed them through their exile, and promised them freedom from their fears and strength for their weakness. *"I will uphold you with My righteous right hand"* (v. 10) is the promise that all of His power is at their disposal to fulfill His purpose.

Second, God gives them the **Promise of His Deliverance** (vv. 11–13). No longer will the people of Israel have to fear the enemy nations that want to destroy them. The LORD of Hosts will fight their battles for them and bring their enemies not just to shame and disgrace but to *"nothing, as a nonexistent thing"* (v. 12b). Backing up this promise is the power of "I AM" with the strength of His right hand, saying, *"Fear not, I will help you"* (v. 13).

Third, God gives them the **Promise of His Empowerment** (vv. 14–16). Realistically identifying their loss of self-esteem, God calls them *"you worm Jacob."* As exiles in Babylon, the people of Jacob's house had been relegated to the lowest strata of society. For the most part, they grovelled like worms at the feet of their captors, disenfranchised as citizens, despised as aliens, and detested as worshipers of Yahweh. All of this will change. For the first of many times in Isaiah, God identifies Himself to Israel as *"your Redeemer"* and then backs up the new title with the quality of His character, *"the Holy One of Israel."* Redemption is always radical, but never more radical than the promise that Israel will be changed from a *"worm"* into *"a new threshing sledge with sharp teeth"* (v. 15). After more than one hundred years of cowering under the boot of the oppressor, the house of Jacob will be the sharp-edged instrument of truth that threshes, winnows, and scatters the nations. Any thought of self-glorifying triumph, however, is quickly dispelled by the balance of rejoicing in the righteousness and justice of the Lord so that they can *"glory in the Holy One of Israel."*

Fourth, God gives His people the **Promise of His Transformation** (vv. 17–20). Justice is always the outcome when God empowers His people as servants. The *"poor and needy"* come first in His promise of transformation. Some of the exiles in the first and second deportations of 597 and 587 B.C. had succeeded in business and gained a measure of social standing. Those in the third deportation of 581 B.C., however, had come from the lower and poorer classes of people who were used as slave labor in Babylon for massive building projects in the city. Perhaps God has these people in mind when He speaks to them first with the assurance that their cry of suffering had been heard and that He has not forsaken them. For them, in particular, and for His people in general, God will transform the dry, desolate, wild, and lifeless desert into rivers, fountains, pools, and springs of water that will create fertile soil in which the cedar, acacia, myrtle, oil, cypress, pine, and box trees will grow.

Isaiah often uses the metaphor of the desert to represent desolation and death due to sin. In these instances "water" becomes the source of life from the hand of God that turns the desert into a garden. For the Israelites who had subsisted on survival margins in the spiritual desert of Babylon for more than one hundred years, the promise would be as refreshing as a drink of cool water while traveling through Death Valley in midsummer heat. God's promise of transformation is given for a purpose. He wants His people to *see* the evidence, *know* the facts, *consider* the implications, and *understand* the meaning of what the Lord has done and what the Holy One of Israel has created (v. 20).

The contrast between the heathen nations and the house of Jacob is clear. God summons the heathen nations to His cosmic court to challenge their gods, but for the people of Israel, He calls them to be His Servant Nation with all of the promises necessary to fulfill their chosen role.

THE TRIAL OF THE GODS (41:21–29)

21 "Present your case," says the LORD.
   "Bring forth your strong reasons,"
      says the King of Jacob.
22 "Let them bring forth and show us
      what will happen;
   Let them show the former things,
      what they were,
   That we may consider them,
   And know the latter end of them;
   Or declare to us things to come.
23 Show the things that are to come hereafter,
   That we may know that you are gods;
   Yes, do good or do evil,
   That we may be dismayed
      and see it together.
24 Indeed you are nothing,
   And your work is nothing;
   He who chooses you is an abomination.
25 "I have raised up one from the north,
   And he shall come;
   From the rising of the sun he shall call on My name;
   And he shall come against princes as though mortar,
   As the potter treads clay.
26 Who has declared from the beginning,
      that we may know?
   And former times, that we may say,
      'He is righteous'?
   Surely there is no one who shows,
   Surely there is no one who declares,
   Surely there is no one who hears your words.
27 The first time I said to Zion,
   'Look, there they are!'
   And I will give to Jerusalem one
      who brings good tidings.
28 For I looked, and there was no man;

> I looked among them,
>> but there was no counselor,
> Who, when I asked of them,
>> could answer a word.
> 29 Indeed they are all worthless;
>> Their works are nothing;
>> Their molded images are wind and confusion.
>>> *Isaiah 41:21–29*

GOD'S SUMMONS (41:21)

After a recess from the session when the Lord called Israel to its chosen role as His Servant Nation and backed up His call with the power of His promises, He returns to a second session of the cosmic court. Heathen nations who worshiped false gods stood trial in the first session. Now God summons the false gods themselves to stand before Him and present the *"strong reasons"* for their case. Employing the delicate and dangerous technique of a master debater, God offers to hear the case of the false gods according to their ground rules.

GOD'S TEST (41:22–24)

The first point of contest is the omniscience of false gods. Rather generously, God offers to let them show their ability to predict what will happen, to recall the past, foretell human history, and show the hereafter. Omnipotence, then, becomes the second point of contest. To prove that they are really gods, the Lord asks them to show that they have the power to do good or evil. Of course, false gods that cannot speak have no answer. So, in the deafening silence, God concludes that the false gods are *"nothing,"* their work is *"nothing,"* and anyone who chooses them is an *"abomination"* (v. 24).

GOD'S PROOF (41:25–28)

Despite the silence of the false gods, the order of the day in court gives God the opportunity for rebuttal. Staying with the ground rules of predicting what will happen, recalling the past, foretelling the future, and showing the hereafter, He makes His case. Beginning with current events and the conquests of Cyrus, God predicts that Cyrus will come to Babylon acknowledging the name of God and conquering the city with ease (v. 25b). Then, as proof of His eternal existence, God asks, *"Who has declared from the beginning, that we may know? And former times, that we may say, 'He is righteous'?"* (v. 26a). No one other than God has shown the future, declared its happenings, and been proven right.

The rise and conquests of Cyrus comprise the case in point. Long before the soothsayers and sorcerers of Babylon heard of Cyrus, God had spoken the good news through Isaiah to His people in Zion first and then to the city of Jerusalem. One more time, in fairness to the false gods, God says that He looked for someone to speak on their behalf. Had they predicted the rise of Cyrus, or did they know of his coming? Silence closes the case.

GOD'S VERDICT (41:29)

The verdict is not flattering. Invoking His own omniscience and omnipotence, God pronounces the triple sentence upon the false gods and the graven images that represent them. They are worthless for seeing, knowing, considering, and understanding; they are powerless to produce any works of substance; and they are represented by *"molded images"* that are empty of thought and devoid of purpose. God has spoken to condemn idols and to comfort Israel. As the living and true God of Israel, He is the Lord of history who will redeem His people.

NOTES

1. Smith, *Expositor's Bible, Volume II,* 118.

PART EIGHT

The Vision Verified

Isaiah 42:1–48:22

CHAPTER TWENTY

The New Order

Isaiah 42:1–43:28

"Behold" is Isaiah's word for either introducing a new theme or developing distinctive dimensions to one that he has introduced earlier. "Behold! My Servant" is a commanding call of expectation for a new insight into the vision that God gave to His prophet. Not that the servant theme is totally new to his prophecies. Looking backward, we see the connection with chapter 11 when the concept of the servant was introduced without specifically using the name. Looking forward, we see that chapter 42 is the first of four servant songs that are pivotal in the Book of Isaiah (42:1–29; 49:1–6, 50:39, and 52:13–53:12). Still, God speaks through His prophet to let us know that with His specific announcement of "My Servant," He is declaring "new things" (42:9). The theological message of Isaiah is new with the shift of emphasis from the sovereignty of God (theology) to the salvation of the world (soteriology). The person whom God calls "My Servant" is also new. While God has called Israel as His Servant Nation (42:8–20) and such individuals as Abraham, Moses, David, and even Nebuchadnezzar and Cyrus as His servant persons, "My Servant" in the Servant Songs is distinctly the Messiah. We understand, then, why God brings us to attention with the cry, "Behold!" As the ultimate word of comfort for His children in exile, He shows them His Servant who will be their Savior.

INTRODUCING THE NEW SERVANT (42:1–4)

1 "Behold! My Servant whom I uphold,
My Elect One in whom My soul delights!
I have put My Spirit upon Him;

> He will bring forth justice to the Gentiles.
> 2 He will not cry out, nor raise His voice,
>   Nor cause His voice to be heard in the street.
> 3 A bruised reed He will not break,
>   And smoking flax He will not quench;
>   He will bring forth justice for truth.
> 4 He will not fail nor be discouraged,
>   Till He has established justice in the earth;
>   And the coastlands shall wait for His law."
>
> *Isaiah 42:1–4*

AFFIRMING HIS RELATIONSHIP (42:1)

Before telling us what His Servant is like or what He will do, God affirms His own commitment to the One He has called. First, He affirms His *relationship* to His Servant. By claiming Him as *"My Servant,"* God reveals an intimate and loving relationship not unlike a Father and Son. With full confidence in His Servant, God promises to *"uphold"* Him by the strength of His omnipotent hand. In contrast with the Servant Nation of Israel, who rebelled against their relationship with God, His New Servant will be obedient to the death.

Second and deeper yet, God affirms His *choice* of the New Servant. God is proud to claim this person as His *"Elect One,"* the One whom He handpicked. Again, His choice of the Servant Nation of Israel had led to the disappointment we remember from the Parable of God's Vineyard (ch. 5). This time, rather than disappointment, God emphasizes that He is the One *"in whom My soul delights."*

Third, God affirms His *investment* in His New Servant. He endues Him with His Own Spirit—the Spirit of wisdom, understanding, counsel, might, knowledge, and fear of the Lord (11:2)—in order to *"bring forth justice"* based upon righteousness to the whole world, including the Gentiles. Israel, the Servant Nation, had also been chosen for the purpose of being the light of the world. Instead, they rejected the Spirit of the Lord, lost their purpose, and ended up being part of the darkness rather than serving as God's light. The New Servant, however, will be the shining light of God's redemptive purpose.

If history has an echo chamber in which God's words of the past reverberate into the future, we can hear the same affirmations at the time of Jesus' baptism. "You are My beloved Son, in whom I am well pleased" (Mark 1:11) carries the same claims of relationship, choice, and identification. As I wrote in *The Communicator's Commentary on Mark*, God said to His Son at the baptism, "You belong to Me, I love You, and I am proud of You." Is there any doubt that the New Servant in the Book of Isaiah is the Beloved Son in the Gospel of Mark?

DISTINGUISHING HIS CHARACTER (42:2–4)

After God's commitment comes a picture of the character of His Servant. By using the negative to describe what His Servant will *not* be like, God sets up the framework for a comparison with Cyrus, the Persian king, whom He has also called "My shepherd" (44:28). First, *He will not use His voice to establish His authority* (v. 2). We are all acquainted with persons who like to hear the sound of their own voices. Those who are visible public figures in high office are particularly vulnerable to the charge. They must be giving speeches, making pronouncements, and grabbing the headlines to retain their image of authority. An ancient king, such as Cyrus, would not have had the advantage of the mass media, but we can envision him riding at the forefront of his troops, shouting commands, or entering a city that he had conquered with a triumphant shout. God's New Servant, however, will *"not cry out, nor raise His voice, nor . . . be heard in the street"* (v. 2). Meekness is the word often used to summarize the way He will approach the world. Not to be confused with weakness, He will be stronger than the bombastic world leader because His authority is in His character more than in His command.

Second, *He will not use force to accomplish His purpose* (v. 3). A *"bruised reed"* is an analogy for persons who are weak and helpless; *"smoking flax"* represents persons who are broken and vulnerable. Whenever force is used to accomplish a purpose, violence spreads to innocent victims who are weak and vulnerable. In our century, the violence of warfare is most vividly seen in the pictures of the children of Hiroshima burned beyond recognition by nuclear fire, the brother and sister of Vietnam fleeing naked from napalm flames, and the bloodied boy of Yugoslavia who is denied medical aid as a victim of "ethnic cleansing." Cyrus, the conquering hero, left similar victims in the wake of his victories. In contrast, God's New Servant will turn the values of the world upside down by making the "bruised reed" of weak persons and the "smoking flax" of broken people His first priority. On His banner will be the motto "Justice for Truth" and the sign of His victories will be strength for the weak and healing for the broken.

Third, *He will not stop until His goal is achieved* (v. 4). Persistence is a virtue of effective leadership. Biographies of great leaders, such as Winston Churchill and Abraham Lincoln, reveal a history of failure and discouragement from which they had to recover on the way to success. In the end, they both died without knowing the outcome for which they gave themselves. Churchill saw victory in Europe, but he did not see the end of the Cold War. Lincoln, on the other hand, did not live to see victory for the North in the Civil War or the emancipation of the slaves in the South. Failure, discouragement, and death are part and parcel of the human condition. Cyrus, for instance, did not see his ambition to conquer the world fully realized and died under the judgment of God for the sin of pride. God's New Servant, however, will be the example of obedience that is persistent and consistent. Endued with the zeal of the energy of the Lord, he will not quit because of obstacles or give up because of exhaustion. Nor will He die until He has "finished the work" that His Father gave Him to do (John 17:4).

According to Isaiah, the New Servant's twofold goal is to set things right by bringing justice to the earth and teaching God's Law to the "coastlands" or the Gentiles (v. 4b). Although God has not yet shown Isaiah that His New Servant will achieve these goals through suffering, we already know that His work as a leader cannot be accomplished without sacrifice. The comparison with Cyrus stands out most forcibly at this point. Whereas Cyrus brought a measure of justice to his empire by law with his decree allowing deported people, including the Jews, to return to their homelands, God's New Servant will bring full justice to all the earth through grace and by the righteousness of His character. The difference, then, is most evident in the response of the "coastlands" or the Gentiles. They cowered in terror as they awaited the coming of Cyrus and his conquering horde, but they waited in hope for the coming of God's New Servant and His teaching of the Law.

EMPOWERING THE NEW SERVANT (42:5–13)

5 Thus says God the LORD,

Who created the heavens
    and stretched them out,
Who spread forth the earth
    and that which comes from it.
Who gives breath to the people on it,
And spirit to those who walk on it:
6 "I, the LORD, have called You in righteousness,
And will hold Your hand;
I will keep You and give You as a
    covenant to the people,
As a light to the Gentiles,
7 To open blind eyes,
To bring out prisoners from the prison,
Those who sit in darkness from the prison house.
8 I am the LORD, that is My name;
And My glory I will not give to another,
Nor My praise to graven images.
9 Behold, the former things have come to pass,
And new things I declare;
Before they spring forth
    I tell you of them."
10 Sing to the LORD a new song,
And His praise from the ends
    of the earth,
You who go down to the sea,
    and all that is in it,
You coastlands and you inhabitants of them!
11 Let the wilderness and its cities
    lift up their voice,
The villages that Kedar inhabits.
Let the inhabitants of Sela sing,
Let them shout from the top of the mountains.
12 Let them give glory to the LORD,
And declare His praise in the coastlands.
13 The LORD shall go forth
    like a mighty man;
He shall stir up His zeal
    like a man of war.
He shall cry out, yes, shout aloud;
He shall prevail against His enemies.

Isaiah 42:5–13

Both Cyrus and the New Servant were commissioned by God to be "anointed" instruments for the fulfillment of His purpose. In support of Cyrus, God gave him a sense of His judgment upon Babylon and a spirit of justice for the release of His people. Still, a certain distance remained between God and Cyrus, His instrument. The King of Persia permitted the worship of Yahweh, but never gave Him more than lip service; he obeyed God as an objective instrument obeys the hand that wields it, and his rule by force carried him to extremes for which he, too, was judged.

God's relationship to His New Servant is different in kind as well as degree. Under the aegis of His name Yahweh, or "I am the Lord," God defines His unique relationship as Creator, Caller, Caregiver, Covenant-keeper, and Commissioner to His New Servant. Out of this relationship comes the resources for the transformation of the *"new things"* that God will declare.

A NEW ENERGY (42:5)

It is one thing to be an obedient servant struggling in your own strength, and quite another to be empowered with the energy of the master to do the work of his bidding. God puts all of His energy as creator of the universe, maker of the earth, and giver of life to its inhabitants behind the work of His Servant. All things, then, become possible. No obstacle of environment, history, culture, or person can stand in the way of His creative purpose. Divine energy will fuel the zeal of the New Servant in His redemptive purpose just as God pursued so vigorously His judgment upon Babylon.

A NEW RIGHTEOUSNESS (42:6a)

The character of Cyrus was independent of his call to be the instrument of judgment upon Babylon. Although he could be characterized as an enlightened despot, he was still a pagan with dictatorial ways. For God's New Servant, however, character is the basis for the call. Personal righteousness will be consistent with social justice. Consequently, He will come with the promise of being more than an instrument in the hand of God. He will walk and serve hand in hand with God! Along with the energy of creation and the

439

righteousness of character, God will be the caregiver for His New Servant.

A NEW COVENANT (42:6b)

In the original covenant that God made with the children of Israel, He used words to state its premise and signs to seal its promise. Although the covenant is a relationship between friends rather than a contract between adversaries, both sides enjoy privileges and assume responsibilities. The people of Israel broke the covenant relationship and rejected their role as the Servant Nation by rebelling against God. He, however, never violated one word or promise that He had given to them. In fact, He announces in this passage that, rather than cancel the old covenant, He will give them a new covenant in the person of His New Servant. Such a commitment is unprecedented in human history; the Incarnation is prefigured among the "new things" that God will do.

A NEW CHARGE (42:6c–7)

Throughout the book of Isaiah, God has never wavered in His purpose to bring the light of truth to the Gentiles, to open their eyes, and set them free. Israel had been chosen as His Servant Nation to be the instrument for the accomplishment of His purpose. Disobedience had caused Israel to forfeit its role and lose its identity in exile. The charge, then, passed to God's New Servant. As with Israel, He too is called to righteousness, empowered to serve, and given as a covenant to the people for the specific purpose of succeeding where the Servant Nation had failed. Under commissioning by God, He will do the *"new thing."* His charge is to be the person who brings light to the Gentiles, who opens blind eyes to the truth and frees imprisoned souls from their bondage.

NEW THINGS (42:8–9)

To reinforce the revelation of His New Servant, God puts His character behind His promises. *"I am the LORD"* is a statement that defies all comparisons of name, glory, and praise (v. 8). On the basis of that name, God cries out *"Behold"* once again. As He introduced His New Servant with "behold" at the beginning of this chapter, so He now commands our attention to announce the *"new things"* that He will do. They are not new in the sense of being novelties or fads. Grounded in the proof that *"former things have come to pass,"* God promises to show through the prophecies of Isaiah the new things that He will do.

Technological advancement progresses on a *J* curve. At the bottom of the *J*, technological development moves slowly along a relatively flat line. But as a series of new inventions comes together, there is a breakthrough in technology that starts the *J* curve on the upward line. Discovery after discovery takes place with speeding development until a technological revolution has taken place. The microchip is an example. Computer technology struggled along a relatively flat line for years with huge mainframes and complicated wiring systems. With the discovery of the microchip, however, massive electronic circuits were reduced to microscopic dimensions. The breakthrough sped computer technology upward on the *J* line to a revolution in the industry with almost unlimited potential. God's "new things" are similar except in one phase. The new things are consistent with everything He has done or promised in the past, but, like the coming of the New Servant, there is a jump on the *J* curve where He breaks through with a miracle and springs upward with the miracle of the Incarnation.

A NEW SONG (42:10–13)

New things need a new song. When the announcement of the Servant peaked with God's declaration of *"new things"* that would *"spring forth,"* the prophet was already on the verge of singing. As he breaks forth in a hymn of praise to Yahweh, all of the ends of the earth are invited to join in the singing. The voices of the coastlands, in particular, are asked to join in the praise. Cyrus had struck terror into their hearts and stilled their singing, but announcement of God's New Servant is cause for singing. Joining with them will be sailors, nomads, villagers, and city dwellers from the sea to the wilderness and from the coastlands to the mountain top. The diversity itself will give the chorus a special sound as it sings glory to the Lord and praise to His name. With a roll of drums and fanfare of trumpets, the coastlands will know that the LORD of Hosts has gone to war on their behalf and prevailed against their common enemies (vv. 12–13).

A military air is not inconsistent with the graciousness of God's New Servant. In preparation for His coming, God will continue to work through Cyrus for the defeat of Babylon, archenemy of the nations. The *"zeal"* or energy that God will give to Him is at one and the same time justice for the weak and judgment for the wicked. We will better understand the dilemma of God's passion for justice and judgment as we hear Him speak from His own heart.

THE PASSION OF GOD (42:14–17)

14 "I have held My peace a long time,
   I have been still and restrained Myself.
   Now I will cry like a woman in labor,
   I will pant and gasp at once.
15 I will lay waste the mountains and hills,
   And dry up all their vegetation;
   I will make the rivers coastlands,
   And I will dry up the pools.
16 I will bring the blind by a way
      they did not know;
   I will lead them in paths
      they have not known.
   I will make darkness light before them,
   And crooked places straight.
   These things I will do for them,
   And not forsake them.
17 They shall be turned back,
   They shall be greatly ashamed,
   Who trust in carved images,
   Who say to the molded images,
   'You are our gods.'

Isaiah 42:14–17

Israel's fear that God had abandoned them in exile has been alleviated by words of comfort based upon the evidence of "former things that have come to pass" or the proof that He is the Lord of history. Objective evidence now gives way to an insight into God's personal involvement in the suffering of His children. Like a parent whose heart is torn by a prodigal child, the Lord speaks to us from the depths of His soul. In earlier chapters we learned of His eternal power and wisdom. Now, we learn of His eternal passion. God too has feelings.

THE PAIN OF PATIENCE (42:14)

God's first desire is to fulfill His redemptive purpose. While His holiness required judgment against sin, He had to restrain Himself from speeding the time line for the deliverance of His people. For those of us who are Type A personalities and driven by the tyranny of time, we understand the pain of God's impatience. Perhaps the greatest frustration is to wait until a process is complete, or people are ready, before taking action. It is much easier to short-circuit the process or bypass the people to get the job done. Yet, maturity of leadership will tolerate the pain of patience in order to assure the larger purpose and the higher good.

Likening His long period of waiting to a woman coming to full term in her pregnancy, God says, *"Now, I will cry like a woman in labor, I will pant and gasp at once"* (v. 14b). These words are freighted with meaning that ripples through the ages and into eternity. Most immediately, they mean that God suffers when we suffer. Israel assumed that they suffered all alone in exile. "No," according to God, "I have suffered with you through the humiliation of deportation and the persecution of exile. You thought that I had abandoned you, but in truth, I felt with you every sign of humiliation and every stab of pain."

God's sensitivity to pain is just as all-feeling as His strength is all-powerful and His knowledge is all-wise. To think that He not only suffers with us but feels our pain even more deeply than we do is demonstrated by Christ's suffering in the Garden of Gethsemane. When He struggled with the decision of the cross, His agony is an emotion best described as the anguish that tears apart the soul, and His sweat becoming like "great drops of blood" is a physical reaction of intense pain. For God to *"cry," "pant,"* and *"gasp"* like a woman in labor over the suffering of His people in exile expresses the same sensitivity of soul that Christ experienced in His passion.

In addition to the words of comfort for the children of Israel, God's participation in pain introduces Isaiah's new theological theme of the

Suffering Servant. Earlier Old Testament theology established the truth that "without the shedding of blood, there is no remission of sins." Animal sacrifices served as the means for forgiveness in the worship of the Israelites. But now God lifts the curtain of revelation to reveal that He too suffers. From here, the curtain will rise again to show that God's redemptive purpose will mean that His Servant must suffer and die for the sins of the world. Although we are ahead of our story, Isaiah is known for introducing a theological theme that he expands in detail in a later prophecy.

THE INITIATIVE OF LOVE (42:15–17)

God is a doer. He does not speak the passion of His love without following with action. True to form, He gives His weak and weary children in exile the promise that He will take the initiative in their return to Jerusalem. Exercising the power of miracles, He will clear the way of obstacles, lead the way along unknown paths, light the way for their walk, and stay with them all the way to their destination. With such a gracious promise for the children of Israel and all future generations of spiritual exiles who want to return home, we can understand why God also says that those *"who trust in carved images"* will be turned back and made *"greatly ashamed."* Only the living Lord can take the initiative of love.

THE TRIAL OF ISRAEL (42:18–25)

18 "Hear, you deaf;
   and look, you blind, that you may see.
19 Who is blind but My servant,
   Or deaf as My messenger whom I send?
   Who is blind as he who is perfect,
   And blind as the LORD's servant?
20 Seeing many things,
      but you do not observe;
   Opening the ears,
      but he does not hear."
21 The LORD is well pleased for His righteousness' sake;
   He will magnify the law
      and make it honorable.

22 But this is a people robbed
    and plundered;
   All of them are snared in holes,
   And they are hidden in prison houses;
   They are for prey, and no one delivers;
   For plunder, and no one says, "Restore!"
23 Who among you will give ear to this?
   Who will listen and hear for the time to come?
24 Who gave Jacob for plunder,
    and Israel to the robbers?
   Was it not the LORD,
   He against whom we have sinned?
   For they would not walk in His ways,
   Nor were they obedient to His law.
25 Therefore He has poured on him the fury of His anger
   And the strength of battle;
   It has set him on fire all around,
   Yet he did not know;
   And it burned him,
   Yet he did not take it to heart.

Isaiah 42:18–25

Against the obedience and the faithfulness of God's New Servant, Israel must be called to judgment for its failure to fulfill its calling as God's Servant Nation. Another trial scene comes before us as God summons the court, makes His case, invites interrogation, and pronounces the verdict. Coming full cycle to the first session of the cosmic court in Isaiah 1:2, God again brings His own children before the judgment bar. In the first session, God indicted His children for rebellion; in this session, He charges them with being blind and deaf to the truth, which, in turn, caused them to fail as His chosen people and His servant nation.

THE SUMMONS OF ISRAEL (42:18–20)

"Hear, you deaf; and look, you blind" is God's summons to Israel for trial. Isaiah had been faithful to his prophetic calling. Yet, as God had told him at the time of his commissioning, the people closed their eyes and stopped their ears as he spoke. By rejecting the prophet's message, they disobeyed the Word of God and denied their Servant

role. A blind servant whose duty is to see, and a deaf messenger with the responsibility to hear, are doubly useless, especially if the blindness and the deafness is self-imposed.

THE CASE AGAINST ISRAEL (42:21–22)

Israel's sin of refusing to hear God's Word and see God's vision is aggravated by comparison with the obedience of the New Servant. In contrast with the Lord's disappointment at the rebellion of His children and their refusal to honor His Law, He is well-pleased with the character of righteousness and the spirit of justice exemplified by His New Servant (v. 21). Consequently, their own stubbornness left God no alternative but to let them be plundered, robbed, trapped, and deported without an apparent sign of hope (v. 22).

THE INTERROGATION OF ISRAEL (42:23–24)

Before summarizing His case, God stops to ask questions of the defendants. "Is anyone willing to listen?" "Does anyone understand?" "Will anyone confess their sin?" "Will anyone acknowledge the God of the house of Jacob, the Holy One of Israel, the LORD of Hosts?" Silence follows. No one will walk in His ways, and no one will be obedient to His Word. The court awaits the verdict.

THE VERDICT AGAINST ISRAEL (42:25)

For those who asked the question "Why should Israel be sent into exile?" the answer has been given. Despite all that God could do to nourish them as children and warn them of judgment for their sins, they persisted in being blind and deaf. *"Therefore He has poured on him the fury of His anger and the strength of the battle; it has set him on fire all around, yet he did not know; and it burned him, yet he did not take it to heart"* (v. 25). Sad words, indeed, because they carry double meaning for those whom God has called as His servants. For the Servant Nation of Israel, the fury of His anger has come down upon them and they still do not know or understand what it means. For the Servant Person whom He has called, it means that the fury of God's anger will be vented on Him for the sins of the people. Out of the trial of Israel will come the theme of the Suffering Servant.

THE ROOTS OF REDEMPTION (43:1–28)

1 But now, thus says the LORD, who created you, O Jacob,
And He who formed you, O Israel:
"Fear not, for I have redeemed you;
I have called you by your name;
You are Mine,

2 When you pass through the waters,
    I will be with you;
And through the rivers,
    they shall not overflow you.
When you walk through the fire,
    you shall not be burned,
Nor shall the flame scorch you.

3 For I am the LORD your God,
The Holy One of Israel, your Savior;
I gave Egypt for your ransom,
Ethiopia and Seba in your place.

4 Since you were precious in My sight,
You have been honored,
And I have loved you;
Therefore I will give men for you,
And people for your life.

5 Fear not, for I am with you;
I will bring your descendants
    from the east,
And gather you from the west;

6 I will say to the north, 'Give them up!'
And to the south,
    'Do not keep them back!'
Bring My sons from afar,
And My daughters from the ends of the earth—

7 Everyone who is called by My name,
Whom I have created for My glory;
I have formed him,
    yes, I have made him."

8 Bring out the blind people
    who have eyes,
And the deaf who have ears.

9 Let all the nations be gathered together,
And let the people be assembled.
Who among them can declare this,

And show us former things?
Let them bring out their witnesses,
    that they may be justified;
Or let them hear and say, "It is truth."

10 "You are My witnesses," says the LORD,
"And My servant whom I have chosen,
That you may know and believe Me,
And understand that I am He.
Before Me there was no God formed,
Nor shall there be after Me.

11 I, even I, am the LORD.
And besides Me there is no savior.

12 I have declared and saved,
I have proclaimed,
And there was no foreign god among you;
Therefore you are My witnesses."
Says the LORD, "that I am God.

13 Indeed before the day was, I am He;
And there is no one who can deliver out of My hand;
I work and who will reverse it?"

14 Thus says the LORD, your Redeemer,
The Holy One of Israel;
"For your sake I will send to Babylon,
And bring them all down as fugitives—
The Chaldeans, who rejoice in their ships.

15 I am the LORD, your Holy One,
The Creator of Israel, your King."

16 Thus says the LORD,
    who makes a way in the sea
And a path through the mighty waters,

17 Who brings forth the chariot and horse,
The army and the power
(They shall lie down together,
    they shall not rise;
They are extinguished,
    they are quenched like a wick):

18 "Do not remember the former things,
Nor consider the things of old.

19 Behold, I will do a new thing,
Now it shall spring forth;
Shall you not know it?
I will even make a road in the wilderness

And rivers in the desert.
20 The beast of the field will honor Me,
    The jackals and the ostriches,
    Because I give waters in the wilderness
    And rivers in the desert,
    To give drink to My people,
        My chosen.
21 This people I have formed for Myself;
    They shall declare My praise.
22 "But you have not called upon Me,
        O Jacob;
    And you have been weary of Me,
        O Israel.
23 You have not brought Me the sheep
        for your burnt offerings,
    Nor have you honored Me
        with your sacrifices.
    I have not caused you to serve
        with grain offerings,
    Nor wearied you with incense.
24 You have bought Me no sweet cane with money,
    Nor have you satisfied Me
        with the fat of your sacrifices;
    But you have burdened Me
        with your sins,
    You have wearied Me
        with your iniquities.
25 "I, even I, am He who blots out your transgressions for
        My own sake;
    And I will not remember your sins.
26 Put Me in remembrance;
    Let us contend together;
    State your case,
        that you may be acquitted.
27 Your first father sinned,
    And your mediators have transgressed against Me.
28 Therefore I will profane the princes of the sanctuary;
    I will give Jacob to the curse,
    And Israel to reproaches.

                                        Isaiah 43:1–28

"But now" is God's way of drawing the contrast between His condemnation of Israel at the end of chapter 42 and His promise of "new things" as a word of comfort to His people. The two radically opposed themes are not inconsistent with the character of God. As Isaiah has taught us, His punishment and His promise are two sides of the same coin. His holiness requires punishment for sin, and His love will not let Him give up on the sinner. "But now" also reveals the ultimate purpose of God. Even though His people have been condemned to exile because of their sins, He is constantly at work on their redemption so that they fulfill their destiny as "light of the world." This chapter teaches us that whatever God does, He is always moving toward our redemption. "But now" is the word of transition between the truth of God's fury against sin (42:25) and the truth of His desire to redeem (43:1). For a moment at least, we turn the pages from the Old Testament to the New Testament and find in this chapter the theological roots of our Christian faith.

THE NEW CREATION (43:1)

What God did in the first creation, He will now do in a new creation with His people of Israel. In fact, He will go beyond the first creation by bringing the creative cycle to its perfection. He says to Israel, "I *created* you, *formed* you, *redeemed* You, and *named* you because *You are Mine."* In the capsule of one verse, the theology of redemption is complete. As God called the earth into existence and then gave it form, so He created Jacob as a body and shaped it into the nation of Israel. This is where the first creation stops. Even though sin contaminated natural creation, it still awaits its day of redemption when God will create the new heavens and a new earth. For Israel, God has advanced the day of its redemption as a promise for the future of all humankind and the natural order. God's naming of Israel is also a special act of His new creation. Like a father and mother giving their child its name at the time of dedication or baptism, God gives Israel His own name as members of the family. To be named the "children of God" reveals a family relationship not unlike Christians who are members of the Body of Christ. "You are Mine" is God's word of comfort that Israel neither deserved nor expected. As with us, only grace can redeem, and only love can give a name.

450

We should not be surprised by the love story that follows the creation cycle. With God willing to claim Israel as His kin, it is natural that He will be present with them through every crisis of life. Reminiscent of His promise to the exiles coming out of Egypt, God assures Israel of His personal presence. Whether through waters that might over-whelm them, rivers that might sweep them away, fire that might consume them, or flames that might scorch, God says *"I will be with you"* (v. 2a).

A love story comes to mind. Several years ago, a carload of Campus Crusade staffers were swept away to their death in the flash flood of the Thompson River in Colorado. One of the staffers was Kathy Loomis, daughter of Charles Loomis who was Chairman of the Board of Loomis Armored Cars in Seattle, Washington. Two or three weeks after the tragedy I met Chuck in the lobby of a downtown hotel. Black circles ringed sad eyes that stared at me as we met. When I expressed my grief and assured him of my prayers, Chuck pulled words from his broken heart that will never be forgotten. "Dave," he said, "the hurt goes deep, but God's love goes deeper."

God gave the same promise to Israel. They would not be immune to trial and tragedy as they passed through waters, rivers, fire, and flames, but they would know that He was with them and that His love would go deeper than their hurt. When God says, *"Fear not,"* He means it.

Isaiah slips into legal language when he uses the term *"ransom"* (vv. 3–4). A strict business transaction for the freedom of slaves is implied when God says, *"I gave Egypt for your ransom, Ethiopia and Seba in your place"* (v. 3b). In our day, we have developed a distaste for the Iran-Contra Affair in which highly-placed officials secretly traded guns as ransom for hostages. Unless we see *ransom* in its redemptive context, the same distaste will be in our mouth as we think about God trading people for people.

When the legal language of ransom is elevated to the spiritual meaning of redemption, we understand that Isaiah is giving Israel an understandable analogy to let them know how much they mean to God. Egypt, Ethiopia, and Seba represent a way of saying that Israel is worth more than the whole world to God. Certainly, this is the meaning when God goes on to say, *"You were precious in My sight, you have been honored, and I have loved you"* (v. 4). No price of ransom is too high for members of our family who are precious, honored, and loved.

THE NEW GATHERING (43:5–7)

As further proof of God's loving relationship with His children, the promise of redemption includes the world's greatest family reunion. Due to a worldwide dispersal of its people, Israel had lost its identity as a nation. "But now" God will fulfill His promise and bring His family home from east, west, north, and south—every corner of the earth.

Literally, the gathering of God's family may stretch in meaning from the return of the exiles from Babylon to the contemporary Zionist movement that brings Jews from across the earth to their homeland in Israel. Militancy and violence, however, have no place in God's plan for the homecoming. When He calls His sons and daughters home, He means those who are called by His name and created for His glory (v. 7). To bear His Name and give Him the glory assumes personal righteousness and social justice that leaves no room for vicious motives and inhuman acts.

THE NEW WITNESS (43:8–13)

Isaiah returns to the familiar scene of the cosmic court where God summons the nations of the world to stand trial. An edge of sarcasm is evident in the courtroom when God calls blind and deaf people to see and hear the case of the false gods versus Yahweh. The implication is that even those who cannot see or hear know that the argument for false gods is pointless. Issuing again the invitation to rebuttal, God asks for any witness among the assembled nations who can testify to the fact that the idols made by human hands can predict the future. The real contest, then, is between Yahweh, the Creator, and idols, the created.

When no witness comes forward, God calls His new witness to the stand—none other than Israel itself. As the Servant Nation created and formed by God, Israel will witness to the fact that it knows, believes, and understands that *"I am He"* is uncreated and unequaled (v. 10). Furthermore, Israel will testify to the truth that He, and He alone, can deliver them from exile and save them from their sins (v. 11). Best of all, what God declares, He will do (v. 12). Israel, out of the experience of exile, is firsthand evidence that no foreign gods can make that claim.

To sum up His case, God points one more time to Israel and declares, *"Therefore, you are My witnesses . . . that I am God"* (v. 12b). Such confidence must be based upon redemptive power. Israel has been rebellious, unfaithful, and embarrassing to God. Yet, He is willing to risk His case upon human beings who are redeemed. Pastors often tell the story of Jesus returning to heaven and telling the archangel that He left Peter and the disciples with the responsibility for communicating the gospel to the world. Skeptically, the archangel asks, "But if they fail, do you have other plans?" Jesus answers with confidence, "No, I have no other plans." God's confidence in Israel, the disciples, and the Church today is based on the fact that He has no other plans.

THE NEW EXODUS (43:14–21)

Emphatically now, God comes before Israel as its Lord, Redeemer, and Holy One. Power, salvation, and holiness belong uniquely and unequivocally to Him. Having distinguished Himself from false gods by predicting the future and then bringing history to pass, He now illustrates His claim by announcing a new exodus. As the nemesis of Israel and the obstacle to His purpose, Babylon must fall before deliverance can begin. God leaves no doubt about the downfall of the evil empire. He foresees the crack troops of Babylon running like fugitives until they reach the distant sea and taking to ships with a sigh of relief (v. 14b).

History may have repeated itself in Operation Desert Storm. When Saddam Hussein sent his crack regiments, the Republican Guard, into battle against the American and allied forces, they fled in panic or surrendered in fear. News media showed before and after shots of Hussein's troops. Before the battle, they marched with spit and polish precision in front of the reviewing stand of the dictator. After the battle, they shuffled through the desert sand with their hands on their heads and defeat in their eyes. If a newscaster had been present when Cyrus swept down upon Babylon, the picture might have looked the same.

Deliverance for Israel follows the downfall of Babylon. Punctuating each of His promises to do "new things" with such a powerful declaration as, *"I am the LORD, your Holy One, the Creator of Israel, your King"* (v. 15), God proceeds to announce a new exodus. Reminding His children that He made a way through the sea and a path through the waters in the first Exodus and then closed the waters to drown the pursuing armies of Egypt, God dares to publish the word of a new exodus. Always before, He had told His children to remember the deliverance of their forefathers and foremothers from bondage in Egypt. While it is still good to remember the past, God tells them He will do a "new thing" that they will know for themselves.

Again, the theology of redemption comes to the forefront. When the truth is put in a quip, we say "God has no grandchildren." We mean that redemption cannot be inherited, it must be experienced. God promises the children of Israel their own deliverance from bondage. He will make a road in the wilderness for them to walk, rivers in the desert for them to drink, and safety from wild animals for them to travel. Why? The theme of the new creation comes back, *"This people I have formed for Myself; they shall declare My praise"* (v. 21). No longer needing to look back upon history as proof of God's covenant with them, the new exodus would write a new script for their journey of faith.

THE NEW MERCY (43:22–28)

As quickly as a change of sets in a dramatic performance, the scene changes again. Although God is pledged to deliver His people in the new exodus, the fact remains that they are still disobedient and unfaithful. The Lord reaches deeply into His own heart again to confess that Israel has burdened and wearied Him with their stubborn rejection of His love. A series of "nots" sets up the negative nature of their response to Him. They have *not* called upon Him in prayer, brought to Him their tithes and offerings, honored Him with acceptable sacrifices in worship, offered Him the sweet spirit of gratitude along with their money, or honored Him with the abundance of their sacrifices. In other words, their heart was not in their ritual, and their spirit was not in their sacrifices. Yet, God had never asked too much of them. His burden was easy and His yoke was light. But they had put upon Him the burden of their sins and the weariness of their iniquities (v.

24b). The role of servant had been reversed. Israel had been called of God to be His Servant Nation. They were not "caused to serve" Him, but given the choice of free will. When they chose to rebel, the burden of their sin shifted to God and He became their servant. With all of the profound truth of the New Testament theology of redemption, we sense the cross that God is already carrying.

Love is full of surprises. Just when Isaiah takes us to the edge of hopelessness, God has another "new thing" for us to hear. With all of the love of His being, He declares, *"I, even I, am He who blots out your transgressions for My own sake; and I will not remember your sins"* (v. 25). How can this be? Israel deserves the unrequited wrath of God for burdening Him with its sins and wearying Him with its iniquities. All of the ransom of Egypt, Ethiopia, and Seba will not pay the debt. Nothing but grace—the unmerited favor of God—can explain God's declaration of new mercy for His people. This truth is reinforced by the reality that God forgives sins for His sake, not for ours. Forgiveness is in the nature of God's character. To blot out transgressions and forget sin is absolutely contrary to human nature. As a perceptive child put it, "If I were God and had been treated the way He has been treated, I'd have kicked this old world to pieces a long time ago." We know how the child felt. It is hard for us to forgive and even harder to forget those who sin against us. The world can be thankful that we are not God.

One more reversal closes God's case. Returning again to legal language in a courtroom setting, God urges Israel to produce any evidence of merit by which the nation should be acquitted by law rather than forgiven by grace. Hearing no response, God rules from the bench that sin has been present among His people from the time of their first father Abraham and throughout their history in the priests and princes of the nation. For this reason, His children must understand why the punishment of exile was necessary and why the forgiveness of sins is a "new thing."

CHAPTER TWENTY-ONE

Saga of Salvation

Isaiah 44:1–45:25

As Israel rises in the glory of God's promise of "new things," Babylon looms against the horizon as the major obstacle to the fulfillment of His promise. Building upon the proof that Yahweh is the Lord of History and Israel is His Servant Nation, Isaiah turns his attention to the downfall of Babylon and its false gods under the hand of Cyrus, the pagan king, who is strangely and wondrously anointed by God as "My shepherd."

REAFFIRMING HIS PROMISES (44:1–5)

1 "Yet hear now, O Jacob My servant,
And Israel whom I have chosen.
2 Thus says the LORD who made you
And formed you from the womb,
    who will help you:
'Fear not, O Jacob My servant;
And you, Jeshurun,
    whom I have chosen.
3 For I will pour water on him
    who is thirsty,
And floods on the dry ground;
I will pour My Spirit on your descendants,
And My blessing on your offspring;
4 They will spring up among the grass
Like willows by the watercourses.'
5 "One will say, 'I am the LORD's';
Another will call himself
    by the name of Jacob;

Another will write with his hand,
'The LORD's.'
And name himself
by the name of Israel.

Isaiah 44:1–5

GAMBLING ON GRACE (44:1)

At the close of Isaiah 43, God had rested His case against Israel. In the court of divine law, every shred of evidence pointed to the verdict *guilty* and justified the sentence of exile in the land of Babylon. "But now, listen," God says. In one short phrase, the contrast of the ages is drawn. From the heights of divine justice we see the depths of divine love.

Like the father of a prodigal son who receives the son home with open arms, God sums up His forgiving love in the names, *"O Jacob, My servant, and Israel whom I have chosen."* Jacob is the esteemed family name that God still honors. But with even greater honor, He still claims the house of Jacob as *"My servant."* Despite their sin, God is willing to risk His witness of servanthood in the world upon the lineage of a redeemed scallywag. And God is not yet done. He also reclaims their national name *"Israel"* and dares to add *"whom I have chosen."*

Carl F. Henry, the prominent theologian, once said that God is history's greatest gambler. He staked the salvation of the world upon a carpenter and twelve fishermen. Centuries before the incarnation, however, God shows us His willingness to gamble upon a rebellious people who are still capable of being redeemed. To call the rebel house of Jacob "My servant," and claim the exiled nation of Israel as the one "whom I have chosen" is a gamble against all odds—until you consider the intervention of divine grace.

POURING OUT HIS BLESSING (44:2–4)

God's generosity can never be matched. For the fear-filled people of Israel, He repeats again and again the assurances that He created them, shaped them, and will help them (v. 2a). To seal this vow, God calls Israel by the name that He gave to Moses along with His original promise to His people but has held in reserve until this time. The

Lord says, *"Fear not O Jacob My servant; and you, Jeshurun, whom I have chosen"* (v. 2b). In Moses' valedictory address to the whole assembly of Israel just before he died, he recited the words of the song that traced God's relationship with Israel from promise to punishment and back to promise again. *Jeshurun* is a name of endearment that God gives to His people whom He nourished and enriched with His love. But alas, "Jeshurun grew fat and kicked, you grew fat, you grew thick, you are covered with fat; then he forsook God who made him, and scornfully esteemed the Rock of his Salvation" (Deuteronomy 32:15).

Only one hope remains. After Moses blesses the tribes of Israel in his final words, he leaves them with a promise:

> There is no one like the God of Jeshurun,
> Who rides the heavens to help you, . . .
>
> The eternal God is your refuge,
> And underneath are the everlasting arms; . . .
>
> Then Israel shall dwell in safety,
> The fountain of Jacob alone,
> In the land of grain and new wine; . . .
>
> Happy are you, O Israel!
> Who is like you,
> people saved by the LORD,
> The shield of your help
> And the sword of your majesty!
>
> *Deuteronomy 33:26–29*

How many times had the children of Israel in exile wistfully sung this Song of Moses? The name "Jeshurun" would be an instant cue that God had a special message for them. Like a hymn, song, or chorus that is given to us by the Spirit of God in moments of deep distress, the children of Israel would begin humming the tune and singing the verse with new hope for their deliverance.

Is it any wonder that Isaiah 44:3–4 has inspired memorable songs of hope throughout the centuries. Even now, if Isaiah is quoted, "For I will pour water on him who is thirsty, And floods upon the dry ground," we start to hum the familiar tune of the chorus and add the verse, "Open your heart for the gift I am bringing, while you are seeking Me I will be found." With the promise of the outpouring of the Spirit, the water of salvation can still turn the dry ground of sin into a field of green grass with willows beside the coursing streams (v. 4).

NAMING HIS CHILDREN (44:5)

In response to God's blessing, the children of Israel will reclaim the names that identify their special relationship to God. What is in a name? A name not only gives us our identity, it tells to whom we belong. After the outpouring of the Spirit of God upon them, the Israelites would proudly take four names that linked them to God. First and foremost, they would take the *spiritual name*, "I am the LORD's." No doubt remains. To say, "I am the LORD's" is to tell the whole world whom you trust, whom you obey, and whom you serve. Second, the Israelites will reclaim the *parental name* of their father Jacob. No longer will they be ashamed of their parentage. As members of the family in the house of Jacob, they will confess at a time when, like their father, they were deceitful and unredeemed. But also like their father, during the exile they had wrestled with God and met Him face to face. Now, with pride, they announce to the world that they too are part of redemptive history and lineage through which the Messiah will come. Third, the Israelites will take the *relational name* of "love" and write it on their hands. In the cultural context of Isaiah's time, young lovers printed the name of the one they loved on the palm of their hand with indelible ink. Today, young lovers wear halves of gold hearts around their neck with the name of their lover inscribed on the back so that all will know to whom they have given their heart. Likewise, the Israelites would be equally quick to identify with the lover of God who opens the hand to reveal the name "*The LORD's*." Although tattoos are distasteful to most of us, we might imagine an Israelite having the name of the Lord etched in the skin to show the permanence of his love. Fourth, the exiles in Babylon would reclaim their *national name* as "*Israel*." During their captivity, they had become a people without a name. Their history was almost forgotten, their homeland was gone, and their future appeared to be hopeless. To retake the name "Israel" is to reclaim their identity as the servant nation chosen by God to be the "light of the world."

All of God's promises come into focus in these four names. By returning to God and trusting in Him, a hapless and hopeless people will be restored in spiritual faith, parental pride, relational love, and national purpose. The same promises are open to any nation, church, or person wallowing in the dust of decline. With the outpouring of God's spirit, there will be water for the thirsty and floods upon the dry ground.

RECALLING HIS NAME (44:6–8)

6 "Thus says the LORD, the King of Israel,
　And his Redeemer, the LORD of hosts:
　'I am the First and I am the Last;
　Besides Me there is no God.
7 And who can proclaim as I do?
　Then let him declare it
　　and set it in order for Me,
　Since I appointed the ancient people.
　And the things that are coming and shall come,
　Let them show these to them.
8 Do not fear, nor be afraid;
　Have I not told you from that time,
　　and declared it?
　You are My witnesses.
　Is there a God besides Me?
　Indeed there is no other Rock;
　I know not one.'"

Isaiah 44:6–8

Isaiah's prophetic rhythm continues to move from the grace notes of redemption to the minor chords of judgment. Dominance, however, belongs on the side of the oracles of salvation in chapters 40–66. In fact, when the oracles of judgment are sounded against Babylon in the next few chapters, it is always in the context of God's salvation for Israel and the world.

GOD'S NAME (44:6a)

We stand on the bridge between Israel's redemption and Babylon's downfall in Isaiah verses 6–8. The character of God is again the base upon which the bridge is built. He is the God whom the heathen call "LORD" (44:5) and He is the God who challenges the folly of worshiping idols (44:9–23). By now, His titles are familiar to us. We have met Him as the "LORD" of history, the "King of Israel," the "Redeemer" of His children, and the conquering "LORD of Hosts." Each of them has been declared by God, tested in the cosmic court, and witnessed by Israel in its past and current history.

GOD'S NEW NAMES (44:6b–7)

To these familiar names, God gives Himself two new names. He says, *"I am the First and I am the Last"* (v. 6b). All eternity is encompassed in this title and all of time and space, humanity and history become His footstool. Reaching back to the opening verse of Genesis, "In the beginning, God" and forward to the end of time, we hear the voice declaring, "I am the Alpha and the Omega, the Beginning and the End" (Revelation 21:6). A direct challenge to the idols of Babylon is forecast in this name. As in earlier challenges, God asks, *"And who can proclaim as I do?"* If idols can speak, let them make their declaration. If they can foresee the future, let them show *"things that are coming and shall come"* (v. 7). "I am the First and I am the Last" is the name of God with which the idols must contend.

GOD'S NEW NAME FOR ISRAEL (44:8)

Turning then to Israel, God gives Himself a name especially for them. With double emphasis now, He says to them for the fourth time, *"Do not fear, nor be afraid"* (v. 8a). Behind this assurance is the second new name that God gives Himself. He is their *"Rock"*—meaning the immovable object in the midst of a stormy sea or a weary land. With their father David, Israel could now sing, "The LORD is my rock and my fortress and my deliverer; My God, my strength, in whom I will trust" (Psalm 18:2–3a). What more comfort can God give to His children? By His grace He is their Redeemer, and by His strength He is their Rock.

ASSERTING HIS SOVEREIGNTY (44:9–20)

9 Those who make a graven image,
       all of them are useless,
    And their precious things shall not profit;

They are their own witnesses;
They neither see nor know,
    that they may be ashamed.

10 Who would form a god or cast a graven image
That profits him nothing?

11 Surely all his companions would be ashamed;
And the workmen, they are mere men.
Let them all be gathered together,
Let them stand up;
Yet they shall fear,
They shall be ashamed together.

12 The blacksmith with the tongs works one in the coals,
Fashions it with hammers,
And works it with the strength of his arms.
Even so, he is hungry,
    and his strength fails;
He drinks no water and is faint.

13 The craftsman stretches out his rule,
He marks one out with chalk;
He fashions it with a plane,
He marks it out with the compass,
And makes it like the figure of a man,
According to the beauty of a man,
    that it may remain in the house.

14 He hews down cedars for himself,
And takes the cypress and the oak;
He secures it for himself among the trees of the forest.
He plants a pine,
    and the rain nourishes it.

15 Then it shall be for a man to burn,
For he will take some of it
    and warm himself;
Yes, he kindles it and bakes bread;
Indeed he makes a god
    and worships it;
He makes it a carved image,
    and falls down to it.

16 He burns half of it in the fire;
With this half he eats meat;
He roasts a roast, and is satisfied.
He even warms himself and says,
"Ah! I am warm,

I have seen the fire."
17 And the rest of it he makes into a god,
His carved image.
He falls down before it
and worships it,
Prays to it and says,
"Deliver me, for you are my god."
18 They do not know nor understand;
For He has shut their eyes,
so that they cannot see,
And their hearts,
so that they cannot understand.
19 And no one considers in his heart,
Nor is there knowledge
nor understanding to say,
"I have burned half of it in the fire,
Yes, I have also baked bread on its coals:
I have roasted meat and eaten it;
And shall I make the rest of it an abomination?
Shall I fall down before a block of wood?"
20 He feeds on ashes;
A deceived heart has turned him aside;
And he cannot deliver his soul,
Nor say, "Is there not a lie in my right hand?"

Isaiah 44:9–20

Two trials involving idolatry have already been held in Isaiah's prophecy. In chapter 40:18–23, nations that worshiped stood before the bar of justice in the cosmic court. Then, in chapter 42:21–29, the false gods themselves had to stand trial. In each case, the verdict turned on God's questions, "To whom then will you liken God? Or what likeness will you compare to Him?" (40:18). Out of these trials came the verdict that idols are worthless and their worshipers are foolish. But even more important, the verdict confirmed God's declaration, "I am He"—immortal, invisible, and incomparable (41:4b). In the confidence of this declaration, He has predicted and performed before Israel as its King and Redeemer and before both Israel and the world as Lord of History and Lord of Hosts (44:6). False gods and their worshipers, however, stood dumb and without anyone to witness for them. Now, the makers of idols are addressed by God.

Another trial scene before the cosmic court is not pictured, but rather, God is directly addressing Israel in a speech with a very specific intention. By describing how the idols are made, He wants to show the folly of them in order to assure Israel that He and He alone has the power to deliver His children from Babylon.

Why does God give so much attention to idolaters, idols, and idol making as part of the salvation oracles? One answer is that Babylon had the reputation as the world center of idol making and idol worship. The same exquisite construction that went into the palaces and gardens of the city went into the idols as well. Israel would have been awed by the sight of these statues standing in public squares and being carried at the head of triumphal marches of the victorious Babylonian armies. Moreover, we know that the children in exile had contaminated their worship of Yahweh with prayers and offerings to these idols (Jeremiah 50:38). Although they might have rationalized their actions by saying that they had not broken the first commandment because they still kept Yahweh first or the second commandment because they had not made the idols themselves, God would not accept their feeble logic. If the nature of this speech is any indicator, idolatry among Israel was a major problem with which God had to deal. Yet, making idols is so fraught with folly that it does not deserve the logic of a legal trial. God only needs to laugh idolatry out of court by showing the absurdities of idol making.

HOW CAN USELESS IMAGES BE PRECIOUS? (44:9–11)

"Precious things" is a play on words by God. In the minds of His hearers, He is referring back to His word of love to Israel, "you were precious in My sight" (43:4) and His name of endearment for Israel, "Jeshurun" or darling (44:2b). The contrast between people and statues is obvious. Human beings are endowed with intrinsic value by their creation as persons in the image of God. Statues, however, have no value in themselves because they have neither life nor personality. Their only value is instrumental, meaning their usefulness. Measured against this standard, they become *"their own witnesses."* Gods are expected to see and know, but when the graven images stand with sightless eyes and silent tongues, they testify to their own uselessness. With their makers, they are *"ashamed together"* (v. 11b). The

absurdity is obvious in God's question of the idol makers, *"Who would form a god or cast a graven image that profits him nothing?"* (44:10).

HOW CAN THE CREATOR BE HUNGRY AND THIRSTY? (44:12)

Building on the ludicrous with an edge of sarcasm, God advances the comparison between Himself as Creator and the idol makers as human craftsmen. The question is, "How can the creator of idols feel hunger, thirst, and fatigue while making the image of a god who never gets hungry, thirsty, and tired?" As Creator of the universe, Yahweh never needed food or water to revive His strength. His resources are inexhaustible.

HOW CAN PHYSICAL MATERIAL BE TRANSFORMED INTO A GOD? (44:13–17)

More detail is given about idol making as the craftsman goes about the painstaking work of creating an idol that is an exact replica of human features, a beautiful image of human personality, and a handhewn product made of the best woods of the forest. But before beginning his work, the craftsman confronts a dilemma. The same wood that is best for making idols is also the best kindling for a fire to bake bread. A clash comes between human hungers: physical hunger for food and spiritual hunger for God. To resolve the dilemma, the craftsman uses half the wood for baking bread and half for making an idol. Folly builds upon folly when the craftsman first fills his stomach, warms his hands over the fire, and expresses gratitude for its glow (v. 16). Second priority for the use of the wood is given to carving an idol. After it is complete, the craftsman bows before it with prayer, *"Deliver me, for you are my god"* (v. 17). In the numbing silence that follows, the craftsman should know that the wood in the fire served him better than the wood in the idol.

Hidden in the parable of the craftsman is the fundamental question, "How can a human being create a subhuman object out of physical matter and transform it into a superhuman god?" The question exposes the absurdity of idols and the stupidity of the idol maker.

HOW CAN A BLIND, DEAF, AND DUMB STATUE BE A WITNESS? (44:18–20)

God's speech culminates in the expectation that a god will have a witness for his words and deeds among his worshipers. Because the false gods have not predicted the future or performed miraculous works, their representation in graven images is the only witness that can be called. Statues, however, do not know, understand, see, hear, or think. Even the lifeless computers of our day have more intelligence than a Babylonian idol. At least the computer can feed back what is fed into it, but an idol gives no response whatsoever.

Turning to the craftsman as a witness is no better. If he exercises his human capacity to reason and know, he will come to the conclusion that *"he feeds on ashes"* (v. 20a). His own heart has deceived him, the idol cannot deliver him, and he cannot admit that he is the maker of a lie. The stupidity of idol making and the absurdity of idol worship are fully exposed.

REDEEMING HIS PEOPLE (44:21–28)

21 "Remember these, O Jacob,
And Israel, for you are My servant;
I have formed you,
    you are My servant;
O Israel, you will not be forgotten by Me!
22 I have blotted out, like a thick cloud,
    your transgressions,
And like a cloud, your sins.
Return to Me, for I have redeemed you."
23 Sing, O heavens,
    for the LORD has done it!
Shout, you lower parts of the earth;
Break forth into singing,
    you mountains,
O forest, and every tree in it!
For the LORD has redeemed Jacob,
And glorified Himself in Israel.
24 Thus says the LORD, your Redeemer,
And He who formed you from the womb:
"I am the LORD, who makes all things,
Who stretches out the heavens all alone,
Who spreads abroad the earth by Myself;
25 Who frustrates the signs of the babblers,
And drives diviners mad;
Who turns wise men backward,

And makes their knowledge foolishness;
26 Who confirms the word of His servant,
And performs the counsel of His messengers;
Who says to Jerusalem,
  'You shall be inhabited,'
To the cities of Judah,
  'You shall be built,'
And I will raise up her waste places;
27 Who says to the deep, 'Be dry!
And I will dry up your rivers';
28 Who says of Cyrus,
  'He is My shepherd,
And he shall perform all My pleasure,
Even saying to Jerusalem,
  "You shall be built,"
And to the temple,
  "Your foundation shall be laid." '

Isaiah 44:21–28

The Plea to Remember (44:21–23)

Grace takes another leap beyond human comprehension when God adds another "new thing" to His words of comfort for Israel. After calling them to *"remember"* that He who created, formed, redeemed, and named will not forget them, God pleads for Israel to return to Him as the witness to His word and of His work in the world. Again, all of His unmerited love is behind His plea. To think that God could look at a rebellious nation in exile and see it as the masterpiece of redeeming grace is beyond our human comprehension. Yet, in the ministry of Jesus we see the transformation again and again. He looked at a prostitute and saw a woman of God; he called a cheating tax collector to be a disciple; and he touched a leper with a hand of healing. The roster of rejects who became His witnesses continues through history until it includes each of us. God is willing to risk His own integrity before the world in the witness of those whom He has redeemed.

When the rest of God's creation sees the witness of His new creation, all of the heavens and the earth will break out with singing and shouting (v. 13). From the top of the heavens to the bottom of earth and with all the mountains and forests in between, the song will be heard,

467

"the Lord has redeemed Jacob, and glorified Himself in Israel" (v. 23b). In the song will be one final note of irony about the absurdity of idol making. All of the forests and *"every tree in it"* will join in the singing. Even the wood from which idols are made knows the true God!

THE PROMISE OF DELIVERANCE (44:24–28)

All of God's words of comfort come into focus with one final, *"Thus says the Lord, your Redeemer"* (v. 24a). The questions, "To whom will you liken God? Or what likeness will you compare to Him?" have been indisputably answered for Israel and the world. On the declaration *"I am the Lord, who makes all things,"* God now tells Israel what He will do for their return to Judah and the restoration of Jerusalem. First, He will frustrate all of the signs of sorcerers and make foolish all of the knowledge of false prophets who foresee disaster in Israel's return to Judah. Second, God Himself will confirm the word of His prophet and the counsel of His messenger with the proof of His personal presence for their journey. Third, He will give them the promise that they will safely reach their destination and will see Jerusalem inhabited and Judah rebuilt out of the waste of its current condition. Fourth, the Lord will go before His people in the new exodus as the sapper who prepares the way through all of the obstacles ("waters") as He did in the Exodus from Egypt. Fifth, He will call Cyrus as His shepherd to *"perform all My pleasure."* His pleasure is to bring down Babylon and free the exiles with the unbelievable command, *"Even saying to Jerusalem, 'You shall be built,' and to the temple, 'Your foundation shall be laid'"* (v. 28).

The key to these promises is God's motivation. "All My pleasure" is another way of reminding Israel that God will deliver Israel for His own sake, in the way that He chooses, and to the end of His world-saving purpose. No wonder the heavens and the earth will sing. With a glimpse into the heart of God, we have seen that redemption is the essence of His character.

CHOOSING HIS INSTRUMENT (45:1–25)

1 "Thus says the Lord to His anointed,
   To Cyrus, whose right hand I have held—
   To subdue nations before him

And loose the armor of kings,
To open before him the double doors,
So that the gates will not be shut:

2 'I will go before you
And make the crooked places straight;
I will break in pieces the gates of bronze
And cut the bars of iron.

3 I will give you the treasure of darkness
And hidden riches of secret places,
That you may know that I, the LORD,
Who call you by your name,
Am the God of Israel.

4 For Jacob My servant's sake,
And Israel My elect,
I have even called you by your name;
I have named you,
    though you have not known Me.

5 I am the LORD, and there is no other;
There is no God besides Me.
I will gird you,
    though you have not known Me,

6 That they may know from the rising
    of the sun to its setting
That there is none besides Me.
I am the LORD, and there is no other;

7 I form the light and create darkness,
I make peace and create calamity;
I, the LORD, do all these things.'

8 "Rain down, you heavens, from above,
And let the skies pour down righteousness;
Let the earth open,
    let them bring forth salvation,
And let righteousness spring up together.
I, the LORD, have created it.

9 "Woe to him who strives
    with his Maker!
Let the potsherd strive
    with the potsherds of the earth.
Shall the clay say to him who forms it,
    'What are you making?'
Or shall your handiwork say,
    'He has no hands?'

10 Woe to him who says to his father,
    'What are you begetting?'
  Or to the woman,
    'What have you brought forth?'"

11 Thus says the LORD,
  The Holy One of Israel,
    and his Maker:
  "Ask Me of things to come concerning My sons;
  And concerning the work of My hands,
    you command Me.

12 I have made the earth,
  And created man on it.
  It was I—
  My hands that stretched out the heavens,
  And all their host I have commanded.

13 I have raised him up in righteousness,
  And I will direct all his ways;
  He shall build My city
  And let My exiles go free,
  Not for price nor reward,"
  Says the LORD of hosts.

14 Thus says the LORD:
  "The labor of Egypt
    and merchandise of Cush
  And of the Sabeans, men of stature,
  Shall come over to you,
    and they shall be yours;
  They shall walk behind you,
  They shall come over in chains;
  And they shall bow down to you.
  They will make supplication to you,
    saying, 'Surely God is in you,
  And there is no other;
  There is no other God.'"

15 Truly You are God, who hide Yourself,
  O God of Israel, the Savior!

16 They shall be ashamed
  And also disgraced, all of them;
  They shall go in confusion together,
  Who are makers of idols.

17 But Israel shall be saved by the LORD
  With an everlasting salvation;

You shall not be ashamed or disgraced
Forever and ever.
18 For thus says the LORD,
Who created the heavens,
Who is God,
Who formed the earth and made it,
Who has established it,
Who did not create it in vain,
Who formed it to be inhabited:
"I am the LORD, and there is no other.
19 I have not spoken in secret,
In a dark place of the earth;
I did not say to the seed of Jacob,
'Seek Me in vain';
I, the LORD, speak righteousness,
I declare things that are right.
20 "Assemble yourselves and come;
Draw near together,
You who have escaped from the nations.
They have no knowledge,
Who carry the wood of their carved image,
And pray to a god that cannot save.
21 Tell and bring forth your case;
Yes, let them take counsel together.
Who has declared this from ancient time?
Who has told it from that time?
Have not I, the LORD?
And there is no other God besides Me,
A just God and a Savior;
There is none besides Me.
22 "Look to Me, and be saved,
All you ends of the earth!
For I am God, and there is no other.
23 I have sworn by Myself;
The word has gone out of My mouth in righteousness,
And shall not return,
That to Me every knee shall bow,
Every tongue shall take an oath.
24 He shall say,
'Surely in the LORD I have
      righteousness and strength.
To Him men shall come,

                    And all shall be ashamed
                    Who are incensed against Him.
              25 In the LORD all the descendants of Israel
                    Shall be justified, and shall glory.'"

                                                        Isaiah 45:1–25

Shock waves must have reverberated through Israel with Isaiah's announcement that Cyrus, the militaristic and pagan King of Persia, had been named by God as "My shepherd" and honored by God as the one who would say to Jerusalem, "You shall be built" and who would speak to the temple, "Your foundation shall be laid" (44:28). Isaiah himself must have choked on his own words as he thought about the severe warnings that he had given the children of Israel against entangling alliances with foreign nations. Expressing an air of concern, he might well have asked, "How can God enter into an alliance with a pagan king to deliver His people after punishing them with exile for putting their trust in foreign nations?" God answers that question in chapter 45. Without apology, He announces His choice of Cyrus, answers those who criticize His choice, and asks His people to see the spiritual end of a mysterious means.

COMMISSIONING CYRUS, HIS SHEPHERD (45:1–4)

Addressing Cyrus directly, the Lord recognizes him as a king who comes to his coronation ceremony. The ritual begins with an announcement of the name, Cyrus. Greatness is inferred in the naming of a king, and Cyrus is no exception. History records Cyrus's own people honoring him with the name Father because of his benevolence; Babylonians whom he conquered called him Liberator because he freed them from a despot; and Greeks would call him Master and Lawgiver because of his wisdom in ruling. God adds to those titles of deference by calling him "anointed."

Debate still swirls among scholars over the meaning of *"anointed"* as applied to Cyrus. Because the word means Messiah, there are those who want to limit the prophecy of Isaiah to the time of its current history and identify Cyrus, not Jesus, as the one whom God names as "My shepherd" throughout the text. The argument comes through a naturalistic framework that refuses to see the supernatural at work in prophecy or the spiritual meaning of God's purpose in human history.

Most scholars, however, would agree that the anointing of Cyrus is consistent with the commissioning of kings (1 Samuel 16:6), prophets (Psalms 105:15), and priests (Leviticus 4:3) for the special task given them by God. In this context, Cyrus is anointed by God as a messiah for the specific purpose of freeing Israel from Babylonian bondage. As a king received his authority by royal commissioning, so Cyrus received his assignment by divine anointing.

Following the naming and anointing in a coronation ceremony for an ancient king, the new ruler then grasped the hand of his god as a gesture for divine help. Cyrus, we know, took the hand of the Persian deity Marduk at the time of his coronation. Whether he knew it or not, God had already reversed the process, taken the initiative, and grasped the right hand of the one whom He has called "My shepherd" to show that He empowers him to accomplish his designated task.

Still consistent with the coronation ceremony, the new king is extolled for his conquests that are yet to come. In Cyrus's case, nation after nation will fall under his attack, kings will loosen their armor as a show of surrender, and the double doors of fortress cities will be opened wide for his triumphal entry. Cyrus may think that his victories come from his own power, but in truth, God has prepared the way by making the *crooked places straight*," removing the obstacles in his path in order to speed him on to victory. Most specifically, then, God will *break in pieces*" the impenetrable bronze gates and iron bars protecting Babylon and give him the *treasures of darkness and hidden riches*" that have been cached in *secret places*" under the city (vv. 2–3a).

God now begins to state His reasons for the anointing of Cyrus for the downfall of Babylon. First, but not foremost, the Lord says, "*That you may know that I, the* LORD, *who calls you by your name, am the God of Israel*" (v. 3b). Cyrus paid respect to many gods. As noted earlier, he grasped the hand of Marduk at the time of his coronation. When he announced the release of exiled people, he did not limit his decrees to Israel alone. Rather, to all the exiles from many nations, he commanded them to return home and restore the worship of their local gods. Furthermore, in the Cyrus Cylinder, a preserved record of Cyrus's exploits, he does not specifically acknowledge the God of Israel as the one for whom he served as an instrument or the one from whom he received his power. Yet, in 2 Chronicles 36:23, the biblical record leaves no doubt about a specific decree from Cyrus that fulfilled Isaiah's prophecy:

> Thus says Cyrus king of Persia: "All the kingdoms of the earth the LORD God of heaven has given me. And He has commanded me to build Him a house at Jerusalem which is in Judah. Who is there among you of all His people? May the LORD his God be with him, and let him go up!"
>
> *2 Chronicles 36:23*

Josephus, historian of ancient times, puts the weight of evidence upon the biblical record by noting that Isaiah's prophecy had an influence upon Cyrus's decree.[1] Although Cyrus did not know God, the Lord knew him personally by name and chose him as the instrument for making His name known: first, to Cyrus himself (v. 3); second, to the nations of the world (v. 6); and third, to all creation (v. 8). In each case, the foundation premise is *"I am the LORD, and there is no other"* (vv. 5–6).

Justifying His Choice (45:5–8)

Hidden in these declarations of God's sovereign and exclusive nature is the paradox that confounds the human mind. God says, *"I form the light and create darkness, I make peace and create calamity"* (v. 7). Immediately, the question is asked, "Is God the author of evil?" From Job in his suffering to the Holocaust of the Jews and the starvation of Africans, the question keeps being asked. Theologically, we struggle with the dilemma of believing that God foreordains human history while giving His humanity a free will for choice. We can push to one extreme or the other and get an answer. With extreme Calvinism, we can deny human freedom in favor of God's sovereignty or with extreme Arminianism we can deny God's sovereignty in favor of human freedom. Another option is to take the path of the philosopher William Brightman who could resolve the suffering and death of his wife only by positing the premise of a limited God who did not have full power over evil.

Isaiah gives us another option, the option of faith. Whenever our human mind tries to comprehend the nature of God, we are forced into the framework of our limited knowledge and finite understanding.

This is true not just for the problem of evil but for all elements of eternal truth, whether heaven and hell, love and hate, grace and justice, or punishment and promise. Faith, then, accepts God's Word when He says, "I make peace and create calamity" because of the foundational premise, "I, the LORD, do all these things" (v. 7b). While God cannot be the author of evil, He is the Lord of history and includes evil in the forces under His control and uses calamity as an instrument to achieve His redemptive purpose. Obviously, He is preparing the way to answer the question, "Why did God anoint a pagan as His instrument to deliver Israel from exile?" Meanwhile, all creation begins to sing the praises of God. While human beings wrestle with the paradox of good and evil, the heavens and the earth rejoice in the knowledge that God's purpose is to pour righteousness from the raining skies and salvation from the opening earth (v. 8).

QUIETING HIS CRITICS (45:9–13)

Irony greets us again as Israel criticizes what creation celebrates. Evidently, Isaiah's announcement had provoked critics among the exiles who questioned God's anointing of Cyrus as their deliverer. Against them God cries "Woe," and defends His position from the standpoint of His role as Creator of all things and Lord of all history.

Knowing of the close-knit nature of the Jewish family and God's command against ethnic contamination, we can understand why the Israelites questioned the choice of Cyrus. He was not a Jew by birth, a king in the lineage of David, or a believer in the Lord of Israel. Again, it appeared as if God was doing everything against which He had warned them. No longer is the debate over the philosophical paradox of good and evil. God's consistency is at stake.

We must note that God never ignores or punishes persons who ask honest questions. The answer He gives may not be one we want, but He does respect human intelligence and responds with more than an arbitrary decree. Three times now, God has said "I am the LORD" (44:24; 45:5; and 45:6). He will say it three more times as the argument advances (45:18, 21, and 22). These are not casual statements. God is couching all of His reasons for the choice of Cyrus with His role as Creator of all things and Lord of all history. From that perspective, we can understand why He responds to His critics by showing them the absurdity of their position as human beings striving with God as if they had His knowledge and understanding. *"Let the potsherd strive with the potsherds of the earth"* is God's way of saying to His critics, "Argue as humans against humans, but not as humans against God." Four examples follow to illustrate the absurdity of their criticism: (1) The clay, as it is being shaped, challenges the potter, *"What are you making?"*; (2) The handiwork created by a craftsman contends that its maker has no hands; (3) The fetus while being conceived demands of the father, *"What are you begetting?"*; and (4) The newborn child questions the mother, *"What have you brought forth?"* Each illustration leads to the conclusion: It is absurd for that which is created to question its Creator or for that which is formed to challenge its Maker without knowing the purpose for which it was created or formed.

Like a parent who answers a child's question "Why?" with the blunt rejoinder, "Because I said so," God might have closed off debate at this point. Instead, He proceeds to explain the second reason why He anointed Cyrus as His shepherd. "For Jacob My servant's sake, and Israel My elect" has already been stated (45:4a). As Creator of the universe and Maker of Israel, the LORD of Hosts has raised up Cyrus *"in righteousness, and I will direct all his ways; He shall build my city and let My exiles go free, not for price or reward"* (v. 13). What more can the critics say? God anointed Cyrus as His shepherd for the sake of the children of Israel, their freedom, and their future. As strange as it may seem, Cyrus is an instrument of God's grace.

SHOWING HIS SALVATION (45:14–25)

Israel's role in God's redemptive plan comes forward with new emphasis following its deliverance from exile by Cyrus. People of nations known for their resources—Egypt's ingenuity, Cush's commerce, and Sabea's men of stature—will submit themselves to Israel in recognition that the one and only God is in the nation that had been known as a worm (41:14). Although the language of the text has a militant tone of conquest, the submission of the nations to the God of Israel is voluntary. They turn from their idols to the true God by recognizing His presence in His people and through the witness of their salvation. Like a latent seed in a dead plant during the wintertime, God has hidden Himself "in" Israel during its rebellion and exile. But through the deliverance of Cyrus, He will be revealed through the witness of the nation to the *"everlasting salvation"* of the Lord. Never again will Israel be ashamed or disgraced (v. 17). The humiliation will belong to the idolaters and idol makers whose gods cannot save them.

Still addressing the children of Israel in exile, the Lord goes on to remind them that His presence was never hidden from them and His word was never *"spoken in secret"* (v. 19a). What He said to them, He did, and what He promised to them, He fulfilled (v. 19b). So calling His people to come closely together, God offers the idolaters another chance to prove that their gods can save them. But alas, again they have failed to predict emerging events or show prescience for the future. Always touching base on the proof of His greatness and uniqueness, the Lord declares, *"And there is no other God besides Me, a just God and a Savior"* (v. 21). Israel has known His justice; soon it will know His salvation.

One more reason is given for the anointing of Cyrus as the shepherd of God and deliverer of Israel. In the progression of His redemptive purpose, God shouts aloud, *"Look to Me, and be saved, all you ends of the earth! For I am God, and there is no other"* (v. 22). The ultimate purpose for the choice of Cyrus is revealed and who can argue against it? God raised up Cyrus and anointed him for the sake of the salvation of the whole world. With the assurance of an oath, the Lord vows that what He has predicted will come to pass (v. 23). *"Every knee shall bow, [and] every tongue shall take an oath"* confessing the name of the Lord and finding in Him *"righteousness and strength"* (vv. 23b and 24a). Israel, then, will no longer be limited to a chosen people and a specific location. For all who trust in the Lord and confess His name will be the *"descendants of Israel,"* justified by grace and giving God the glory.

What started out as a moment in time with the anointing of Cyrus has expanded into a full-blown picture of God's eternal purpose in human history. Cyrus was chosen for the sake of his acknowledgment of the Lord of heaven, for the sake of Israel's deliverance from bondage to be God's witness, and for the sake of the whole world in confessing the Lord as Savior. Edward J. Young, in his work *The Book of Isaiah, Volume III,* also sees a theological progression in God's purpose when he writes, "Monotheism, true conversion, and universalism go together."[1] He means God's repeated declaration "I am the Lord, there is no other" leads to true conversion by faith for all to the ends of the earth who confess His name. To paraphrase Young, it might be said that "True monotheism, true conversion, and true universalism go together." True monotheism means acknowledgement of the Lord of Heaven, true conversion means voluntarily and individually confessing His name, and true universalism means the spiritual body of believers who are justified by grace and give Him the glory.

NOTES

1. E. J. Young, *The Book of Isaiah, Volume III* The New International Commentary of the Old Testament, (Grand Rapids: Eerdmans, 1972), 216.

CHAPTER TWENTY-TWO

The Burden of Love

Isaiah 46:1–48:22

Isaiah continues to write in the "prophetic present." Through the eyes of the Lord who predicts and publishes the "new things to come," Isaiah foresees events in history far beyond his lifetime. Having predicted the rise of Cyrus as the anointed servant of God to deliver Israel, he moves in time to the eve of Cyrus's attack upon Babylon. Perhaps the critics of God's appointment of a pagan king have taken their toll. As the moment of crisis approaches, the faith of the Israelites begins to weaken and, as doubts arise, they cast a longing look at the Babylonian gods, which become a rallying point for the people in the pomp and ceremony of their worship. To these Israelites whom God calls the "stubborn-hearted," Isaiah has a message of tough love.

THE BURDEN OF FALSE GODS (46:1–13)

1 Bel bows down, Nebo stoops;
   Their idols were on the beasts and on the cattle.
   Your carriages were heavily loaded,
   A burden to the weary beast.
2 They stoop, they bow down together;
   They could not deliver the burden,
   But have themselves gone into captivity.
3 "Listen to Me, O house of Jacob,
   And all the remnant of the house of Israel,
   Who have been upheld by Me from birth,
   Who have been carried
      from the womb:

4 Even to your old age, I am He,
And even to gray hairs I will carry you!
I have made, and I will bear;
Even I will carry, and will deliver you.

5 "To whom will you liken Me,
    and make Me equal
And compare Me,
    that we should be alike?

6 They lavish gold out of the bag,
And weigh silver in the balance;
They hire a goldsmith,
    and he makes it a god;
They prostrate themselves,
    yes, they worship.

7 They bear it on the shoulder,
    they carry it
And set it in its place, and it stands;
From its place it shall not move.
Though one cries out to it,
    yet it cannot answer
Nor save him out of his trouble.

8 "Remember this,
    and show yourselves men;
Recall to mind, O you transgressors.

9 Remember the former things of old,
For I am God, and there is no other;
I am God, and there is none like Me,

10 Declaring the end from the beginning,
And from ancient times things that are not yet done,
Saying 'My counsel shall stand,
And I will do all My pleasure.'

11 Calling a bird of prey from the east,
The man who executes My counsel,
    from a far country.
Indeed I have spoken it;
I will also bring it to pass.
I have purposed it;
I will also do it.

12 "Listen to Me, you stubborn-hearted,
Who are far from righteousness:

13 I bring My righteousness near,
    it shall not be far off;

My salvation shall not linger,
And I will place salvation in Zion,
For Israel My glory.

Isaiah 46:1–13

THE GODS WE CARRY (46:1–2)

With the approach of Cyrus' advancing army, the Babylonians turn naturally to their two most prominant gods, Bel and Nebo, for help. Bel is the father or lord of Babylonian gods and the equal of Marduk with the name often merged as Bel-Marduk. King Belshazzer, for instance, took his forename from Bel in order to lay claim upon the title, "Lord." Nebo is the son of Bel whose name identified him as the "god of prophecy" with the special gift of intelligence and the particular task of keeping the record of the gods. King Nebuchadnezzar identified himself with Nebo when he framed the first part of his name. Both of these gods became the center of attention for an annual festival of Akitu that reached its peak with a processional march from the Gate of Ishtar, past the wonder of the Hanging Gardens, and to the temple for concluding worship. At the head of the processional, Bel and Nebo were carried in carts and pulled by beasts of burden. Because of their size and weight, they might well have wearied the animals before the long march was over. Without any power of their own, Bel and Nebo bow and stoop in dependence upon the strength of animals and become a burden for those who carry them.

Another reading of the burden of Bel and Nebo is to envision the flight of the Babylonians from Cyrus' advancing army. A nation fell when its gods fell. To avoid total defeat, then, the Babylonians would retreat carrying their gods with them. But the dead weight of the idols dragged in slow-moving carts by plodding beasts would become a burden for the Babylonians. Instead of their gods saving them, the gods would become a major factor in their defeat.

All false gods that we carry become dead weights to defeat us. A bumper sticker on the back of a car reads, "The one who dies with the most toys wins." A comic countered that false notion by saying, "The only thing I haven't seen on a Los Angeles freeway is a hearse towing a U-haul trailer." Whether the false god we carry is toys or things, we can neither take them with us when we die nor count on them to save us while we live. Sooner or later, our false gods become burdens that weary us and contribute to our defeat.

THE GOD WHO CARRIES US (46:3–4)

Isaiah has spent so much time comparing the God of Israel with the idols of pagan nations that we might be forgiven for assuming that he will repeat himself when God gives him the imperative to sound, *"Listen to Me, O house of Jacob, and all of the remnant of the house of Israel"* (v. 3). But if we take that attitude, we will miss an insight into the heart of God that equals the initial promise of deliverance for His people. Around the familiar declaration, "I am He," God draws the comparison between Himself and the Babylonian gods, Bel and Nebo. While they are the dead gods who must be carried as a burden by their worshipers, the Lord is the living God who carries the burden for His people. Another new dimension has been added to the role of God as Creator, Maker, Redeemer, and Deliverer of Israel. He is also their Burden Bearer. What a promise! From birth and infancy to old age and gray hairs, or as some might say, "from womb to tomb," God gives the assurance, *"I will carry you"* (v. 4). Earlier, He had given the promise that what He creates, He will care for. Now, He extends His vow to say, *"I have made, and I will bear; even I will carry, and will deliver you"* (v. 4b).

No more radical contrast could be drawn between the gods of Babylon and the God of Israel. Instead of saving their followers, the gods of Bel and Nebo will become a burden contributing to the defeat of Babylon. But the living Lord of Israel will be the Burden Bearer from beginning to end for His people and He will deliver them victoriously as He has promised. The greatest difference, however, is the love and compassion of God that Bel and Nebo can neither show nor give.

THE TEST OF THE GODS (46:5–7)

On the basis of the evidence comparing Himself with the gods of Babylon, God asks, *"To whom will you liken Me, and make Me equal and compare Me, that we should be alike?"* (v. 5). Three separate questions make up a test of the gods. "To whom will you liken Me?" is a test of the image of the god. In the graven images of Bel and Nebo, the idol makers tried to portray visually the qualities of the god. Somehow, the distinction between Bel the father god had to be distinguished from Nebo the son god. But what are the facial expressions of "I am He"? How do you carve the representation of His justice and love in the same face? The goal, of course, was to produce a god whom they could love and worship. "Liken," then, implies an *affective* response.

"To whom will you make Me equal?" is the second test of a choice between gods. Bel and Nebo contested for position with other gods in the Babylonian pantheon. When Bel and Marduk came up equal, they had to settle the contest by merging their names into Bel-Marduk. Thus "equal" here suggests a *volitional* choice.

"To whom will you compare Me?" is yet another test of the gods. This time God is asking if He can be compared to any human being. Babylonian kings took on the names of Bel and Nebo in competition with their gods, but who can take the name "I am He" and invite comparison? "Compare" then infers a *cognitive* conclusion based upon intelligent decision making. In total, the threefold test of the gods involves the heart, will, and mind of Isaiah's hearers. God is saying that His uniqueness can be put to the test by any part of human personality and the answer will be the same. "I am He"—none is like Me, equal with Me, or compared to Me.

The conclusive results of the three-fold test lead God to give us another insight into His unique nature. Advancing a step in the idol-making process, He reminds the Israelites who are tempted to trust in Babylonian gods that, after creating, forming, and carrying their idol, the makers *"set it in its place, and it stands; from its place it shall not move"* (v. 7). Within those words is God's promise that He will lead them on their journey of destiny back to Judah and Jerusalem. And not just leading out in the front of the company. When they cry for help, He will answer them, and when they are deep in trouble, He will save them. Their Burden Bearer will be their File Leader; their File Leader will be their Protective Escort. All of this while Bel and Nebo are tottering on a pedestal, deaf and dumb.

THE PLEASURE OF GOD (46:8–13)

With the case of Bel and Nebo settled, God uses strong imperatives to bring the doubting and fearful Israelites to attention. *"Remember this, and show yourselves men"* is a challenge to their cowardice, and *"recall to mind, O you transgressors"* is a directive against their stubborn refusal to believe. He has said that He raised up Cyrus for the sake of the king, the sake of Israel, and the sake of the world. Yet the Israelites rejected His explanation and continued in the rebellion that got them into trouble in the first place. But not even their stubbornness can frustrate the timing and purpose of God. *"My counsel shall stand, and I will do all My pleasure"* signals the end of the debate and the close of the argument. Although they will not hear, He will act. Cyrus, like *"a bird of prey from the east"* will swoop down upon Babylon and execute his command from God. The Lord of History has stepped forward in power. What He has said, He will do; and what He has purposed, He will complete (v. 11).

Another forceful imperative singles out the rebels among the Israelites. Condemning them as the *"stubborn-hearted, who are far from righteousness,"* God shows that He is even more intent on accomplishing His purpose. With Cyrus coming near, His purpose is about to be fulfilled. Spiritual language takes over the oracle as God speaks of *"My righteousness"* and *"My salvation."* Despite the stubbornness and continuing sin of Israel, God will still save and use them for His glory. Through them, the true Messiah will come and *"place salvation in Zion,"* not by physical location but by personal faith. The God of grace has spoken again. Whether with the Israelites or with us, stubbornness and unrighteousness do not deter the God of grace. He still wants to save us and use us for His glory.

THE BURDEN OF PRESUMPTUOUS SINS (47:1–15)

1 "Come down and sit in the dust,
   O virgin daughter of Babylon;
   Sit on the ground without a throne,
   O daughter of the Chaldeans!
   For you shall no more be called
   Tender and delicate.
2 Take the millstones and grind meal.
   Remove your veil,
   Take off the skirt,
   Uncover the thigh,
   Pass through the rivers.

3 Your nakedness shall be uncovered,
Yes, your shame will be seen;
I will take vengeance,
And I will not arbitrate with a man."

4 As for our Redeemer,
    the LORD of hosts is His name,
The Holy One of Israel.

5 "Sit in silence, and go into darkness,
O daughter of the Chaldeans;
For you shall no longer be called
The Lady of Kingdoms.

6 I was angry with My people;
I have profaned My inheritance,
And given them into your hand.
You showed them no mercy;
On the elderly you laid your yoke very heavily.

7 And you said, 'I shall be a lady forever,'
So that you did not take these things to heart,
Nor remember the latter end of them.

8 "Therefore hear this now,
    you who are given to pleasures,
Who dwell securely,
Who say in your heart,
'I am, and there is no one else besides me;
I shall not sit as a widow,
Nor shall I know the loss of children';

9 But these two things shall come to you
In a moment, in one day:
The loss of children, and widowhood.
They shall come upon you in their fullness
Because of the multitude of your sorceries,
For the great abundance of your enchantments.

10 "For you have trusted in your wickedness;
You have said, 'No one sees me';
Your wisdom and your knowledge have warped you;
And you have said in your heart,
'I am, and there is no one else besides me.'

11 Therefore evil shall come upon you;
You shall not know from where it arises.
And trouble shall fall upon you;
You will not be able to put it off.

And desolation shall come upon you suddenly,
Which you shall not know.
12 "Stand now with your enchantments
And the multitude of your sorceries,
In which you have labored from your youth—
Perhaps you will be able to profit,
Perhaps you will prevail.
13 You are wearied in the multitude of your counsels;
Let now the astrologers, the stargazers,
And the monthly prognosticators
Stand up and save you
From these things that shall come upon you.
14 Behold, they shall be as stubble,
The fire shall burn them;
They shall not deliver themselves
From the power of the flame;
It shall not be a coal to be warmed by,
Nor a fire to sit before!
15 Thus shall they be to you
With whom you have labored,
Your merchants from your youth;
They shall wander each one to his quarter.
No one shall save you.

Isaiah 47:1–15

After the fall of the false gods, Bel and Nebo, the proud city of Babylon comes next. Mixing the sounds of a taunting song dipped in sarcasm with the lament of a funeral dirge, God addresses Babylon as the corporate symbol of evil. Its reputation as a world-class city known for its architectural wonders, cultural refinements, commercial power, and accumulated wealth gave its citizens a haughty sense of pride. But with the downfall of its gods and the imminent threat of Cyrus's army, the city shows its vulnerability. Babylon has no moral core for survival. By the time Cyrus arrives, all of the assumptions upon which its pride was built have been judged false under the judgment of God.

THE PRESUMPTION OF IMMUNITY (47:1–4)

Two signs of humiliation mark the downfall of Babylon. "*Come down and sit*" is the call that pulls the city from its heights and predicts how far it will fall. *"Sit in the dust"* is a sign of impending destruction. Whenever Isaiah uses the metaphor of dust following the judgment of God, he means death. *"Sit on the ground without a throne"* signifies the loss of identity and the isolation of the city after Cyrus's attack. How far the mighty have fallen!

Behind the downfall is a false assumption that Babylon is immune to external attack. Perceiving itself as a *"tender and delicate"* virgin who had never been violated, the Babylonians felt that their protective systems of religion, wealth, military might, knowledge, and allied nations would be their invincible defense against enemy attack. In vivid language, God traces the disgrace of the "virgin," one step at a time. From exquisite debutante, she will become a slave girl grinding meal between millstones; from noble dame, she will be shamed by a lifted veil and an exposed face; from sophisticated lady, she will remove her skirt and bare her thigh for menial work or immoral reasons; and from pampered woman, she will pass through the rivers of suffering just ahead. Worst of all, from the finery of the gowns that hide her true character, she will be seen naked and exposed for what she really is. When the facade of artificial defenses are stripped away, Babylon's shame will be uncovered. Almost brutally, God says, *"I will take vengeance, and I will not arbitrate with a man"* (v. 3b). We might fault God for such vicious language against Babylon except that He used the same words to describe His judgment against His own people for their sin (3:16–26).

Perhaps anticipating the reply of critics who cite God for cruel and unjust punishment, Isaiah inserts the reminder to Israel that He is their Redeemer with the will to save them, the LORD of Hosts with the power to save them, and the Holy One of Israel with the character to complete their salvation.

THE PRESUMPTION OF SOVEREIGNTY (47:5–9)

Dame Babylon has already been consigned to the disgrace of sitting in the dust. Now, her humiliation continues as the Daughter of the Chaldeans is relegated to *"sit in silence, and go into darkness."* Her arrogance has peaked in the self-conceived image of being *"The Lady of Kingdoms"* or Queen of the Earth. Having taken such a presumptuous title, it is a short step to the pompous claim, *"I shall be a lady forever."* Assuming the attributes of being sovereign and eternal, Dame Babylon put herself into competition with God.

A sinner is well-identified by the assumption that he or she will live forever. How many AIDS victims have we heard testifying to the fatal assumption, "It can't happen to me"? Or how many members of the Yuppie generation go into deep debt for cars, houses, and boats with the assumption that their current affluence will continue undiminished in the future? The contradiction is puzzling. While living for the moment as if they would soon die, they also live for tomorrow as if they will live forever. Self-deception is a product of sin.

To the sin of defying the Lordship of God, Dame Babylon also added the flaunting of His command. God had chosen Babylon to punish His people for their sins. He did not do this easily or lightly. Consistent with His holiness, when His love met their sin, it flashed with righteous anger that caused deportation for His chosen people and destruction for His holy city. Reluctantly, God gave His people and His city over to Babylon for punishment. But when He did, Babylon's self-pride took them beyond the bounds of mercy to commit acts of cruelty against elderly citizens of Jerusalem who represented the innocent, helpless, and unarmed victims of warfare. How can God be the Lord of history and still permit such atrocities? The conundrum of foreknowledge and free will confronts us again. As we concluded earlier, the uneasy balance between divine sovereignty and human freedom can be maintained only by the faith that eternal truth is a paradox that still escapes the finite mind. Not unlike Adam and Eve in the Garden of Eden, God gave them their boundaries, but did not stop them from exercising their free will and falling into sin. Babylon, the symbol of evil, took the same path.

Babylon's presumptive sins of competing with God as sovereign and eternal culminated in the ultimate blasphemy, *"I am, and there is no one else besides me"* (v. 8). The image of Dame Babylon as a virgin now shifts to the image of a woman who is enjoying her prime years as a wife and a mother. Smugly, she says in her heart, *"I shall not sit as a widow, nor shall I know the loss of children"* (v. 8b). With the sense of absolute sovereignty goes the assumption that the blessings of life can be preserved and increased forever.

Babylon might be considered the prototype of our Western culture. Unlimited technological progress and ever-increasing economic growth are foundational to our success and our security. Like Babylon, we assume that we will never know the grief of seeing the death of our technological partner nor feel the loss of our economic children. Also, like Babylon, our false assumption may soon be tested. As we speed toward a world economy, the ripple effect of our interlocking relationships will mean that we rise or fall together. Advancing technology, as well, may become an albatross around our neck. The START II treaty between the United States and the Commonwealth of States in the old Soviet Union may reduce the overkill potential of nuclear weapons in the superpowers, but expose the vulnerability of the world to despots such as Saddam Hussein, whose catch-up technology will soon include nuclear capability. The Western world cannot assume immunity from technological widowhood today and economic childlessness tomorrow. We are not God.

Double calamity is predicted for Babylon because of its blasphemy. Anticipating the swift and decisive attack of Cyrus, God informs the city that the *"loss of children, and widowhood"* will come *"in a moment, in one day"* with *"their fullness"* (v. 9). Advancing the image of Dame Babylon one more step, she is now described as a voluptuous woman whose seductive body is the result of her wealth and prosperity and whose security is found in the *"sorceries"* of Chaldean magic and the *"enchantments"* of Babylon's culture. Sex played a major role in Babylonian religion and culture. Ishtar, the sex goddess, held an honored place in the pantheon of gods, and orgies in her name were sanctified in temple worship. Isaiah is kinder to Dame Babylon than John, the Revelator. In blunt language, John calls Babylon, "The Mother of Harlots" (Revelation 17). When the city that played God and worshiped sex falls, its nakedness will be exposed to show "a habitation of demons, a prison for every foul spirit, and a cage for every unclean and hated bird" (Revelation 18:2).

THE PRESUMPTION OF AUTONOMY (47:10–11)

With the downfall of its gods and the rise of its arrogance, the rotting inner core of Babylon is unmasked. Morally, the city felt as if it had become a law unto itself. Three symptoms of this presumptive sin are readily identified. First, without the trust in idols, Babylon must resort to confidence in its own wickedness. Sooner or later, every sinner becomes trapped in the tangled web of sin. Rather than escaping from evil, or using its devices at will, the sinner becomes a victim of wickedness, having to count upon one sin to cover another until sin becomes the way of life. Babylon had reached that point. Second, with the assumption that Babylon had become the God "I Am," the corporate body of the city took on the notion that no all-seeing eye observed their sins and, therefore, it was accountable to no one but itself. The greatest moral tragedies follow in the wake of such an assumption. Whether it is Babylon, Berlin, Baghdad, or Boston, whenever the policies of a city are enacted in secrecy to cover wrong-doing, innocent and helpless people suffer and moral decay sets in. Although "sunshine laws" are onerous for public proceedings, they have the merit of helping to keep the issues above the table and to make civil servants accountable. Third, without moral absolutes against which to make judgments, Babylon had twisted its rational processes to justify its sins and had come to the blasphemous conclusion, *"I am, and there is no one else besides me"* (v. 10b). All sinners must be masters of rationalization. Even if they do not have the advantage of special revelation through God's Word, they cannot escape the evidence of the Godhead in the natural law of creation (Romans 1:20) or the twinges of conscience from the light of the moral law within (John 1:9). A perversion of truth is necessary to justify sin and mollify guilt.

Point for point, God responds to Babylon's assumption that it is morally autonomous. Evil will come upon evil as Babylon is subjected to the calamities of: (a) a surprise attack; (b) inadequate defenses; and (c) sudden destruction (v. 11). To paraphrase the proverb, "He who lives by the sword dies by the sword," Babylon will learn the moral "She who lives by evil will die by evil."

THE PRESUMPTION OF SORCERY (47:12–15)

When all else fails, Babylon will turn to its *"enchantments"* and its *"sorceries"* (v. 12). People who feel as if their destiny is out of their control and do not want to trust in God are ready candidates for the occult. Silicon Valley in California, for instance, is populated by educated, wealthy, and refined people whose genius creates miracles of hardware and software in the computer industry. But just beneath the core of their success and security is a moral and spiritual vacuum that is often filled by cultic movements. New Age philosophy, Eckanar, scientology, transcendental meditation, astrology, and other cultic and occult movements thrive in the Valley. Not unlike Babylon, a God-shaped vacuum must be filled by either the Lord of Creation or the lord who is created.

In contrast with the blind, deaf, and dumb idols of Babylon, at least the seers and sorcerers can see, hear, and speak. But after years of hearing their wise seers talk in hypothetical circles and make predictions that never come true, the people of Babylon are weary of their rambling (v. 13). By their own admission, they have peeled off another layer of hope from the onion of their confidence and exposed the rotting inner core.

But God is fair. He invites Babylon to let their astrologers, star gazers, and monthly prognosticators *"stand up and save you"* (v. 1). Alas, they too are helpless. Like the stubble of a dead bush, they will explode into flames with just a touch from the fire of judgment. Biting sarcasm draws a comparison between the stubble of the sorcerers and the wood of the idols. At least the wood from the idols could be used to build a fire to warm the hands. The stubble of the sorcerers will produce only a flash fire that dies quickly into ashes without cooking the dinner or warming the hands of its followers.

Babylon has one last hope for deliverance. Perhaps the network of commercial relationships with other nations will bring them to its aid. After all, if Babylon falls as the center of the network, the whole commercial system will follow. But no, economic motives are a poor basis upon which to build relationships in which one partner takes a risk for another partner. The profit motive dominates and limits the risk of self-giving. Babylon will learn the lesson: When the fall of the city is inevitable, the merchants will flee and seek their profits elsewhere. To use the language of the marketplace, the bottom line is drawn. Dame Babylon will sit in the dust, shamed by her nakedness, stripped of her resources, and abandoned by her friends. She understands when God says, *"No one shall save you"* (v. 15b).

THE BURDEN OF UNGRATEFUL PEOPLE (48:1–22)

1 "Hear this, O house of Jacob,
    Who are called by the name of Israel,
    And have come forth from

491

the wellsprings of Judah;
Who swear by the name of the LORD,
And make mention of the God of Israel,
But not in truth or in righteousness;
2 For they call themselves after the holy city,
And lean on the God of Israel;
The LORD of hosts is His name:
3 "I have declared the former things from the beginning;
They went forth from My mouth,
    and I caused them to hear it.
Suddenly I did them,
    and they came to pass.
4 Because I knew that you were obstinate,
And your neck was an iron sinew,
And your brow bronze,
5 Even from the beginning
    I have declared it to you;
Before it came to pass
    I proclaimed it to you,
Lest you should say,
    'My idol has done them,
And my carved image
    and my molded image
Have commanded them.'
6 "You have heard;
See all this.
And will you not declare it?
I have made you hear new things from this time,
Even hidden things,
    and you did not know them.
7 They are created now
    and not from the beginning;
And before this day you have not
    heard them,
Lest you should say,
    'Of course I knew them.'
8 Surely you did not hear,
Surely you did not know;
Surely from long ago your ear was not opened.
For I knew that you would deal very treacherously,
And were called a transgressor from the womb.
9 "For My name's sake I will defer My anger,

And for My praise I will restrain it from you,
So that I do not cut you off.

10 Behold, I have refined you,
    but not as silver;
I have tested you in the furnace of affliction.

11 For My own sake, for My own sake,
    I will do it;
For how should My name be profaned?
And I will not give My glory to another.

12 "Listen to Me, O Jacob,
And Israel, My called:
I am He, I am the First,
I am also the Last.

13 Indeed My hand has laid the
    foundation of the earth,
And My right hand has stretched out the heavens;
When I call to them,
They stand up together.

14 "All of you, assemble yourselves, and hear!
Who among them has declared these things?
The LORD loves him;
He shall do His pleasure on Babylon,
And His arm shall be against the Chaldeans.

15 I, even I, have spoken;
Yes, I have called him,
I have brought him,
    and his way will prosper.

16 "Come near to Me, hear this:
I have not spoken in secret from the beginning;
From the time that it was, I was there.
And now the Lord GOD and His Spirit
Have sent Me."

17 Thus says the LORD, your Redeemer,
The Holy One of Israel:
"I am the LORD your God,
Who teaches you to profit,
Who leads you by the way you should go.

18 Oh, that you had heeded My commandments!
Then your peace would have been like a river,
And your righteousness like the waves of the sea.

19 Your descendants also would have been like the
    sand,

And the offspring of your body
 like the grains of sand;
His name would not have been cut off
Nor destroyed from before Me."
20 Go forth from Babylon!
Flee from the Chaldees!
With a voice of singing,
Declare, proclaim this,
Utter it even to the end of the earth;
Say, "The LORD has redeemed
His servant Jacob!"
21 And they did not thirst
When He led them through the deserts;
He caused the waters to flow from the rock for them;
He also split the rock,
 and the waters gushed out.
22 "There is no peace," says the LORD, "for the wicked."
Isaiah 48:1–22

After all of God's reasoned explanation of His redemptive purpose, Israel continues to be hypocritical, skeptical, and stubborn. But
with Cyrus approaching the gates of Babylon, time is of the essence.
So, God commands Israel to *"hear this"* one more time before taking
decisive action.

Faculties in higher education are notorious for their endless debate. As
scholars with a gift for working with ideas and weighing the details,
the tendency is to talk until all parties are heard and every option is
explored. Then, if everyone is not satisfied and the proceedings run
true to form, the issue will be referred to a committee for further
study before a recommendation is made. Among college presidents,
the quip is often repeated, "Nothing ever happens in a faculty meeting until the President defines the 'sense of the meeting.'"

God's discussions with Israel in chapters 40–48 sound a bit like a
faculty meeting. His initial purpose was to give comfort to His people
by forecasting the downfall of their bondmaster, Babylon, and the return to their beloved Jerusalem. At God's announcement that He had
chosen the pagan Cyrus, king of Persia, as His anointed servant for
delivering His people, critics arose to challenge His wisdom and His
judgment. Nothing that God can say will convince them. But ever so
patiently, God walks through each element of truth once again before

making His final appeal of love to His people and commands them to flee from Babylon before Cyrus unleashes his firestorm.

THE HYPOCRISY OF ISRAEL (48:1–2)

No nation on earth ever enjoyed the privileges that God bestowed on Israel. They were created by His power, formed by His hand, chosen as His instrument, and redeemed for His purpose. In return for their obedience, every promise of blessing was given. In response to His love, the bonds of the spiritual community would be forged. And, through their seed, the whole world would be saved. But the saddest words of tongue or pen are these: It might have been.

The prophet's picture of Israel in exile just before Cyrus attacked Babylon is a sad portrait of hypocrisy. God now avoids calling His people Israel. Instead, He commands them, *"Hear this, O house of Jacob"* (v. 1a). Jacob, of course, is the name of the patriarch known for his treachery until he was redeemed. In the name Jacob, then, we foresee what God intends to say to hypocritical Israel and what He must do to save them .

Hypocrites in every generation follow the pattern of Israel. First, they still take the name of God's people, whether it is *Israel* in the sixth century B.C., or *Christian* in the twentieth century A.D. (v. 1b). Second, they still claim the spiritual heritage of their birth whether of ethnic origin or family membership (v. 1c). Third, they still swear by the name of God whether in solemn oaths or personal pledges (v. 1d). Fourth, they still make mention of the God of Israel whether in religious worship or theological discussion. All of their gestures, however, are pretense because they reject the truth of God's Word in their mind and lack the righteousness of God's Spirit in their heart. Yet, they still claim membership in the spiritual community of Zion (v. 2a) and *"lean"* upon the God of Israel when they need Him. How shameful! After all that God has done for His people, they want all of their privileges but none of their responsibilities.

THE SKEPTICISM OF ISRAEL (48:3–5)

Skepticism is different from an honest doubt. A skeptic is a person who finds a reason to reject any argument with which he or she does not agree. An honest doubter, on the other hand, is sincere in motive, candid in questions, and open to options. Isaiah may have had his doubts about God's anointing of Cyrus, for instance, but he was willing to listen to God's explanation and trust Him by faith when he did not understand all of the answers. His skeptical counterparts among the children of Israel came to their questions from the opposite point of view. They used the anointing of Cyrus to confirm their lack of faith in God's promises, excuse their hypocrisy, and justify their enchantment with idols. While they might have claimed to be neo-Israelites, in God's mind they were still hypocrites.

To deal with their skepticism, God reveals the tactics He used. Exercising His predictive powers, He dared to announce the events of history before they happened and then brought them to pass on a timetable of surprise because He anticipated the stubbornness of the Israelites (v. 4a). Like my Scandinavian ancestors, the Jews also had a reputation for stiff necks and hard heads (v. 4b). So God deliberately predicted events in the history of Israel and brought them to pass so quickly that the skeptics did not have time to say, *"My idol has done them, and my carved image and my molded image have commanded them"* (v. 5). Israel had no excuse for the worship of idols that could neither predict nor perform.

THE TREACHERY OF ISRAEL (48:6–8)

Treachery is a companion to skepticism. When specious arguments fail to carry the skeptic's case, a bag of tricks must be opened. One of those tricks is to claim that there is nothing new under the sun. A person who professes to know everything is an arrogant bore. Recently, I heard two young people talking about a mutual friend who had alienated them by being a know-it-all who constantly upstaged them on any subject they talked about. In fact, he would set them up on a subject just to prove his superior knowledge. I heard one of the young persons say, "I felt used and demeaned."

God had to anticipate the tricks of pseudo-Israelites when He announced, "Behold, I will do a new thing." With the anointing of Cyrus, for instance, He did not follow His usual pattern of declaring "former things from the beginning" as He did with prophecy of the Exodus. Instead, He held the announcement until the last minute in order to foil Israelites who were looking for an excuse not to trust Him. Because the anointing of Cyrus caught the exiles totally by surprise, no one could scoff at the news and say, "Of course, I knew it all along." Even the most calloused of critics would have to confess that only God foresaw the coming of Cyrus. The tricksters had been outsmarted.

THE PATIENCE OF GOD (48:9–11)

The patience of God is another miracle of grace. While He had every reason to vent His rage against the hypocritical, skeptical, stubborn, and treacherous Israelites, God informs Israel that He defers His anger and restrains His wrath, not for their sake, but for the sake of His *"name"* and His *"praise,"* (v. 9). Again, He would have been fully justified to cut off Israel and leave them in the dust of death along with Babylon's idols, but no, He chose to refine them in the *"furnace of affliction"* through Babylonian exile with the knowledge that they would still not come out of the fire with the purity of silver (v. 10). Still, He will not be turned from His purpose. *"For My own sake, for My own sake,"* God says, *"I will do it."* Otherwise, His holy name will be profaned, and His glory given to someone else.

God's patience has run its course. Although His beloved children have become His bitter enemy, He will deliver them because salvation is the essence of His nature. "For My own sake," is not a show of self-justification. To be true to Himself, God will deliver His people to save His world.

THE PLAN OF GOD (48:12–19)

God's impassioned appeal to His people is summarized in a series of statements that attest to the righteousness of His decision to proceed with the deliverance of Israel for His own sake. Returning to the touchstone of His uniqueness, He attests, *"I am He, I am the First, I am also the Last"* (v. 12b). From that base, He advances to His role as Creator and Controller of the heavens and the earth (v. 13). He then is the One who can call Israel and all nations into an assembly to confirm His prediction that Cyrus is His anointed servant, whom He loves, whom He raised up, and whom He will prosper (vv. 14–15). Whispering into His hearers' ears, then, God says that they should not be surprised because He is eternal and His word is sure. The coming of Cyrus is an ever-present and accomplished event on the timeless screen of eternity (v. 16).

With Cyrus at the gates of Babylon, God pauses for a reflective moment. Remembering His role as the good teacher and sure guide for Israel, a sigh of disappointment issues from God's heart. *"Oh, that you had heeded My commandments!"* is another way of speaking the saddest words of tongue or pen: It might have been. Israel might have known the *shalom* of His peace like a river flowing steadily through its soul, and the promises of His righteousness rolling endlessly like the waves of the sea (v. 18). Israel did not have to lose its identity; Jerusalem did not have to be destroyed; Judah did not have go into exile. If only they had borne the easy yoke of God's commandments, they would already have seen the promise to Abraham fulfilled. Instead of being a dispersed and diminished people in exile, their descendants and their offspring would have been like the sands of the seashore, too numerous to count. God would have been faithful to them, if they had been faithful to Him.

THE SHOUT OF GOD (48:20–22)

The time has come. With unmistakable clarity and urgency, God shouts, *"Go forth!"* Israel is commanded to leave the city of Babylon and flee from the Chaldees before the hordes of Cyrus sack the city, slay its army, and capture its citizens. Despite the urgency of the command, they are not to flee in panic, but with the song of redemption on their lips, *"The LORD has redeemed His servant Jacob!"* (v. 20b). Faith will then take on the journey that will remake history. In the new exodus from Babylon as in the old exodus from Egypt, the children of Israel will be assured of God's constant presence and His miraculous saving acts. In the midst of the desert, which symbolized their death in exile, God will give them the miracle of fresh water as the symbol of their new life in Him.

But for the wicked of their number whose hypocrisy, skepticism, stubbornness, and treachery will keep them from the journey, the promise does not hold. For them, the Lord says, *"There is no peace."*

The prophecies of deliverance are complete. Beginning with the good news of deliverance for the exiles in Babylon, rising on the surprise of God's anointing of Cyrus as His shepherd, slumping under the stubbornness of Israel, the prophecies peak with God's faithfulness to His own nature and to His own ultimate purpose. Where sin abounds, grace abounds much more (Romans 5:20).

PART NINE

The Vision Incarnate

Isaiah 49:1–57:21

CHAPTER TWENTY-THREE

The Servant Lord

Isaiah 49:1–26

Isaiah's vision progresses in time and theme as he opens another chapter in his prophecy. The time is the period following Cyrus's conquest of Babylon when the Israelites, both in exile and at home, await the new exodus and the restoration of Jerusalem. Specific historical events, however, fade into the background as the major theme of salvation takes on the spiritual meaning of redemptive history. At the center of that history is the role of the Messiah, God's chosen Servant through whom redemption will come, not just for Israel but for the people of all nations, including the Gentiles. Isaiah never loses sight of God's glorious purpose for the one He anoints as His Messiah. Immediately, the voice of the Servant is heard crying out, "Listen, O coastlands, to Me, and take heed, you peoples from afar!" (49:1). All nations and all people are called to hear the good news of salvation that the Servant will bring. Much is to be said about the means to that end, but the end is never forgotten. As we study the text and work our way through the details, the grand vision of God for His Servant, the Messiah, must be kept constantly in view: *"I will also give You as a light to the Gentiles, that you should be My salvation to the ends of the earth"* (49:6b).

HIS PROPHETIC ROLE (49:1–6)

1 "Listen, O coastlands, to Me,
   And take heed,
      you peoples from afar!
   The LORD has called Me
      from the womb;

> From the matrix of My mother
>   He has made mention of My name.
> 2 And He has made My mouth like a sharp sword;
>   In the shadow of His hand He has hidden Me,
>   And made Me a polished shaft;
>   In His quiver He has hidden Me."
> 3 "And He said to me,
>   'You are My servant, O Israel,
>   In whom I will be glorified.'
> 4 Then I said, 'I have labored in vain,
>   I have spent my strength for nothing and in vain;
>   Yet surely my just reward is with the LORD,
>   And my work with my God.' "
> 5 "And now the LORD says,
>   Who formed Me from the womb
>   to be His Servant,
>   To bring Jacob back to Him,
>   So that Israel is gathered to Him
>   (For I shall be glorious in the eyes of the LORD,
>   And My God shall be My strength),
> 6 Indeed He says,
>   'It is too small a thing that You should be My Servant
>   To raise up the tribes of Jacob,
>   And to restore the preserved ones of Israel;
>   I will also give You as a light
>   to the Gentiles,
>   That You should be My salvation
>   to the ends of the earth.' "

Isaiah 49:1–6

The Servant has already been introduced to us. In the first of four servant songs, God personally presented Him with the unforgettable announcement, "Behold! My Servant whom I uphold, My Elect One in whom My soul delights! I have put My Spirit upon Him; He will bring forth justice to the Gentiles" (42:1). What more needs to be said? In a capsule summary, we learn about the call and character of the Servant, His unique relationship to God, and the specific purpose of His servanthood. Certainly, the question, *why* is answered, but nothing is said about *how* except that God will put His Spirit upon Him. Other servant songs are needed to fill in the details and answer the question, *how*. We await, then, three other servant songs that follow.

But who is the Servant? Not all scholars agree that Isaiah is writing about the Messiah in the person of Jesus Christ. No one argues that Cyrus, whom God anointed as "My shepherd," is the subject of the song. His deed of deliverance is done and his role as servant is over. Isaiah does not mention his name again. Many scholars, however, contend that the corporate nation of Israel is the Servant to whom Isaiah refers. Their argument is both theological and textual. Theologically, they are not ready to accept the thought that Isaiah could predict forward with a prescience requiring divine inspiration. Like proverbial dominoes, to admit the supernatural in one instance of revelation is to admit it in many other instances as well. If, for instance, Isaiah's prediction of Jesus Christ is accepted, His virgin birth, divine-human nature, sacrificial death for the forgiveness of sins, and resurrection all become issues with which they must deal. Consequently, they hang heavily upon the statement in 49:3 when God is quoted as saying, "You are My servant, O Israel." As an isolated text, the case seems closed. In context, however, the evidence shifts heavily toward the argument that the Servant is an individual and specifically, the Messiah. To reconcile the apparent conflict from a textual viewpoint, other scholars see the Servant Person as the personification of the Servant Nation. They were both called and commissioned for the same task, to be the "light of the nations" for the salvation of the world. Israel, the Servant Nation, failed because of sin, so the call and commission passed to Jesus Christ, the Servant Person who would not fail. Seen in this light, God might well say to Jesus Christ, "You are My Servant, O Israel." The position we take for this commentary is that the Servant of Isaiah 49:3 is (a) a person; (b) Jesus Christ, the Messiah; and (c) one with Israel, the Servant Nation, in being the instrument of God's redemptive purpose.

His Call (49:1)

Speaking for Himself, the Servant calls the *"coastlands"* and *"peoples from afar"*—Isaiah's way of including all the nations and people of the earth—to hear the testimony of His call and commissioning. His words come to us as the second of the four servant songs that highlight chapters 48–56. In His testimony we learn first of His **call** to be a prophet (v. 1). Significantly, while He is born, He is not created. This fact argues for the individuality of the Servant and His distinction from Israel. Earlier passages that described Israel as God's Servant always began with God as the one who created and formed the nation. The Messiah is called *"from the womb"* and mentioned by name before birth. Our mind reaches back to Isaiah's earlier prophecy, "The virgin shall conceive and bear a Son, and shall call His name Immanuel" (7:14). As Immanuel, "God with us," His call is to personify God's new covenant with His people; His name identifies His office as the Messiah and His vocation as the Servant.

HIS PREPARATION (49:2)

No one can doubt that the Servant's primary task is to speak the Word of God. His identity with Jesus Christ is reinforced by His primary task. As Jesus "came preaching," so the Servant spoke the Word. And Jesus' preaching matched the character of prophetic preaching described by the Servant in Isaiah. His Word had the double-edged strength of a *"sharp sword"* following years of preparation *"in the shadow of His hand,"* and the single-point precision of a *"polished shaft"* hidden in the *"quiver"* of His parables.

Preparation for prophetic preaching has not changed. To be effective, the contemporary prophet must be thoroughly equipped with the Word of God as a sharp sword. Sharpness comes from being persons of one Book who use inductive study to let the Word of God speak for itself through the agency of the Holy Spirit. Complementing the personal study, prophetic preachers must also be students of careful exegesis (analysis of the text), sound hermeneutics (interpretation of the text), and systematic theology (organization of beliefs) in order to be effective. To escape the dangers of intellectual preaching without passion, then, the contemporary prophet must be *"hidden"* in the shadow of His hand, nurtured in such spiritual disciplines as prayer and fasting in reflective solitude with God alone. From the desk of study and the closet of prayer, the prophetic preacher must then walk out into the streets of the city to communicate the Word of God with the precision of a "polished shaft" to the many needs of the people. Without this full-orbed preparation, prophetic preaching will be dull, shallow, and pointless.

HIS WORK (49:3)

With the Servant's call and commissioning comes the reality of His **work** as a prophet. At a distance and over a period of time, we tend to romanticize the work of a prophet. We think of a person who is charismatic in personality, undaunted in spirit, and held in awe by the people. But by His own testimony, the Servant tells us otherwise. Far more important than a charismatic personality is the evidence that the work of the Servant is *reflective of God's character*. *"You are My Servant, O Israel, in whom I will be glorified"* (v. 3) indicates that the work of the Servant is reflective of the glory of God, not of His own personality. Earlier, when we were studying the character of God, we determined that wherever God touched down in human history, His work reflected the glory of His righteousness and His justice. The work of the Servant, then, becomes the mirror image of the character of God. Whatever the Servant does will reflect righteousness and justice. When Jesus said that He came to do the will and work of His Father, He made it clear that He would find no glory in Himself, but only as He glorified God.

True and false prophets are sorted out on this test of servanthood. Elmer Gantry and all charlatans who followed him would instantly fall out as true prophets of God. While they might mouth the words, "Give God the glory!" only the most gullible are fooled. Their work is for their own glory, and the name of God is invoked for their own praise. On the other hand, the work of the true prophet takes precedence over personality. The results of the work have the glow of His glory while the charisma of the personality fades into the background. "To God be the Glory" is the motive as well as the motto of a true prophet of God.

His Renewal (49:4)

Whatever glamour is attached to the work of a prophet is quickly dispelled when the Servant confesses His discouragement and His need for **renewal** by God's strength. *"I have labored in vain, I have spent my strength for nothing and in vain"* (v. 4a). To be a prophet is not only work without worldly honor, it is physically exhausting and emotionally draining. Isaiah had been forewarned by God that his word would fall upon deaf ears and his vision would be hidden to blind eyes. The Servant of God, even with the good news of salvation, will be subject to the same discouraging response. Slowly but surely, God is revealing the truth that the Messiah will also be His Suffering Servant. Eventually we know that this hard truth became the turning point for the masses who followed Jesus and for His disciples as well. All of us want to share in the glory of His ministry, but none of us wants to participate in His suffering. Anyone who has preached the gospel or witnessed to unbelievers, however, knows that there is no escape from exhaustion and discouragement. Whether we like it or not, servanthood and suffering are inseparable for the prophet of God. Faithfulness to truth, not freedom from opposition, is God's expectation for His servants.

To the maturity of faithfulness must be added the maturity of reward. Immature servants need increasing rewards to remain faithful. Whether in the tangible evidence of visible results, or the intangible reinforcement of outward praise, most of us depend upon external rewards to bolster our morale and renew our energies. Only the most mature among us can find renewal in the intrinsic reward of the work itself, knowing that doing God's will is sufficient satisfaction to maintain and renew the level of energy for the work. Although the Servant admits exhaustion and discouragement, He also testifies, *"Yet surely My just reward is with the LORD, and My work with God"* (v. 4b). Quite in contrast with unfaithful Israel, which refused to believe the external evidence of God's blessings in the past, the Servant's *"just reward"* is to be in the presence of God and to do His work.

HIS GOAL (49:5–6)

"And now, the LORD says" is the Servant's statement of the reason He is called to be a prophet. As the agent of the Lord, He is given short-term and long-term goals for His work. The short-term goal is *"To bring Jacob back to Him, so that Israel is gathered to Him"* (v. 5). Most immediately, He will be instrumental in the deliverance of Israel from Babylon and their return or "gathering" in Jerusalem. The purpose is self-evident. Despite its initial rebellion and continuing obstinacy, God will bring His chosen people back to Zion in order to fulfill His redemptive purpose for the world through the "seed of Jesse."

With utter confidence in God's intention, the Servant has no doubt about His role in the deliverance. He testifies, *"For I shall be glorious in the eyes of the LORD and My God shall be My strength"* (v. 5b). Israel's work and promise are now His. As God chose the children of Israel and made His covenant with them, He foresaw His reflective glory in their work and promised them the power to do the task. They failed, but the Servant will not. The house of Jacob cannot bring itself back, and Israel cannot gather itself to Him. Only the Messiah, an individual person, can accomplish the task. In the cycle of prophecy, these events may refer to current events as well as to Old Testament history. The "gathering" of Israel is happening again as Jews from across the world return to their homeland. Whether they acknowledge it or not, their gathering is in the plan of God for salvation through His Servant, the Messiah.

Israel cannot be arrogant. Although privileged as God's choice to be His Servant Nation, it took the Babylonian exile to show that it was not exempt from judgment for sin. Now, it also must learn that God's promise of return from exile and the restoration of Jerusalem is not an end in itself. With rather startling words, the Servant testifies that God has told Him, *"It is too small a thing that You should be My Servant to raise up the tribes of Jacob, and to restore the preserved ones of Israel"* (v. 6).

A critic once said, "The Church is caught in the thickness of thin things." He might have been paraphrasing Isaiah 49:6. Prophets who are called of God can also be criticized for getting "caught in the bigness of small things." When a survival mentality for a local congregation, a defensive posture by Christians in the public square, a paranoid emphasis upon preserving the purity of the Body, or a success syndrome built upon growth in numbers and dollars dominate the work of a prophet, God will say, "It is too small a thing that You should be My Servant." Prophets have something bigger to do.

No task can be larger, more challenging, and more meaningful than God's goal for His Servant. *"I will also give You as a light to the Gentiles, that You should be My salvation to the ends of the earth"* (v. 6b). While the charge is as pointed as the "polished shaft" of a swift arrow speeding toward the bull's-eye, it goes far beyond the privileged people of Israel to engage the heathenish Gentiles and far beyond the borders of the minuscule nation of Israel to encompass the ends of the earth. As we know from hindsight, Jesus Christ never got caught in the "bigness of small things." Whether in His preaching to the masses, His teaching of the disciples, or His commission to believers of all generations, He gave Himself to be the "light to the Gentiles" and to bring "salvation to the ends of the earth."

HIS PROPHETIC CONFIRMATION (49:7–13)

7 Thus says the LORD,
   The Redeemer of Israel,
      their Holy One,
   To Him whom man despises,
   To Him whom the nation abhors,
   To the Servant of rulers:
   "Kings shall see and arise,
   Princes also shall worship,
   Because of the LORD who is faithful,
   The Holy One of Israel;
   And He has chosen You."
8 Thus says the LORD:
   "In an acceptable time I have heard You,
   And in the day of salvation
      I have helped You;
   I will preserve You and give You
   As a covenant to the people,
   To restore the earth,
   To cause them to inherit
      the desolate heritages;
9 That You may say to the prisoners,
      'Go forth,'
   To those who are in darkness,
      'Show yourselves.'
   "They shall feed along the roads,
   And their pastures shall be on all desolate heights.
10 They shall neither hunger nor thirst,
   Neither heat nor sun shall strike them;
   For He who has mercy on them will lead them,
   Even by the springs of water He will guide them.
11 I will make each of My mountains a road,
   And My highways shall be elevated.
12 Surely these shall come from afar;
   Look! Those from the north
      and the west,
   And these from the land of Sinim."
13 Sing O heavens!
   Be joyful, O earth!
   And break out in singing,
      O mountains!

For the Lord has comforted His people,
And will have mercy on His afflicted.

Isaiah 49:7–13

Edward Land, the inventor of the Polaroid camera, is reputed to have said, "The only task worth doing is one that is well-nigh impossible." The goal of salvation for all people from every corner of the earth is one of those well-nigh impossible tasks. God's Servant took it on, but not alone or in His own strength. The Lord knew that the commissioning of the Servant would not be complete without the confirmation of His personal support for the prophetic call. So, in response to the Servant's testimony, the Lord Himself gives the words of confirmation.

I Will Exalt You as My Chosen One (49:7)

Anticipating the incarnational text in Philippians 2:5–11, which describes the self-emptying, suffering, death and exaltation of Jesus Christ, the Lord identifies the Servant as His chosen One who will suffer as *"the Servant of rulers"* before being exalted as the One before whom all rulers will stand and all princes will bow. The vow is sealed with the signature of the Lord's faithfulness.

I Will Make You My Personal Covenant (49:8–9a)

No shred of doubt is in God's mind about His choice of the Servant. As He had been willing to enter into covenant with Israel and make the nation His light to the world, now God goes a step farther. His Servant will be more than the symbol of His covenant with humanity, He will be the covenant Himself. God's confidence is complete. The Servant Himself will *"restore the earth,"* by redeeming the heathen, freeing the prisoners, and enlightening those in darkness (vv. 8b and 9). The Messiah will do personally what Israel failed to do corporately.

I Will Go Before You as My Gatherer (49:9b–12)

The well-nigh impossible task of gathering all people from all corners of the earth cannot be done without advance and continuing preparation by God's Spirit in the world. So, as part of God's confirmation proceedings, He assures His Servant that He will ready the world for His coming. As the "gathering" begins, food and water symbolic of basic resources will be provided for their journey through the desert; the heat and sun of natural forces will not stop them; the Lord Himself will lead them; miracles such as life-giving water from the rock will assure them; and the obstacles of mountains and valleys will be smoothed to speed them on their way (vv.9b–11).

A chuckle came to me when I read of God's elaborate preparation in confirmation of the work of His Servant. To keep the President's home at Asbury Theological Seminary always ready for receptions and unexpected visitors, a member of the custodial staff comes each Friday for two hours to assist my wife with housecleaning. Dixie has served for almost ten years in this capacity, and although she works with spit-and-polish efficiency, my wife spends most of Friday morning getting ready for her arrival. She cleans, mops, dusts, and washes throughout the house and then leaves a list for Dixie to finish. When I asked her why she did this, she answered, "I wouldn't want Dixie to think we're sloppy!"

God must have felt the same way. Before turning the final work over to His Servant, He prepared the way with such immaculate detail that He could exclaim to Him, *"Look! Those from the north and the west, and these from the land of Sinim"* (v. 12). They are already on the way! From every corner of the compass and as far away as Sinim (a name often given to China, which represented the end of the earth), God shows His Servant that the gathering has begun.

I WILL LEAD CREATION IN PRAISE FOR YOUR WORK (49:13)

Earlier in these oracles, God had given His people a song to sing as they journeyed home. With the great gathering of people from the ends of the earth, all of God's creation will join in the singing. Heavens, earth, and mountains will praise God because the Servant has brought salvation to the human realm. As He promised in the first word of these salvation oracles, His people will be "comforted" and the afflicted will receive mercy.

Ecology is a term usually applied to the environment where everything is connected with everything else. Because the environment is so finely-tuned, we know that pollutants on earth can produce holes in space, and explosions on earth sends shock waves to the stars. Isaiah tells us that ecology may also be applied to the spiritual realm as well. Salvation does not stop when it spreads to the ends of the earth. Because of the connections within creation that caused the universe to groan under the curse of human sin, the same connections will cause creation to sing praises for human salvation. Most appropriately, the Song of Creation is the finale for God's confirmation of His Servant.

HIS PASTORAL ROLE (49:14–26)

14 But Zion said,
    "The LORD has forsaken me,
    And my Lord has forgotten me."
15 "Can a woman forget her nursing child,
    And not have compassion on the son of her womb?
    Surely they may forget,
    Yet I will not forget you.
16 See, I have inscribed you on the palms of My hands;
    Your walls are continually before Me.
17 Your sons shall make haste;
    Your destroyers and those who laid you waste
    Shall go away from you.
18 Lift up your eyes, look around and see;
    All these gather together
        and come to you.
    As I live," says the LORD,
    "You shall surely clothe yourselves with
        them all as an ornament,
    And bind them on you as a bride does.
19 "For your waste and desolate places,
    And the land of your destruction,
    Will even now be too small for the inhabitants;
    And those who swallowed you up will be far away.
20 The children you will have,
    After you have lost the others,
    Will say again in your ears,
    'The place is too small for me;
    Give me a place where I may dwell.'
21 Then you will say in your heart,
    'Who has begotten these for me,

Since I have lost my children
   and am desolate,
A captive, and wandering to and fro?
And who has brought these up?
There I was, left alone;
But these, where were they?'"

22 Thus says the Lord GOD:
"Behold, I will lift My hand
   in an oath to the nations,
And set up My standard for the peoples;
They shall bring your sons in their arms,
And your daughters shall be carried on their shoulders;

23 Kings shall be your foster fathers,
And their queens your nursing mothers;
They shall bow down to you
   with their faces to the earth,
And lick up the dust of your feet.
Then you will know that I am the LORD,
For they shall not be ashamed
   who wait for Me."

24 Shall the prey be taken from the mighty,
Or the captives of the righteous be delivered?

25 But thus says the LORD:
"Even the captives of the mighty
   shall be taken away,
And the prey of the terrible be delivered;
For I will contend with him who
   contends with you,
And I will save your children.

26 I will feed those who oppress you
   with their own flesh,
And they shall be drunk with their own
   blood as with sweet wine.
All flesh shall know
That I, the LORD, am your Savior,
And your Redeemer,
   the Mighty One of Jacob."

Isaiah 49:14–26

Poor Israel. Having heard the commissioning of the Servant and
His confirmation by God, even the faithful people of Zion felt the rise

of old fears and new doubts. Did the coming of the Servant mean that God had given up on Israel? Did God's promise to Abraham for their spiritual destiny still hold? Did God have the power to deliver them from their captors? Each of these questions is answered by God with a salvation oracle for His people. By addressing them as "Zion," we know that He is giving assurance to the remnant in Israel who make up the spiritual body of faith. Even those who believe have honest doubts.

THE FEAR OF BEING FORGOTTEN (49:14–20)

"But Zion said, 'The LORD has forsaken me, and my Lord has forgotten me'" is a negative statement of lost hope. When the conjunction *but* begins a sentence, all that proceeds it is altered. A parent, for instance, says to a child, "I love you, *but* you must behave." In the mind of the child, love becomes conditional upon behavior and therefore loses its unconditional nature. Israel must have experienced some of the same feeling when God announced His Servant, who would be Israel and would fulfill the purpose on which His chosen people had defaulted.

No greater expression of God's love can be found in Holy Scripture, short of Christ's death, than the multifaceted response to reassure His people. A love poem of fourteen lines has the same theme as Elizabeth Barrett Brownings celebrated sonnet, "How do I love thee? Let me count the ways." God says the same thing to Israel as He counts the ways He loves them.

Three different images spell out God's love. The first is the image of a mother's love. *"Can a woman forget her nursing child, and not have compassion on the son of her womb?"* (v. 15a). No one would dispute the rhetorical answer. A mother would never forget her child, but even if she did, God would never forsake His chosen children. Shifting from the love of the mother to a young man's love, God says, *"I have inscribed you on the palms of My hands."* Israel would have been acquainted with two customs in Babylon. Idol worshipers tattooed the name of their god on their palms as an ever-present symbol of their worship, and young men in love also tattooed the name of their beloved on their palms as a symbol of faithfulness. Believers in Zion would have been visibly moved by the thought of a tattoo on God's palm that read I-s-r-a-e-l. Every time God opens His hand, then, He sees the reminder of His people in bondage and the walls of His city in ruins. The tattoo will never let Him forget them or fail in His promise to deliver them and restore Jerusalem.

The third image is the bride's love (v. 18). Like a bride who looks up the aisle and beams with love as she sees the bridegroom coming to her, God asks Israel to *"lift up your eyes"* and see the gathering of her sons coming home. As a bride wears her wedding ornaments, those who are coming home from the far corners of the earth will be the jewels that Israel will wear. Out of these images will come the proof that God has not forgotten His children. The promise to Abraham is still good. Into the wasteland of Judah and the ruins of Jerusalem will come a new wave of sons and daughters who will be so plenteous that the land will be too small to hold them. Israel lost generations of children in the exile, but they will be replaced by new generations of children who will burst the boundaries of the tiny nation and test the limits of its old covenant.

THE FEAR OF BEING CHILDLESS (49:21–23)

Because of lingering guilt and years in exile, even the faithful of Israel grovel in low self-esteem. As much as they may want to believe that God's promise to Abraham will be fulfilled in new generations of children (numerous as the stars of the sky and the sands of the sea), they feel like a widow who has lost her children, her home, and her relatives. To be told that she will bear and bring up more children than she can count is to prompt her logical questions, *"Who has begotten these for me?"* and *"Who has brought these up?"* (v. 21). God answers with another oracle of salvation. Raising His hand for all nations to see, He takes an oath on His word and lifts a banner for all people. He tells Israel that she will be the spiritual mother for the children of faith who will be brought to her by parents of all nations and nourished by kings and queens of those nations who serve as foster fathers and nursing mothers for Zion's coming generations. Just as every knee shall bow before God's Servant and confess His name, so the kings and queens will bow in the dust at the feet of Israel to acknowledge the Lord (v. 23a). For those who are faithful in Israel, then, God gives the promise that they will not be ashamed by Him or of themselves (v. 23).

THE FEAR OF BEING ANNIHILATED (49:24–26)

One more fear resides deep in the heart of Israel's faithful people. As desperately as they want to believe that their God can deliver them, they cower daily under the whimsical rule of an Eastern despot. Fully honest, they ask whether or not the tyrants of the earth will give up their *"prey"* and set the *"captives"* free. God's response comes in a final oracle of salvation that seems too brutal for civilized spirits. By making Himself the one who personally contends with the power of the tyrants, He assures the *"captives of the mighty"* and the *"prey of the terrible"* that he will forcibly free them, deliver them, and save them (v. 25). Violence will be required because these tyrants respond only to violence.

During the Cuban Missile Crisis in the early 1960s, all efforts at diplomacy failed to move the Soviet dictator. Not until President Kennedy stood eyeball-to-eyeball with Khrushchev and matched him missile for missile did the dictator back down. Envisioning a similar showdown between God and the tyrants holding His people captive, we are told that the "terrible" will suffer the same consequences of violence that they have wrought on God's children. After Jerusalem had been besieged and sacked by the Babylonians, the survivors became so desperate and deranged that they ate their own children. As revolting as it may be, God will make the plight of the tyrants so desperate that they too will become cannibals, eating human flesh and drinking human blood. But before we condemn the barbarians of the past, we need to read a twentieth-century newspaper. Just the other day a press release told of cannibalism among the tyrants in Red China who ate their enemies, not because they were starved but as a show of vengeance. Sinful human beings, whether in the sixth century B.C. or the twentieth century A.D., are capable of sub-human acts.

God has only one purpose in the overthrow of tyrants. He wants to free His people so that *"All flesh shall know that I, the LORD, am your Savior, and your Redeemer, the Mighty One of Jacob"* (v. 26b). Israel is assured that it still has a vital role in God's plan to be the "light to the Gentiles" through His Servant, the Messiah.

CHAPTER TWENTY-FOUR

The Teaching-Learning Servant

Isaiah 50:1–52:12

Salvation continues to be Isaiah's theme as the portrait of the Servant begins to fill out with the features of one who goes through the teaching and learning of suffering in order to save. In the commissioning of the Servant, we saw how God set before Him the goal of being His "light to the Gentiles" and His "salvation to the ends of the earth" (49:6b). Emphasis was put upon the character of the Servant or *what* he would be. The question of *how* He would accomplish His task was addressed only in general terms. Now in chapters 50:1–54:17, Isaiah answers the question *how* with a depth of poetic, but realistic, passion that only God can reveal. The script unfolds as the first part of an epic story. By His own choice, the Servant will suffer to deliver Israel and restore Jerusalem so that Zion will be poised to fulfill its chosen role as the instrument for world redemption. But first will come the suffering of the Servant and the redemption of Israel, and the restoration of Jerusalem. Hard lessons are to be learned.

THE TEACHING-LEARNING ENVIRONMENT (50:1–3)

1 Thus says the LORD:
"Where is the certificate of your
mother's divorce,
Whom I have put away?
Or which of My creditors is it
to whom I have sold you?
For your iniquities you have sold yourselves,
And for your transgressions your
mother has been put away.
2 Why, when I came, was there no man?

> Why, when I called,
>   was there none to answer?
> Is My hand shortened at all that it cannot redeem?
> Or have I no power to deliver?
> Indeed with My rebuke
>   I dry up the sea,
> I make the rivers a wilderness;
> Their fish stink because there is no water,
> And die of thirst.
> 3 I clothe the heavens with blackness,
> And I make sackcloth their covering."
>
> *Isaiah 50:1–3*

A student must be free from fear in order to learn. Otherwise, fear will dictate a defensive response, stifle creativity, and squash the rising hopes for the future that learning will stimulate.

Fear still resides in the faithful people of Israel. God has answered three of their fears that came out as troubling questions in chapter 49:14–26. With oracles of salvation, He assured them of His love (vv. 15–20), His promise (vv. 22–23), and His power (vv. 25–26). One question still lingers in their minds—perhaps the most fearful question of all—"How can sinful Israel be delivered from the law?" For the faithful, deliverance from human tyrants is easier than deliverance from divine justice. As long as the fear of the law hangs over their heads, Israel cannot be free to learn.

THE RELATIONSHIP OF LOVE (50:1a)

God speaks to their fear of the law with the heart of a loving husband and father. In ancient Israel, a husband had exclusive power to hand an unfaithful wife a writ of divorce (Deuteronomy 24:1–4). Upon receipt of the document, she had no right of appeal or recourse. The faithful of Israel had this fear for themselves because of the sin of the nation. Their respect for the law, with its irrevocable and nonnegotiable standard of justice, added a sense of hopelessness to the fear. In response, God asks the question, *"Where is the certificate of your mother's divorce?"* (v. 1a). Without a bill of divorcement, God assures them that despite their sin He has not broken the relationship. Their learning will take place in a relationship of love.

519

THE CLIMATE OF FREEDOM (50:1b)

A related fear for the faithful of Israel is the provision in the law for a debtor to sell his children if all other sources for repayment are exhausted (2 Kings 4:1). Because of the size of the debt incurred by their sin, even those who remained faithful feared that the price required by the law exceeded the resources of God. But they failed to remember that God has no *"creditors."* As the word of assurance, then, God asks them to name the one to whom He has sold His children. Because there are no creditors, His relationship to His children in Israel remains unbroken, and they are free from the debt of their sin.

Israel is victimized, then, by its own sin. The questions about God's bill of divorcement and debtor sale of His children are misdirected. God says, *"For your iniquities you have sold yourselves, and for your transgressions your mother has been put away"* (v. 1b). Again, we are reminded that sin carries the seeds of its own destruction. God gets blamed for the consequences of sin and criticized as the author of evil. But if He simply leaves us to our own devices, we bring punishment upon ourselves. More often than not, the chains of fear are self-imposed.

THE DYNAMIC OF GRACE (50:2–3)

Grace now takes over for the law. Despite the original rebellion and continuing stubbornness of Israel, God has the power to redeem and deliver them. Citing the workings of His power in the Exodus from Egypt, He reminds them that He parted the waters of the Red Sea and made the ground so dry that even the fish died of thirst and stank with rot (v. 2b). For good measure, He adds the memories of His power in clothing *"the heavens with blackness"* as the plague of locusts swarmed over Egypt and in causing national mourning when the Angel of God slew all of their firstborn sons. Surely, the same God has the power to deliver His people again. Israel can sing with the eighteenth-century hymn writer, "O to grace how great a debtor, daily I'm constrained to be" (Robert Robinson, 1758, "Come, Thou Fount of Every Blessing").

THE TEACHING-LEARNING PLAN (50:4–11)

4 The Lord GOD has given Me
The tongue of the learned,
That I should know how to speak

520

A word in season to him who is weary.
He awakens Me morning by morning,
He awakens My ear
To hear as the learned.
5 The Lord GOD has opened My ear;
And I was not rebellious,
Nor did I turn away.
6 I gave My back to those
who struck Me,
And My cheeks to those
who plucked out the beard;
I did not hide My face from shame and spitting.
7 "For the Lord GOD will help Me;
Therefore I will not be disgraced;
Therefore I have set My face like a flint,
And I know that I will not be ashamed.
8 He is near who justifies Me;
Who will contend with Me?
Let us stand together.
Who is My adversary?
Let him come near Me.
9 Surely the Lord GOD will help Me;
Who is he who will condemn Me?
Indeed they will all grow old like a garment;
The moth will eat them up.
10 "Who among you fears the LORD?
Who obeys the voice of His Servant?
Who walks in darkness
And has no light?
Let him trust in the name of the LORD
And rely upon his God.
11 Look, all you who kindle a fire,
Who encircle yourselves with sparks:
Walk in the light of your fire and in
the sparks you have kindled—
This you shall have from My hand:
You shall lie down in torment.

Isaiah 50:4–11

Another Servant Song, the third of four, is an oracle of hope for the faithful, but fearful, children of Israel in exile. In a hymn of hope, the Servant himself defines His special relationship with the *"Lord GOD"* and His special role as a disciple (*"the learned"*). Four times in the short song, the Servant refers to the "Lord GOD" (vv. 4a, 5a, 7a and 9a). The double title is unique to this Song and conveys the dual meaning of God's "sovereign control over the nations and His covenant relationship with Israel."[1] Behind the Servant's ministry, then, is all the power of the sovereign "Lord" and all the love of the covenant-making "GOD." With these inexhaustible resources, the Servant identifies Him as the one to whom God has given, *"The tongue of the learned"* (v. 4a). At one and the same time, the Servant is the teacher and the one who is taught (v. 4b). *Disciple* is an accurate translation for this unique teaching-learning relationship, which is also unique to the Book of Isaiah. The same term appeared in Isaiah 8:16–17 when the Lord instructed Isaiah, "Bind up the testimony, seal the law among my disciples." As a disciple, then, the teaching-learning role of the Servant is defined.

THE TEACHING-LEARNING GOAL (50:4a)

God has a singular purpose in giving His Servant the *"tongue of the learned."* By His Own testimony, the Servant says, *"That I should know how to speak a word in season to him who is weary"* (v. 4a). All of Israel would resonate with the sound of those words. As homeless and nameless people wearied by years of exile, no greater words of comfort could be given. Notably, the Servant does not see learning as an end in itself. Many prominent scholars fall into this trap. They become so enamored with the excitement of discovering knowledge that they fail to see its application to human need. When this happens, colleges and universities become ivory towers where erudite scholars endlessly pursue the truth, seldom discover it, and when they do, fail to apply it personally or socially. Some biblical scholars, for instance, can spend a lifetime analyzing the history, literature, and language of the Word without ever experiencing the impact of truth upon their lives. The teaching-learning Servant is our model. He possessed knowledge of the truth and learned how to speak with eloquence so that He could bring the timely Word to those who were weary. Learning of the Word is never an end in itself; we learn the Word to teach those in need.

THE TEACHING-LEARNING PROCESS (50:4b–6)

Three principles are outlined in the Servant's description of His own teaching-learning process. First, He tells us that He *learned by listening*. The Lord GOD, who is His Teacher, awakens Him morning by morning to hear and learn the Word. The daily discipline of listening to God, before speaking on behalf of God, is a lesson that few of us learn. Listening itself is a gift that must be cultivated. Effective leaders are invariably good listeners. Second, the Servant testifies that He *learned by obedience*. When the Lord opened His ear to learn, He reports, *"And I was not rebellious, nor did I turn away."* Quite in contrast with Israel's rebellion and stubbornness, He remained obedient to the Lord and submissive to His teaching. Third, the Servant says that He *learned through suffering*. In the biographies of great people, we encounter episode after episode of failure before ascent to fame. Most will testify to the fact that they learned more from the pain of failure than from the euphoria of success. Through their own suffering, they learned to be sensitive to the suffering of their followers. The Servant goes through a learning experience that is even more painful and humiliating. He became weary under the lashes of a flogging, the indignity of having His beard plucked out, and the shame of being spit upon (v. 6). Yet, from the experience, He learns to speak with compassion as well as competence to those who are weary.

THE TEACHING-LEARNING TEST (50:7–9)

When the Servant faces the final examination for His teaching-learning experience, He does not rely upon Himself. An advocate is needed to carry His case against His adversaries as He is hauled into a court of law. Foreshadowing the trial of Jesus Christ and His response to His accusers, the Servant knows that He can count upon the Lord GOD to help Him as they stand together at the trial. Fully confident that He need not speak for Himself, the Servant sets His *"face like a flint"* and asks only the critical questions *"Who is My adversary?"* (v. 8b) and *"Who is he who will condemn Me?"* (v. 9). Try as they might, His adversaries have no case. In the most picturesque language, they will grow and be moth-eaten, like an old garment, without a single word of condemnation (v. 9b).

THE TEACHING-LEARNING MODEL (50:10)

As a fitting conclusion for the third Servant Song, those who have heard the Servant's testimony are invited to follow His example. For those who fear the Lord, obey His voice, and long for light in their darkness, the Servant is their model for trusting in His Lord and relying upon His God. Both the sovereign power and the covenant love of the Lord GOD will be theirs to take them through their suffering and hold them when they are weary. In turn, they will be disciples to whom the Lord GOD gives the "tongue of the learned" so that they too will know "how to speak a word in season to him who is weary."

The same word of truth from the lips of the Servant that builds trust in those who fear, obey, and seek God, strikes terror into the hearts of those who refuse to participate in the teaching-learning experience of the Lord GOD. They will not learn the Word, listen to His voice, obey His instructions, or submit to His discipline. With unbridled arrogance, they assume that they can have knowledge of the truth without experiencing the source of truth. Such people are as dangerous as sparks thrown upon dry kindling because of the raging fire they kindle to deceive and consume naive people. But in the end, the fires of falsehood they have kindled will be the bed upon which they will lie and die when God permits their sin to be their hell.

George Adam Smith puts this Servant Song into perspective when he outlines three disciplines behind the voice of the prophet: (a) *credibility* of living; (b) *competence* of learning; and (c) *compassion* of listening.[2] Nothing more needs to be said. In the teaching-learning experience of God's chosen Servant, He is that prophet and the Messiah. We need not look for any other.

THE TEACHING-LEARNING CURRICULUM (51:1–52:12)

1 "Listen to Me, you who follow after righteousness,
   You who seek the LORD:
   Look to the rock from which you were hewn,
   And to the hole of the pit
       from which you were dug.
2 Look to Abraham your father,
   And to Sarah who bore you;
   For I called him alone,
   And blessed him and increased him."

3 For the LORD will comfort Zion,
   He will comfort all her waste places;
   He will make her wilderness like Eden,
   And her desert like the garden of the LORD;
   Joy and gladness will be found in it,
   Thanksgiving and the voice of melody.
4 "Listen to Me, My people;
   And give ear to Me, O My nation:
   For law will proceed from Me,
   And I will make My justice rest
   As a light of the peoples.
5 My righteousness is near,
   My salvation has gone forth,
   And My arms will judge the peoples;
   The coastlands will wait upon Me,
   And on My arm they will trust.
6 Lift up your eyes to the heavens,
   And look on the earth beneath.
   For the heavens will vanish away like smoke,
   The earth will grow old like a garment,
   And those who dwell in it will die in like manner;
   But My salvation will be forever,
   And My righteousness will not be abolished.
7 "Listen to Me,
     you who know righteousness,
   You people in whose heart is My law:
   Do not fear the reproach of men,
   Nor be afraid of their revilings.
8 For the moth will eat them up like a garment,
   And the worm will eat them like wool;
   But My righteousness will be forever,
   And My salvation from generation to generation."
9 Awake, awake, put on strength,
   O arm of the LORD!
   Awake as in the ancient days,
   In the generations of old.
   Are you not the arm that cut Rahab apart,
   And wounded the serpent?
10 Are you not the One
     who dried up the sea,
   The waters of the great deep;
   That made the depths of the sea a road

For the redeemed to cross over?

11 So the ransomed of the LORD shall return,
And come to Zion with singing,
With everlasting joy on their heads;
They shall obtain joy and gladness,
And sorrow and sighing shall flee away.

12 "I, even I, am He who comforts you.
Who are you that you should be afraid
Of a man who will die,
And of the son of a man who will be made like grass?

13 And you forget the LORD your Maker,
Who stretched out the heavens
And laid the foundations of the earth;
You have feared continually every day
Because of the fury of the oppressor,
When he has prepared to destroy.
And where is the fury of the oppressor?

14 The captive exile hastens,
    that he may be loosed,
That he should not die in the pit,
And that his bread should not fail.

15 But I am the LORD your God,
Who divided the sea whose waves roared—
The LORD of hosts is His name.

16 And I have put My words in your mouth;
I have covered you with the shadow of My hand,
That I may plant the heavens,
Lay the foundations of the earth,
And say to Zion,
    'You are My people.'"

17 Awake, awake!
Stand up, O Jerusalem,
You who have drunk at the hand of the LORD
The cup of His fury;
You have drunk the dregs of the cup of trembling,
And drained it out.

18 There is no one to guide her
Among all the sons she has brought forth;
Nor is there any who takes her
    by the hand
Among all the sons she has brought up.

19 These two things have come to you;

Who will be sorry for you?—
Desolation and destruction,
    famine and sword—
By whom will I comfort you?
20 Your sons have fainted,
They lie at the head of all the streets,
Like an antelope in a net;
They are full of the fury of the LORD,
The rebuke of your God.
21 Therefore please hear this,
    you afflicted,
And drunk but not with wine.
22 Thus says your Lord,
The LORD and your God,
Who pleads the cause of His people:
"See, I have taken out of your hand
The cup of trembling,
The dregs of the cup of My fury;
You shall no longer drink it.
23 But I will put it into the hand
    of those who afflict you,
Who have said to you,
'Lie down, that we may walk over you,'
And you have laid your body like the ground,
And as the street,
    for those who walk over."
1 Awake, awake!
Put on your strength, O Zion;
Put on your beautiful garments,
O Jerusalem, the holy city!
For the uncircumcised and the unclean
Shall no longer come to you.
2 Shake yourself from the dust, arise,
And sit down, O Jerusalem;
Loose yourself from the bonds
    of your neck,
O captive daughter of Zion!
3 For thus says the LORD:
"You have sold yourselves for nothing,
And you shall be redeemed without money."
4 For thus says the Lord GOD:
"My people went down at first

527

Into Egypt to sojourn there;
Then the Assyrian oppressed them without cause.

5 Now therefore, what have I here," says the LORD,
"That My people are taken away for nothing?
Those who rule over them
Make them wail," says the LORD,
"And My name is blasphemed
  continually every day.

6 Therefore My people shall know My name;
Therefore they shall know in that day
That I am He who speaks:
'Behold, it is I.'"

7 How beautiful upon the mountains
Are the feet of him who brings good news,
who proclaims peace,
Who brings glad tidings of good things,
Who proclaims salvation,
Who says to Zion,
"Your God reigns!"

8 Your watchmen shall lift up their voices,
With their voices they shall sing together;
For they shall see eye to eye
When the LORD brings back Zion.

9 Break forth into joy, sing together,
You waste places of Jerusalem!
For the LORD has comforted His people,
He has redeemed Jerusalem.

10 The LORD has made bare His holy arm
In the eyes of all the nations;
and all the ends of the earth shall see
The salvation of our God.

11 Depart! Depart! Go out from there,
Touch no unclean thing;
Go out from the midst of her,
Be clean,
You who bear the vessels of the LORD.

12 For you shall not go out with haste,
Nor go by flight;
For the LORD will go before you,
And the God of Israel will be your rear guard.

Isaiah 51:1–52:12

By character and credentials, the Servant has been prepared to be a disciple empowered by the Lord GOD with the responsibility for teaching. Imagine, a classroom setting for chapters 51:1–52:12. The teaching sessions are introduced by imperatives that a teacher would use. *"Listen"* (51:1 and 7), *"awake"* (51:9, 17, and 52:1), and *"give ear to me"* (51:4) call the class to attention. In general, the members of the class are the children of Israel, but they are divided between those who are in Babylonian exile and those who remain in Jerusalem. Within these two groups, the class is also divided by the level of spiritual insight. Beginning with those who *"seek the LORD"* (51:1) and moving progressively to those whose mature faithfulness qualifies them as members of the spiritual *"Zion"* (52:1), the Servant addresses the particular problem that each group faces, presents a factual solution to the problem, and concludes with a word of assurance based upon a change of behavior for the learners. From this perspective, six lessons make up the teaching of the Servant: (1) The Lesson of History (51:1–3); (2) The Lesson of Nature (51:4–6); (3) The Lesson of Law (51:7–8); (4) The Lesson of Power (51:9–16); (5) The Lesson of Judgment (51:17–23); and (6) The Lesson of Redemption (52:1–12).

THE LESSON OF HISTORY (51:1–3)

"Listen to Me" is the imperative that brings the class to order. The students are those who *"follow after righteousness"* and *"seek the LORD."* While they may be the faithful and obedient Israelites in exile who make up the remnant that will return to Jerusalem, they are clearly classified as those who are in the early stages of spiritual growth. In the class meetings of John Wesley, the participants were divided between *inquirers* and those who were *convinced.* Inquirers were those persons who hungered and thirsted for righteousness but needed more instruction before they would become fully convinced believers by knowledge and experience. For them, the basics of the Gospel were taught.

Inquirers or seekers is an appropriate description for the members of the class to whom the Servant taught His first lesson. Not yet fully convinced that the Lord can deliver them, they need to hear the most basic of truths. Consequently, their teacher takes them back to their origins. *"Look to the rock from which you were hewn, and to the pit from which you were dug"* (v. 1b) is a call to remember the history of the children of Israel. James Conant, past President of Harvard, said that good teaching always begins with history. If we want to understand who we are today, we need to know who we were yesterday and how far we have come. Likewise, in our spiritual development, we need to begin with a reminder of our past condition, our progress over time, and our current status. Each of us shares the testimony of the backwoods preacher who said, "Thank God, I ain't what I was and I ain't what I will be, but I am what I am." The children of Israel had come from the poorest of the poor and the weakest of the weak to be chosen as God's covenant people. On this fact, they can build their faith.

Even greater encouragement is given to the class of seekers with a second imperative, *"Look to Abraham your father, and to Sarah who bore you"* (v. 2a). Memory will reveal another fundamental fact to them. They are the recipients of God's miraculous promise to the old man Abraham and the barren woman Sarah that He will bless them with a child and increase their numbers beyond count. By remembering the proof of this promise, they will know that the same God can turn the barrenness of their dismal existence in exile into a veritable garden of joy, gladness, thanksgiving, and melody. As a good teacher, the Servant foresees the lesson of origins leading to a change of behavior in His students. The hesitant question of the honest seeker becomes the *"voice of melody"* when the proof of God's covenant and promise in the past is recalled.

THE LESSON OF NATURE (51:4–6)

Another imperative, *"listen to Me,"* calls another class to order. The students are now those who have learned the first lesson of history and responded to the teacher's designation, *"My people"* and *"My nation."* These are learners who have advanced to the level of obedience to the law and the requirements of justice. They do the law, but they do not delight in it. For them, the proof of God at work is in the evidence of social justice for current affairs. Today, they would be advocates for the "social gospel" and activists in political issues such as equal rights for minorities, environmental protection, economic welfare, and educational opportunity. For them, the Servant promises that His *"righteousness is near"* and His *"salvation"* is on the way.

Their preoccupation with temporary affairs and social justice, however, needs to be advanced to a higher level of understanding. Although the work for social justice is essential to the witness of the believer, it can become an end in itself to the neglect of higher spiritual and eternal values. As the balance for students at this level of faith development, the Servant teaches a basic truth about the nature of physical creation and human existence: *"The heavens will vanish . . . the earth will grow old . . . and those who dwell in it will die . . ."* (v. 6a). By way of contrast, the Servant teaches, *"But My salvation will be forever, and My righteousness will not be abolished"* (v. 6b).

Whether we are strong advocates of social issues on the right or the left, the same caution holds. Our work must be done and our witness must be given from the perspective of spiritual and eternal values. As one successful businessman decided, "I want to give myself to something that will outlive me." For those whose faith is expressed primarily at the level of setting things right in the social order, the Servant shows them the next stage of faith development—to see the spiritual and eternal purpose of God.

THE LESSON OF LAW (51:7–8)

The imperative, *"listen to Me,"* is now given to those *"who know righteousness"* and *"in whose heart is My law"* (v. 7a). In this class and at this level of learning, the *seekers* have become *knowers* and those who are *keepers* of the law have become *lovers* of the law. For them, the Servant has the lesson of faithfulness.

Spiritual people are always subject to criticism. They are branded as *fanatics* and *enthusiasts* who have lost touch with the real world. We can understand the sting the faithful Israelites felt from those who reproached and reviled them during the time of exile. When pessimists spread their message of gloom and doom among the people, they were the optimists who foresaw the promise of God for deliverance and called for patience. For them, the Servant has a special lesson from His own experience. He, too, has been subjected to the biting criticism of adversaries who tried to condemn him unjustly (v. 7–9). But they will remember His response. Setting His face like a flint, He refused to be ashamed or disgraced because the Lord GOD stood with Him as His advocate. Those who tried to condemn Him would grow old and die like a moth-eaten garment without proving one single charge against Him. The Servant, then, can teach by the strength of His example. He invites the faithful to identify with Him and be assured that their critics will also fail to condemn them, and like the moth-eaten garment or the worm-eaten wool, they too will grow old and die without proving their charge. In contrast, the righteous in heart will live forever, and they will become teaching-learning servants themselves as they communicate faithfulness from *"generation to generation"* (v. 8b).

THE LESSON OF POWER (51:9–16)

A new and doubly strong imperative is used to open the next class session. *"Awake, awake"* is a loud call with a rising note of urgency. Even those who have the spirit of the law written in their hearts need to be shaken into action. In fact, they can err on the side of inaction if their spirituality becomes an end in itself. Monks who retreated to the desert in early Christian centuries are a case in point. To escape the evils of the world, they isolated themselves in caves, lived in poverty, prayed in solitude, and professed purity. Of course, they soon discovered sin within themselves and realized that the evil of the world was still very much with them. Modern-day mystics tend toward the same error. I recall a religion professor who spent several months in spiritual retreat. When he returned to the campus, he walked and talked with a holy aura, but no longer had an interest in such mundane matters as balancing the budget of his department. I recall using the words of Jesus when I met with him, "This you should have done, but not left the other undone."

For those who retreat into spirituality out of fear for the real world, the Servant has a lesson, crying "Awake, awake." He calls upon the power of the arm of the Lord GOD to act again. A lesson out of the spiritual history of Israel follows. By the power of God, Rahab, the sea monster and author of chaos, had been cut apart, and Satan, the serpent and author of evil, had been wounded. By the power of God, the Red Sea parted, and the dry ground became a road to freedom for the children of Israel as they fled from Egyptian bondage (v. 10). Surely then, the same arm of power can overcome the obstacles and prepare the way for the exiles in Babylon to return home to Zion with a song on their lips and joy on their heads (v. 11).

The music of a military march follows. With all of the stirring words of "The Battle Hymn of the Republic" and the foot-tapping rhythm of "The Stars and Stripes Forever," God gives spiritual people a song of action. They will not fear any mortal being because the Lord their Maker is all-powerful (vv. 12–13). The time has come for their release from exile, and the LORD of Hosts will set them free (vv. 14–15). Moreover, they have the promise of God's Word, the presence of His Spirit, and the power of His creation assuring them of salvation because they are still His covenant people (vv. 16b). As every master teacher leads the students to action, so the Servant has empowered the faithful few with the energy and incentive to lead the new exodus.

THE LESSON OF JUDGMENT (51:17–23)

With the same strong imperative *"Awake, awake!"* the Servant calls another class of students together in a different location. Preparation for the return of the remnant from Babylon needs to be made with the Jews who remained in Jerusalem as well as with those who are in exile. So, to the beleaguered company who suffered a marginal existence among the ruins of Jerusalem, the Servant's word is, *"Stand up, O Jerusalem."* In the most graphic language depicting judgment at the hand of the Lord, the Servant describes their plight as a drunkenness that has gone from drinking, to the *"cup of His fury,"* to draining the dregs of the *"cup of trembling"* until they have passed out and fallen over in a drunken stupor.

Ordinarily, a man would come to mind in such a picture of drunken disgrace. But alas, Jerusalem is described as a woman. The disgrace is even deeper as the analogy continues into the hopelessness of the people of the city. When fathers got drunk and fell over, their sons had the obligation to pick them up and lead them home. For drunken Jerusalem, chosen to be the mother of spiritual Zion, the judgment is so complete that she has no sons to take her by the hand, lift her up, and lead her home. The disgrace is also complete because she has suffered the loss of her land due to *"desolation and destruction"* and the loss of her sons due to *"famine and sword"* (v. 19). The cup of judgment has been drunk and drained.

But through the teaching of the Servant, the Lord GOD has a lesson for His faithful children in Jerusalem. With genuine and personal pathos, the Lord GOD says to those who are suffering the saturation of judgment, *"Please hear this"* (v. 21). By His grace, He promises them that they will no longer drink of the cup of trembling and fury, but the same cup will be given to their enemies to drink. Desolation and destruction will now come upon their enemy's land; famine and sword will now decimate their enemy's sons. To press home the point, the Lord recalls the standard treatment that their Babylonian captors had given them. As a sign of their conquest, the Babylonians forced their prisoners to lie in the dust of the street while they walked over their backs. Now the worm turns, and under the judgment of God the proud people of Babylon will be the ones biting the dust and feeling the boots of the conqueror breaking the bones of their backs.

Although the reversal of judgment seems cruel, we cannot forget the repeated theme of Isaiah in which sin carries the seeds of its own destruction. Consequently, those who live by the sword will die by the sword. So, we should not be surprised to learn that the brutality of the conquering Babylonians will be turned against them with added vengeance by their conquerors. The real purpose of this lesson, however, is not to teach about judgment. Rather, it is a lesson in grace. When God says, *"I have taken out of your hand the cup of trembling, the dregs of the cup of My fury,"* He takes that cup to Himself with all of its implications for the Suffering Servant. When Jesus asked His disciples, "Can you drink the cup that I drink?" (Mark 10:38); when he took the cup at the Last Supper and said, "This is My blood of the new covenant" (Mark 14:24); and when he prayed in the garden, "Take this cup away from Me" (Mark 14:36), He filled out the meaning of this lesson from Isaiah. Drunken and stuporous Jerusalem had no hope within itself and no power to stand, but when God took the cup of fury and trembling to Himself, He put the cup of love and grace to its lips. As His children in Babylon received the promise of power for their return, so His children in Jerusalem received the promise of power for their restoration. In each case, salvation is the common theme.

THE LESSON OF REDEMPTION (52:1–12)

The teaching of the Servant moves to its most advanced level with a repetition of the double imperative, *"Awake, awake! Put on your strength, O Zion"* (v. 1). The class is now made up of the children of Israel in Babylon, Jerusalem, the coastlands, and the farthest parts of the earth who are members of Zion or the spiritual family of God by knowledge, obedience, and faith. For them, the time has come for their deliverance through the return from exile and the restoration of Jerusalem. With poetic beauty, the Servant calls for Zion to "put on your strength" as a young virgin bride puts on her wedding dress. What a contrast with the drunken woman who is unable to stand and has no one to help her! The "captive daughter" is to be set free from her bonds and dressed in the finest of clothes in preparation for meeting her lover and celebrating their marriage.

Grace is again the agent that makes deliverance possible. When the Lord says, *"You have sold yourselves for nothing, and you shall be redeemed without money"* (v. 3), He is confirming the fact that He never gave up on His people. They sold themselves into judgment by their sin, but He still said, "You are My people" (v. 16b). That which is never sold does not need to be repurchased. Of course, there is a price for their redemption, but it is not money. With another indirect reference to the Suffering Servant, the inspired words of Peter are anticipated, "Knowing that you were not redeemed with corruptible things, like silver or gold, from your aimless conduct received by tradition from your fathers, but with the precious blood of Christ, as of a lamb without blemish and without spot" (1 Peter 1:18–19).

To the assurance of grace is given the assurance of power. Notably, when the Servant speaks of grace, the word is, *"For thus says the LORD"* (v. 3). But when He speaks of power, He employs the rare and strong double title, *"For thus says the Lord GOD"* (v. 4). The children of Israel have already suffered under the heels of two oppressors, Egypt and Assyria (v. 4a). In each case, God had bared the arm of His power to deliver them from physical bondage and paralyzing fear. Therefore, in so many words, the Lord GOD says, "I will do it again" so that *"My people shall know My name"* and My nature, *"Behold, it is I"* (v. 6b).

Everyone who has heard Handel's Messiah begins to hum when they read another song of deliverance, *"How beautiful upon the mountains are the feet of him who brings good news"* (v. 7a). Few, however, grasp the full meaning of the song that He gives the people of Zion to sing. Our mind's eye must see through the eyes of the *"watchmen"* (v. 8) looking out from the ruined walls of Jerusalem toward the distant mountains where the faint image of a messenger on the run comes into view. As the runner comes closer, the speed of the gait, the smile on the face, and the note being waved in the air leaves no doubt—the messenger comes to proclaim the *"good news"* of *"peace"* and the *"glad tidings"* of *"salvation."* Within hearing distance now, the shout is heard, *"Your God reigns!"* The watchmen run from their post and into the streets to shout the same good word to all the people. Those who wail will *"break forth with joy"* and those who sorrow will begin to *"sing together"* (v. 9). "Our God Reigns" is the good news of peace and the glad tidings of salvation that breaks through despair with joy and brings a note of song to the lips of sorrowing people.

Urgency takes over the last lesson of the Servant with the multiple imperatives, *"Depart! Depart! Go out from there"* (v. 11a). All of the preparation for deliverance is complete. The time has come to act. Yet, with urgency, there is a caution and a promise. The caution is: *"Touch no unclean thing; go out from the midst of her; be clean; you who bear the vessels of the LORD"* (v. 12b). From earlier oracles, we know that Hezekiah had stripped the temple of the Lord to pay tribute to Babylon. We also know that Isaiah had condemned those in exile who contaminated the worship of Yahweh with the worship of idols. Both of these sins need to be corrected in the return of the remnant. No idols were to be touched, and no bearers of the vessels for the temple were to be contaminated. The purity of Zion is a first concern of God whether for the restoration of His temple in Jerusalem in the sixth century or the renewal of His church in the twentieth century. Our prayers for revival in our day should begin with the separation from competing gods and the cleansing of those who carry His witness.

God's promise adds another "new thing" to the lessons of His salvation. In contrast with the hurried exodus from Egypt, He tells the children of Israel in exile that they will *"not go out with haste, nor go by flight"* (v. 12a). Cyrus's decree will cause them to leave Babylon by orderly march, with the vessels of the temple, in order to restore the worship of their God. For their long and tortuous journey, they are given another promise. The Lord will go before them as their sapper to remove the obstacles and smooth the way. He will also come behind them as their *"rear guard"* to assure their safety. These two dimensions of God's presence—before us and behind us—are all the assurance that is needed to take the risks that God asks of His people.

Each time that we step out by faith to do His will, we are amazed to find that He has prepared the way before us and assured us of His protection for our flank. As a wise counselor once told me during a time of criticism, "If you are being shot at from the rear, you know that you are in front of your enemies and heading in the right direction!" Whether it is obstacles in front of us or enemies behind us, the Lord promises to prepare the way before us and protect the way behind us.

Every contingency has now been covered by the lessons of the Servant for the children of Israel in their generation and for the faithful in Zion for every generation. As with all learning experiences, the evidence of maturity in knowledge and understanding comes when the student tests the learning experientially and experimentally in a new situation. When the faithful children of Israel depart from Babylon and head home toward Jerusalem, they will show that they have learned their lessons well.

NOTES

1. H. M. Wolf, *Interpreting Isaiah* (Grand Rapids: Zondervan, 1985), 210.

2. Smith, *Expositor's Bible, Vol. II*, 335.

CHAPTER TWENTY-FIVE

The Sin-Bearing Servant

Isaiah 52:13–55:13

All of Isaiah's gifts as a prophet and a poet are displayed in the fourth of the Servant Songs. Language that employs rare words for Old Testament prophecy and lyrics that express the deepest of human emotions come together in a Song of Suffering that tells of the meaning of Christ's death and its significance for the world. In the first Servant Song, Isaiah introduced the Servant of the Lord to us by His ultimate mission "As a light to the Gentiles" (42:1–9). The second Servant Song added the insight that He would feel human discouragement, "I have labored in vain," and natural fatigue, "I have spent My strength for nothing and in vain" (49:1–13). Suffering becomes integral to the Servant's role, however, in the third Servant Song when He testifies, "I gave My back to those who struck Me, and My cheeks to those who plucked out the beard; I did not hide My face from shame and spitting" (50:4–9). While the fact that the Servant must suffer is revealed in these first three songs, the reason for His suffering is still unknown. Full explanation is given in the fourth Servant Song under the appropriate title, "The Sin-Bearing Servant."

THE SUFFERING OF THE SERVANT (52:13–53:12)

13 Behold, My Servant shall deal prudently,
   He shall be exalted and extolled
      and be very high.
14 Just as many were astonished at you,
   So His visage was marred more than any man,
   And His form more than the sons of men;
15 So shall He sprinkle many nations.
   Kings shall shut their mouths at Him;

For what had not been told them
    they shall see,
And what they had not heard
    they shall consider.
1 Who has believed our report?
    And to whom has the arm of the
    LORD been revealed?
2 For He shall grow up before Him
    as a tender plant,
    And as a root out of dry ground.
    He has no form or comeliness;
    And when we see Him,
    There is no beauty
      that we should desire Him.
3 He is despised and rejected by men,
    A man of sorrows
      and acquainted with grief
    And we hid, as it were,
      our faces from Him;
    He was despised,
      and we did not esteem Him.
4 Surely He has borne our griefs
    And carried our sorrows;
    Yet we esteemed Him stricken,
    Smitten by God, and afflicted.
5 But He was wounded for our transgressions,
    He was bruised for our iniquities;
    The chastisement for our peace was upon Him,
    And by His stripes we are healed.
6 All we like sheep have gone astray;
    We have turned, every one,
      to his own way;
    And the LORD has laid on Him the iniquity of us all.
7 He was oppressed and He was afflicted,
    Yet He opened not His mouth;
    He was led as a lamb to the slaughter,
    And as a sheep before its shearers is silent,
    So He opened not his mouth.
8 He was taken from prison
    and from judgment,
    And who will declare His generation?
    For He was cut off from the land of the living;

For the transgressions of My people
He was stricken.
9 And they made His grave
with the wicked—
But with the rich at His death,
Because He had done no violence,
Nor was any deceit in His mouth.
10 Yet it pleased the LORD to bruise Him;
He has put Him to grief.
When You make His soul an offering for sin,
He shall see His seed,
He shall prolong His days,
And the pleasure of the LORD shall
prosper in His hand.
11 He shall see the travail of His soul,
and be satisfied.
By His knowledge My righteous
Servant shall justify many,
For He shall bear their iniquities.
12 Therefore I will divide Him a portion with the great,
And He shall divide the spoil
with the strong,
Because He poured out His soul unto death,
And He was numbered
with the transgressors,
And He bore the sin of many,
And made intercession for the transgressors.
Isaiah 52:13–53:12

Human nature shies away from suffering. When suffering comes, we try to explain it as a penalty for sin or a circumstance of chance. Few, if any of us would think of suffering voluntarily for the sin of others or believe that our suffering would save others. Yet, this is precisely what the Servant of the Lord did. In full obedience to the will of the Lord GOD, He made the voluntary choice to suffer for the sins of others and to find His reward in the redemption of others.

SUFFERING THROUGH OBEDIENCE (52:13–15)

No wonder Isaiah opens the Song with the cry, *"Behold, My Servant."* Of all the "new things" that God promised to do in the first Servant

Song, voluntary suffering for the sins of others in order to redeem sinners is the newest of the "new" (42:9). The Servant's decision to suffer is not a matter of blind obedience to the iron will of God. The prophet tells us He made the choice *"prudently"* or as a result of practical wisdom. The wisdom of the choice reflected the Servant's understanding of the big picture of God's redemptive purpose; practical wisdom meant that He fully realized the horrifying consequences that would follow. By His act, He also reversed the sin of Adam and Eve in the Garden when they chose to eat from the tree of life in order to be as "prudent" or as wise as God. Paul, the apostle, saw the implications of these two decisions when he wrote, "For as by one man's disobedience many were made sinners, so also by one Man's obedience many will be made righteous" (Romans 5:19). Although Paul had the hindsight of the resurrection, he sums up the meaning of the first verse of the Servant Song in one sentence.

Astonishment is the only way that humans can respond to the information that the Servant will voluntarily suffer for the sins of others in order to *"sprinkle many nations"* with the symbolic water of purification or righteousness. Although He will suffer pain and humiliation never known before, He will *"be exalted,"* *"extolled,"* and *"be very high"* (52:13a). Without pressing the meaning of these terms too far, the rising level of exaltation in the three stages may well coincide with the resurrection, ascension, and glorification of Jesus Christ, God Incarnate. In any case, the rise of the obedient Servant from the deepest human disgrace to the highest level of divine exaltation cannot be denied. His obedience to suffering and His salvation of the nations will cause kings to shut their mouths in awe as they see what their sorcerers had failed to show them and consider what their wise men had failed to tell them (52:15). Through His obedience, the Servant will suffer until He appears to be less than human, but then His Lord will exalt Him until He is undeniably more than human. In fact, He whom "man despises" and "the nation abhors" will be the one before whom "kings . . . arise" and "princes . . . worship" (49:7).

SUFFERING FROM REJECTION (53:1–3)

Obedience to suffering extracts an incredible price in social esteem from the Servant of the Lord. The depth of His social suffering goes beyond belief, and so much so that the prophet asks, *"Who has believed our report? And to whom has the arm of the LORD been revealed?"* (v. 1). The rhetorical question answers itself. No one can believe that the Servant grew up from such lowly beginnings that His background is likened to a *"tender plant"* or a young shoot that is a nuisance and usually cut off before maturity. Also, like a *"root out of dry ground,"* His background is so blighted that no one can believe that He would be the seed of royal blood in the lineage of Jesse and David (v. 2).

All of the romance that time and distance have created around the beginnings and background of Jesus get a strong dose of reality in the description of the Servant as a "young shoot" and an "impoverished root." Some scholars suggest that Jesus' birth to the virgin Mary scandalized the family and permanently scarred His name. Despite Joseph's gracious act of love to marry the pregnant woman and give her child a name, Jesus never lost the label as the illegitimate son of Mary. Such a "young shoot" would never stand a chance for social recognition. Furthermore, the "impoverished root" may speak more than just the humble beginnings of Jesus in the wretched little town of Nazareth. His designation as a carpenter may be interpreted either as the honorable profession of a craftsman or the abased position of a handyman who does odd jobs around town. Isaiah's description of the background of the Servant comes closest to a shameful birth and an abased position.

Physical features, even in Jesus' time, influenced social esteem. When beautiful people reveal their emotional insecurities or their moral emptiness, we are surprised because we equate beauty with esteem. Ugly people live with the opposite reputation. Our first reaction to a disfigured face is withdrawal. Our second reaction is to devalue the worth of that person on our scale of esteem. Abraham Lincoln suffered from his ugliness throughout his lifetime and even during his tenure as President. Those who knew him, however, saw past the ugliness and through the gentleness of the eyes into the compassion of his heart. At one time, Lincoln is reputed to have responded to a question about his ugliness by saying, "The face you have before forty you cannot help, but the face you have after forty you deserve."

The Servant will not have the advantage of time to communicate the beauty of His person and His personality. To the end of His life, He will know the sorrow and the grief of being *"despised and rejected by men"* (v. 3). Like the shock of the hideous face behind the half mask of the Phantom of the Opera, those who see the face of the Servant will hide their eyes, and without ever knowing the person behind the mask, they will write him off as inhuman. The "sorrow and grief" that the Servant felt from hidden eyes and debasing glares meant that He entertained no masochistic pleasure in His rejection. Just the opposite. With a verve for living, a desire for friends, and a wish for good will, the *"sorrows"* and *"grief"* of the Servant come because of His total rejection.

THE SUFFERING OF PAIN (53:4–6)

Although the suffering of social rejection deeply wounded the Servant of the Lord, the physical beating that He took brings greater pathos from the prophet. The adjectives *"stricken," "smitten," "afflicted," "wounded," "bruised,"* and the nouns, *"chastisement"* and *"stripes"* explain why Isaiah had written earlier, "His visage was marred more than any man, and His form more than the sons of men" (52:14). In the vernacular of our day, the Servant of the Lord was "beaten to a pulp."

But even as we cringe at the thought of His excruciating physical pain, tears of gratitude well in our eyes when we read another set of words that explain why the Servant of the Lord suffered as He did. Counterbalancing the expressions of pain are the words that tell us He suffered for us. Three words speak the meaning of His suffering, *"He has **borne** our griefs and **carried** our sorrows . . . the LORD has **laid** upon Him the iniquity of us all"* (vv. 4a and 6b). Theologians interpret His sin-bearing as the doctrine of *substitution,* meaning that He took our place to bear the judgment of our sin even though He Himself knew no sin. The other side of this truth is the reason for our tears of gratitude. All of His pain is for *"our griefs," "our sorrows," "our transgressions,"* and *"our iniquities."* The Servant not only took our sins upon Himself, but He also took our sorrows. Through the ministry of sorrows, we know that He understands every grief we suffer because He too has felt our pain. And the ministry of bearing our sins and carrying our sorrows does not stop there. Through the *"chastisement"* of the Servant we have *"our peace,"* and through the *"stripes"* of the Servant we are *"healed"* (v. 5). His suffering, then, is not in vain. Contrary to the frustration that we often feel when we try to share the burden of suffering with someone we love, but find ourselves helpless to make a difference, the Servant's ministry of sorrows is effective.

When Matthew recorded his account of the healing ministry of Jesus with those who were physically sick and demon-possessed, he explained the events by quoting Isaiah 53:4, "He Himself took our infirmities and bore our sicknesses" (Matthew 8:17). In sacrificial language, Peter quoted the same text at length when he wrote to comfort Christians throughout the Roman Empire who were suffering persecution for their faith, "Who Himself bore our sins in His own body on the tree, that we, having died to sins, might live for righteousness—by whose stripes you were healed" (1 Peter 2:24). All of this despite the fact that we, like Israel, are sheep that have gone astray (53:6a). Peter expands upon Isaiah's text to seal the effective results of the Servant's ministry of sorrows when he concludes, "For you were like sheep going astray, but have now returned to the Shepherd and Overseer of your souls" (1 Peter 2:25). The suffering of pain is more than a matter of bearing judgment for our sins and carrying the weight of our sorrows. With all of our iniquities "laid on Him," we can stop straying and return home to the Shepherd of our souls.

SUFFERING IN SILENCE (53:7–9)

Human reason explains suffering as a penalty inflicted upon a person who is guilty. Deep within us is a nagging sense of "cash register justice" that rings in a crime and rings out a penalty. As simplistic as it may sound, we must all confess that when we suffer, our first question is, "What did I do wrong?" Job, a righteous man, had this question turned on him by his alleged friends and comforters when he suffered on the brink of death. They probed and probed for the sin in his life. When they failed to confirm their accusations, they left him in disgust as a hopeless case. Although they were reputed to be wise, their doctrine of cash register justice left no room for the suffering of the innocent.

When the Servant of the Lord took on all of our iniquities, He also took upon Himself the penalty of judgment against our sins. A sacrificial tone has already been set in the previous verse of the Servant Song when we are likened to sheep that have gone astray and He is likened to the scapegoat that was sent into the wilderness bearing our sins. As a progression on that theme, the Servant is now likened to a sacrificial lamb going silently to the slaughter or a sheep lying passively in the hands of its shearers (v. 7). Paralleling this image is the vision of a courtroom in which a mock trial is being held. As the Servant bears His physical beatings in silence and refuses to confess sins that He did not commit, His accusers become more and more aggressive in their accusations until He is falsely condemned to die, executed as a criminal, and buried with the "*wicked*" and the "*rich*" after His death (v. 9).

Behind the fiasco, however, is the proof that the Servant suffered in silence because of His sinlessness. No person could pay the penalty for the sins of others if that person had his or her own sins. Although He was falsely accused, unjustly condemned, conveniently executed, and disgracefully buried, not a shred of evidence had been found proving that He had broken civil law by violence or moral law by deceit. Scholars who argue that this Servant Song refers exclusively to the suffering of Israel through its history of holocausts miss the most important point. Suffering in silence is more than gritting the teeth against false accusations. It is the inner peace of innocence that only Jesus Christ, the Servant of the Lord, has known. No one else can pay the penalty for our sin.

SUFFERING FOR REDEMPTION (53:10–12)

Another conundrum that escapes human understanding confronts us when we read, "*Yet it pleased the LORD to bruise Him . . . put Him to grief . . . [and] make His soul an offering for sin*" (v. 10a).   Naturally, we find it difficult to understand how the Lord can find pleasure in the suffering of His Servant. In this context, the pleasure of the Lord is not the glee of whimsy or selfish intent. As Isaiah has taught us repeatedly throughout his prophecy, the Lord's *pleasure* is His good purpose to bring redemption to the world despite the unfaithfulness of Israel and the rejection of His Servant. The suffering of the Servant, then, is a necessary means to a purposeful end. As the Servant is exalted, the Lord GOD is glorified. But even before the end of God's pleasure is known, the Servant will be honored for His obedience and His suffering. The Lord GOD will (1) show Him the "*seed*" of His work in the persons who believe in Him; (2) prolong His days throughout eternity; (3) satisfy Him with the knowledge of seeing the redemptive outcome of His suffering; and (4) share with Him the victories of His conquest over sin and suffering (vv. 10b–12a). With John the Revelator, it is time to stop and sing, "Worthy is the Lamb who was slain to receive power and riches and wisdom, and strength and honor and glory and blessing!" (Revelation 5:12).

Why must the Servant of the Lord be exalted? Because by voluntary choice,*"He poured out His soul unto death,"* and by sinless suffering *"He was numbered with the transgressors"* (v. 12a). Why must the Servant of the Lord suffer? Because by bearing our sins, He and He alone can be our advocate before the throne of the Holy God and our hope for pardon from our transgressions.

THE HERITAGE OF THE SERVANTS (54:1–17)

1 "Sing, O barren,
  You who have not borne!
  Break forth into singing,
    and cry aloud,
  You who have not travailed with child!
  For more are the children of the desolate
  Than the children of the married
    woman," says the LORD.

2 "Enlarge the place of your tent,
  And let them stretch out the curtains of your habitations;
  Do not spare;
  Lengthen your cords,
  And strengthen your stakes.

3 For you shall expand to the right and to the left,
  And your descendants will inherit the nations,
  And make the desolate cities inhabited.

4 "Do not fear,
    for you will not be ashamed;
  Nor be disgraced,
    for you will not be put to shame;
  For you will forget the shame of your youth,
  And will not remember the reproach of
    your widowhood anymore.

5 For your Maker is your husband,
  The Lord of hosts is His name;

And your Redeemer is the Holy One of Israel;
He is called the God of the whole earth.

6 For the LORD has called you
Like a woman forsaken
    and grieved in spirit,
Like a youthful wife when you were refused,"
Says your God.

7 "For a mere moment
    I have forsaken you,
But with great mercies
    I will gather you.

8 With a little wrath I hid My face from
    you for a moment;
But with everlasting kindness I will
    have mercy on you,"
Says the LORD, your Redeemer.

9 "For this is like the waters of Noah to Me;
For as I have sworn
That the waters of Noah would
    no longer cover the earth,
So have I sworn
That I would not be angry with you, nor rebuke you.

10 For the mountains shall depart
And the hills be removed,
But My kindness shall not depart from you,
Nor shall My covenant of peace be removed,"
Says the LORD, who has mercy on you.

11 "O you afflicted one,
Tossed with tempest,
    and not comforted,
Behold, I will lay your stones with colorful gems,
And lay your foundations with sapphires.

12 I will make your pinnacles of rubies,
Your gates of crystal,
And all your walls of precious stones.

13 All your children shall be taught by the LORD,
And great shall be the peace of your children.

14 In righteousness you shall be established;
You shall be far from oppression,
    for you shall not fear;
And from terror,
    for it shall not come near you.

15 Indeed they shall surely assemble,
       but not because of Me.
    Whoever assembles against you
       shall fall for your sake.
16 "Behold, I have created the blacksmith
    Who blows the coals in the fire,
    Who brings forth an instrument
       for his work;
    And I have created the spoiler to destroy.
17 No weapon formed against you shall prosper,
    And every tongue which rises against you in judgment
    You shall condemn.
    This is the heritage of the servants
       of the LORD,
    And their righteousness is from Me,"
    Says the LORD.

Isaiah 54:1–17

The Servant of the Lord has done His work. Having "poured out His soul unto death" and borne the "sin of many," He will now be "exalted and extolled and be very high" (52:13). From His position at the right hand of the Holy God, He will continue to make "intercession for the transgressors" (53:12). Consequently, the theme of Isaiah's prophecy now shifts from the work of the Servant to the salvation that He brings. Chapters 54–56 are oracles of salvation to three different groups of people who are the beneficiaries of the Servant's ministry. Chapter 54 is addressed to those in exile who are faithful to God and represent the spiritual Church in all ages. Chapter 55 is a timeless and universal invitation to those who are spiritually hungry and thirsty for salvation by faith followed by the promise of abundant life. Chapter 56:1–8 extends the invitation and the promise to Gentiles who have been blocked from the blessings of the covenant by religious restrictions that are now superseded by faith.

A significant shift is evident in chapter 54 when "the Servant" as a singular noun disappears from Isaiah's prophecy. From now on, "the servants" of the Servant, or those who carry on His legacy of obedience, faithfulness, and self-sacrifice will be the focus of Isaiah's attention. The key to understanding chapter 54 is found in the conclusion when the Lord says, *"This is the heritage of the servants of the LORD and their righteousness is from Me"* (54:17). Perhaps we can imagine ourselves

548

sitting together as children at the reading of a loving parent's last will and testament. Blessing after blessing is given to us in the legacy.

THE BLESSING OF GROWTH (54:1–3)

Metaphors and contrasts continue to be Isaiah's favorite means of communicating the message of the Servant's salvation. To set up the magnificent blessing that will come to the faithful remnant in Israel who are still in exile as well as to the Church through the ages, Isaiah draws upon the metaphor of a barren woman who has lost hope for having children. Sarah, the barren and aged wife of Abraham, would immediately come to mind for the Jews in Babylonian exile. They would liken themselves to her despair because they had lost hope in God's promise to Abraham that his seed would be as the "sand of the sea, which cannot be numbered for multitude" (Genesis 32:12). For them, God has a special message. Just as the barren woman, Sarah, gave birth to a son who became the father of Israel, so He will bring them from the desolation of their exile to the promise, *"And your descendants will inherit the nations, and make the desolate cities inhabited"* (v. 3). As Sarah's child represented the special promise of God, so the barren body of the faithful will be blessed by sons and daughters who will grow in numbers far beyond the boundaries of Jerusalem and Judah. "Enlarge the place of your tent . . . stretch out the curtains . . . lengthen your cords . . . strengthen your stakes" are the instructions for expanding on all sides to make room for the children of promise who will be born into the family by faith. Once again, one of Isaiah's earliest prophecies resounds in our ears, "Now it shall come to pass in the latter days that the mountain of the LORD's house shall be established on the top of the mountains, and shall be exalted above the hills; *and all nations shall flow into it* (2:2).

Contrary to some opinions, the spiritual body of the Church need not be small to be faithful. Whether it is the New Testament church expanding daily with those who were being saved or the megachurch of the late twentieth century multiplying by thousands overnight, growth should be expected in the Body of the faithful. The crucial question is whether or not the growth comes from those who are children of faith rather than products of popular movements or mass marketing. Jesus had to deal with the issue early in His ministry. After the feeding of the five thousand, the masses wanted to make

Him king. To test their faith, He spoke the hard truth about His death, resurrection, and ascension. With each progressive step calling for greater faith, the masses fell away until only Jesus and His disciples stood alone. To the twelve, He asked, "Do you also want to go away?" Simon Peter spoke for the group when he answered, "Lord, to whom shall we go? You have the words of eternal life" (John 6:67–68).

Truth takes the number of disciples down to a faithful few, but the same truth increases the body of disciples by multiplying numbers and expanding boundaries. Dean Kelley, in his book *Why Conservative Churches Are Growing*, illustrates this fact when he notes the first reason for growth in these churches is a clearly defined set of biblical beliefs that become the basis for preaching, teaching, and witness. Closely related to these beliefs is a discipline for the members that Kelley calls "the power of the gate." Persons come through the gate into membership by the discipline of the church in its theological teaching, spiritual nurture, and moral principles. But the gate swings both ways. If the person rejects the beliefs or the disciplines of the church, membership is forfeited as the gate swings out. Finally, Kelley cites an enthusiastic personal witness by the members of the church as an attraction for outsiders.[1] Isaiah would have concurred. Biblical truth, spiritual discipline, and personal faith are the criteria by which the barren churches bear children and *"inherit the nations"* (v. 3).

THE BLESSING OF GRACE (54:4–8)

Another metaphor of marriage is used to describe the contrast between unfaithful Israel and its inheritance of God's *"everlasting kindness"* (v. 8b). Likening Israel to a woman *"forsaken"* by her husband and *"grieved in spirit"* (v. 6) because of an adulterous act as a young woman, God offers the assurance, *"Do not fear, for you will not be ashamed; nor be disgraced, for you will not be put to shame"* (v. 4a). Isaiah envisions God as the bridegroom of the adulterous young bride. For her sin He has put her away in a separation short of divorce. The exile is that period of separation. Yet, as God sees it from an eternal perspective, He forsook Israel, vented a *"little wrath"* and hid His face from her for just a mere *"moment"* (v. 7). Of course, for those undergoing the suffering of separation, one hundred years in exile is far more than a moment. Pain has a way of making a moment feel like an eternity. Does God really understand our suffering? The answer requires the perspective of God's purpose. Israel suffered in exile because of its stubborn rebellion against God. By every rule of law, Israel should have died in exile. But instead of death, God shortened the time with *"great mercies"* and *"everlasting kindness"* (vv. 7–8). Compared to eternal death, the exile was indeed a mere moment.

Ordinary justice of the Mosaic law dictates divorce for the adulterous bride. But extraordinary grace offers her forgiveness of sin, freedom from fear, and restoration from shame (v. 4). The reason for such great mercy is that her Maker is also her Husband. God is willing to put the reputation of His name, the character of His holiness, and the power of His sovereignty on the line for His bride, the Church. As sad as it seems, scandal is not alien to the Church. In more moments throughout human history than we care to admit, the bride of Christ has brought shame and disgrace to the name of God. How then has the Church continued to be His chosen instrument for the redemption of the world? There is no answer except for "great mercies" and "everlasting kindness." God, the maker of the Church, is also the husband who will not let her go because He has called her, married her, and counts upon her to be the mother of His children.

The Blessing of Peace (54:9–10)

God seldom takes an oath or swears on His name. All He needs to do is say, "I am He" and it will be done. After His judgment upon sin by the flood that wiped out most of His creation, however, God made a covenant with Noah and all flesh on earth. He swore, "Never again shall all flesh be cut off by the waters of he flood; never again shall there be a flood to destroy the earth" (Genesis 9:11). As a reminder to Himself and an assurance to all people on earth, He set a rainbow in the sky as the sign of His covenant. All Israel, faithful or not, knew that God had kept His oath. Although He had punished the sins of Israel by Exile, He had only shown "a little wrath" for "a moment" (vv. 7–8). The exile, as devastating as it was, did not cover the earth or wipe out most of God's creation.

As part of the heritage of His servants, God takes another oath. As He swore that His wrath against sin would never again be shown by a worldwide flood, He goes a step farther to tell His faithful people that He will never again be angry with them or rebuke them (v. 9b). His reference is to the exile. As the flood served a specific purpose in God's relationship with His creation, so the exile served a specific purpose in God's relationship with His Church. Although His oath did not guarantee the Church exemption from human persecution or self-imposed punishment, His anger would never be shown by exile again. As witnesses in a courtroom take their oath on a Bible, so God swears by His own creation. "Til the mountains slide off their base and the hills are picked up and moved away," God assures His faithful people of His everlasting kindness and His covenant of peace.

God's covenant of peace with His Church is as sure as His covenant of preservation with His creation. Neither has ever been canceled; neither has ever been broken. Even when the Church has become the home of martyrs, the covenant of peace has held. God's oath links back to the Servant's suffering. We have peace because of His chastisement (53:5). Following His example, then, we need not defend ourselves under persecution. God will be our Advocate and our adversaries will lose their case because we have done no violence or spoken no words of deceit. Jesus added to our legacy when He promised, "Peace I leave with you, My peace I give to you; not as the world gives do I give to you. Let not your heart be troubled, neither let it be afraid" (John 14:27). God's oath and Christ's gift assure us of the covenant of peace in our spiritual inheritance.

THE BLESSING OF RENEWAL (54:11–13)

Violence has reduced the city of Jerusalem and the church of Zion to ruin and rubble. In picturesque language, Isaiah describes the current condition of the city and the church as *"afflicted"* from within, *"tossed with tempest"* from without, and *"not comforted"* by any word of hope (v. 11). Richard Neibuhr once described the church by saying, "If it weren't for the storm without, you couldn't stand the stench within." Isaiah would have agreed. The church of Zion in exile had the stench of internal sickness and the storm of external opposition.

What a difference the ministry of the Servant makes! From the ruin and the rubble caused by sins within and siege without, God gives the blessing of restoration from the ground up with the most precious of stones. *"Behold"* is the word that calls us to look upon its new splendor.

Sapphires are the foundations, rubies are the pinnacles, crystals line the gates, and all kinds of precious stones make the walls a sparkling mosaic. Is Isaiah exaggerating? Perhaps, but exaggeration may be necessary to show how the sorry plight of the existing city and the exiled church will be transformed into splendor under the blessing of God.

Rebuilding the city of Jerusalem, or the church of Zion, into a place of splendor cannot be an end in itself. A glorious city or church has value only as it is populated by citizens whose lives match the quality of the architecture. Splendor far beyond precious stones will be seen in children who are disciples following the model of the teaching-learning Servant. Although *disciple* is a rare word in the Old Testament, we read its meaning again in God's promise, *"All your children shall be taught by the LORD"* (v. 13). Isaiah's earlier prophecy will be fulfilled when all nations and many people will say, "Come, and let us go up to the mountain of the LORD, to the house of the God of Jacob; He will teach us His ways, and we shall walk in His paths" (Isaiah 2:3). Peace and righteousness will follow as the glory of the city and the Church.

THE BLESSING OF PROTECTION (54:14–17)

As peace will be the comfort for God's people and righteousness will be the cure for its internal affliction, so God's protection will be the buffer against external storm. Release from the fear of oppression, terrorism, and false accusation are freedoms of "the servants" just as they were freedoms of the Servant.

Further assurance is needed by God's people for two particular fears. One is the fear of force that caused the destruction of Jerusalem and drove the children of Israel into exile. For this fear, God returns to His role as the Maker of all humanity, including the blacksmith who is the weapon maker. As the Lord of History, God reminds His people that both the maker and the user of worldly weapons are in His hand. True, He used the Assyrians and the Babylonians to bring judgment upon His rebellious people, but for those who are faithful He gives the assurance that *"No weapon formed against you shall prosper"* (v. 17).

A recent television program sounded the warning that one day soon nuclear arms will be in the hands of the weapons-dealers who are currently selling conventional weapons. With nuclear weapons in the hands of bandit nations or terrorists, the whole world could be held hostage and paralyzed by fear. If it happened, we would understand how the children of Israel felt after the devastation of Jerusalem under Babylonian assault. But even in that event, with the annihilation of civilization as a distinct possibility, people of faith would know that the weapons and their users are under God's control and Luther's sixteenth-century hymn would take on new meaning,

> Let goods and kindred go,
> This mortal life also;
> The body they may kill;
> God's truth abideth still,
> His kingdom is forever.

The other fear to which God gives special attention is the threat of false accusation. Words of condemnation can be more destructive than weapons of force. In response to this fear, God gives an answer that moves people of faith from the defense to the offense. Not only will the false charges fail because of the righteousness of His people, but the Word of truth that they have learned as disciples will be the same sharp sword that the Servant himself will wield (49:3). On this high note of blessing, the Lord says, "This is the heritage of the servants of the LORD, and their righteousness is from Me" (v. 17b). The Servant of the Lord has passed on His legacy to the servants of the Lord—people of faith in all generations from all corners of the earth who are redeemed by the Holy One of Israel.

THE HERITAGE OF STRANGERS (55:1–13)

> 1 "Ho! Everyone who thirsts,
> Come to the waters;
> And you who have no money,
> Come, buy and eat.
> Yes, come, buy wine and milk
> Without money and without price.
> 2 Why do you spend money
>   for what is not bread,
> And your wages
>   for what does not satisfy?
> Listen diligently to Me,
>   and eat what is good,

And let your soul delight itself in abundance.
3 Incline your ear, and come to Me.
Hear, and your soul shall live;
And I will make an everlasting
covenant with you—
The sure mercies of David.
4 Indeed I have given him as a witness to the people,
A leader and commander for the people.
5 Surely you shall call a nation
you do not know,
And nations who do not know you
shall run to you,
Because of the LORD your God,
And the Holy One of Israel;
for He has glorified you."
6 Seek the LORD while He may be found,
Call upon Him while He is near.
7 Let the wicked forsake his way,
And the unrighteous man his thoughts;
Let him return to the LORD,
And He will have mercy on him;
And to our God,
For He will abundantly pardon.
8 "For My thoughts are not your thoughts,
Nor are your ways My ways,"
says the LORD.
9 "For as the heavens are higher than the earth,
So are My ways higher than your ways,
And My thoughts than your thoughts.
10 "For as the rain comes down,
and the snow from heaven,
And do not return there,
But water the earth,
And make it bring forth and bud,
That it may give seed to the sower
And bread to the eater,
11 So shall My word be that goes forth
from My mouth;
It shall not return to Me void,
But it shall accomplish what I please,
And it shall prosper in the thing for
which I sent it.

12 "For you shall go out with joy,
   And be led out with peace;
   The mountains and the hills
   Shall break forth into singing before you,
   And all the trees of the field shall clap their hands.
13 Instead of the thorn shall come up the cypress tree,
   And instead of the brier shall come up the myrtle tree;
   And it shall be to the LORD for a name,
   For an everlasting sign that shall not be cut off."
                                          Isaiah 55:1–13

In the grand finale of the salvation oracles that began with the prologue in Isaiah 40:1–11, the blessings of the Servant's completed work are now extended beyond the children of Israel to people who are foreigners to the faith and strangers to the covenant. No passage in the Old Testament better expresses the love of God than Isaiah chapter 55, which begins with the oft-quoted words, *"Ho! Everyone who thirsts"* (v. 1). In the first half of the chapter, imperatives such as *"come," "buy," "eat," "listen," "seek,"* and *"call"* are used to outline God's plan of salvation for every thirsty soul (vv. 1–7). Affirmations of *"mercy," "pardon," "joy,"* and *"singing"* then seal the invitation with the signs of the Lord's salvation. Chapter 55 may well be considered a pinnacle in Isaiah's prophecy, bringing to fulfillment the spiritual meaning of preceding chapters (1–54) and laying the foundation for all that will follow (56–66).

AN OPEN INVITATION (55:1–5)

As we remember, the Lord God informed His Servant that His role in bringing salvation to Israel alone was "too small a thing for Him" (49:6). God commissioned Him for the larger role and ultimate mission of being the "light to the Gentiles" and "to the ends of the earth" (49:6). Chapter 55 might be entitled "Mission Accomplished." In lyrical language that puts before us the image of God standing with open arms and extending the invitation, "Ho! Everyone who thirsts, come to the waters," we see His love in action. In these words, we also hear the echoes of Jesus' own invitation, "Come to Me, all you who labor and are heavy laden, and I will give you rest" (Matthew 11:28). In each of these invitations, the call is universal, salvation is free, and the results are satisfying.

The Universal Call (55:1a)

For the children of Israel, it would not be easy to invite foreigners or Gentiles to join them in the kingdom of righteousness. As the chosen people of God, they had developed a distinctive identity that tied their ethnicity with their faith. To be a Jew referred both to race and religion. Moreover, throughout their history God had commanded them to keep their ethnic origins and their religious worship pure. Intermarriage and idolatry were contaminants to be avoided at all costs. The purpose for these commandments, however, went beyond ethnic and religious purity as an end in itself. God wanted to keep His people pure so that they could fulfill their chosen servant role of being the light to the Gentiles and bringing the message of redemption to all nations. They could sin at either extreme. If they failed to remain pure in race and undefiled in religion, God could not use them as His instrument for the message of salvation. But if they became so exclusive in race and so restrictive in religion that they refused to include others in God's redemptive plan, God had to find a new Servant for the fulfillment of His purpose.

Israel sinned on both counts. During Isaiah's time, the nation rebelled against God, intermarried with heathen, and mixed idolatry into its religious worship. Later, in Jesus' time, Israel sinned by assuming that they were exclusively chosen by God for salvation and created a religious system based upon regulations rather than faith. Unfortunately, they are not alone. The church also is tempted to sin on one side or the other. Contamination by the world and isolation from the world are like magnetic poles that have the power of attraction in every generation. After more than a decade of close connection with forces on the political right during the 1980s and 1990s, the evangelical church in America may well retreat into isolation as the center of political power shifts to the left during the 1990s and on into the twenty-first century.

Isaiah leaves no doubt. God's purpose is to build a kingdom of righteousness that is inclusive of Jews and Gentiles, chosen children and foreigners, neighbors and strangers. All other plans for affirmative action pale before His ultimate purpose to bring all races, ages, genders, and ethnic origins from every corner of the earth together in a spiritual body created exclusively by trust in God and faith in Christ. "Ho! Everyone who thirsts" is the inclusive call of God to participate in the blessings of salvation provided exclusively by the Servant of the Lord.

The Free Gift (55:1b)

Equal to the marvel of the universal call is the mind-boggling thought that salvation is free. The analogy of the spiritually thirsty people is advanced to the truth that salvation is something that money cannot buy. Again, we find ourselves poised between extremes. Sometimes we overbalance the scriptural teaching, "Work out your own salvation with fear and trembling" (Philippians 2:12) and try to create a religious system of belief, experience, or practice that will earn us our redemption. Or, we make salvation so free that everyone will be saved whether or not they have faith in God or believe in Jesus Christ. I remember the shock of speaking at a world conference of Christians in Nairobi on the subject, "Jesus Christ Alone for Our Salvation." As I spoke, I felt apologetic because the biblical truth seemed so obvious. Afterward, however, I learned that some were upset by my "outdated" preaching on the exclusiveness of Christ. In their drive for inclusiveness with other religions, they had abandoned the first premise of biblical faith.

Isaiah makes no mistake about the meaning of the free gift of salvation provided by the ministry of the Servant. Perhaps with an ear cocked to the interests of the Jews in exile who had prospered as merchants in Babylon, his invitation to *"come to the waters,"* includes those who *"have no money"* and excludes those who thought that they could buy the *"wine and milk"* of abundant life or barter for their benefits. With an insight into revelation far ahead of his time, Isaiah foresees the fact that the price of redemption for all people has already been paid by the Suffering Servant and faith in Him is all that is required to receive the living water of salvation.

The Satisfying Life (55:2–3)

A natural question follows, *"Why do you spend money for what is not bread, and your wages for what does not satisfy?"* To live abundantly is one thing; to live satisfied is quite another. A woman who was married to one of the richest men in America told me that she had everything that money could buy—mansions, jets, diamonds, automobiles, servants, and inclusion in the "400" social register. But her husband, spoiled by riches and steeped in alcoholism, beat her unmercifully during his drunken rages. Finally, after years of abuse, she said that she ran for her life with only the clothes on her back and one diamond ring on her finger. After an uncontested divorce in which she asked for nothing, she restarted her career, met a Christian man, gave her life to Jesus Christ, and found the satisfaction that she had been denied—to be a mother. In her late fifties, she and her husband adopted two small babies and raised them as parents in their sixties and seventies. If you asked her the question, she would answer with Isaiah, *"Let your soul delight itself in [the] abundance"* of the free gift of grace, not in the things that money can buy. How false is the bumper sticker that reads, "He who dies with the most toys, WINS!"

The Royal Covenant (55:4–5)

Literalists among the children of Israel would have been insulted by the thought that God would include Gentiles in the everlasting covenant that He had made with David, the revered king of Judah and the prototype of the Messiah. Yet, God informs all who are thirsty and trust in Him that they will receive the *"sure mercies"* that God had shown to David, they will be *"a witness to the people"* as David led and commanded his people, and they will find unknown nations running to them as David's reign of righteousness and peace served as a model for kings and kingdoms. As God glorified His Servant in the works that He did, so all who trust in Him, whether Jew or Gentile, will be glorified for the witness of their faith and their works. As the royal seed of David will produce the Messiah, so all those who trust in Him will become members of the "royal priesthood," as Peter called the people of God (1 Peter 2:9).

AN URGENT IMPERATIVE (55:6–9)

The free gift of grace does not eliminate all human initiative in the plan of salvation. Urgency is heard in the new imperative, *"Seek the LORD while He may be found, call upon Him while He is near"* (v. 6). Although everyone who hungers and thirsts for righteousness receives the invitation to salvation, God expects the courtesy of an RSVP. Otherwise, the invitation is like the wedding announcement that came to our home and got lost in the shuffle of papers. Weeks later my wife searched in the file for another document and found the wedding announcement with RSVP on the bottom. "Oh no," she exclaimed, "we missed it!" God's invitation to salvation is both timely and timeless. While He invites us again and again, there are golden moments of readiness when He is especially near and easily found. The promptings of the Spirit lead us to those golden moments.

Repentance is the human act that is required for salvation. Foreshadowing New Testament theology, the prophet puts out the double imperative, *"Let the wicked forsake his way, and the unrighteous man his thoughts"* (v. 7). Sin is both doing and being. The wicked man must stop doing sin and the unrighteous man must stop being sinful in his thoughts. To repent of our wicked ways and unrighteous thoughts, we must turn around and go the other way. Jewish theology puts major emphasis upon the actions of a person as the indicator of righteousness. Roman Catholic practice in the sixteenth century had also moved toward the wickedness or righteousness of outward deeds that could be forgiven by confession and indulgences without a change of heart. Martin Luther reacted so strongly against this theological distortion that he contended for salvation by faith alone. Isaiah, however, teaches us that repentance is a turning from the acts of wickedness and the thoughts of sinfulness. With equal vigor, the prophet would repeat his major theme that salvation is both personal righteousness and social justice. By turning from our sin and returning to the Lord, our Maker and our God, the promise of mercy is given, *"For He will abundantly pardon"* (v. 7).

While the Jews emphasized the way a person walked over the thoughts of the heart, God reverses the order when He adds the note, *"For My thoughts are not your thoughts, nor are your ways My ways"* (v. 8). A sense of God's transcendence and immanence comes through this statement. Neither God's thoughts nor His ways are simply human thoughts and ways raised to the divine level. Or, we might say, the supernatural is not just an extension of the natural. There is a distinct break between the thoughts and ways of God and human beings. He thinks as we cannot think, and He acts in ways that we cannot act. Therefore, when He touches down on earth with actions that are His way, there has been a breakthrough from the supernatural to the natural. Conversely, when His ways are done on earth, they are reflective of His thoughts, which the finite mind cannot understand. God's point is that our repentance cannot save us. When the promise was given, "For He will abundantly pardon" (v. 7b), an act of divine intervention took place. From His transcendent thought of human redemption, He bridged the gap through the immanent way of His Servant to save those who seek Him, call upon Him, and repent of their wicked acts and unrighteous thoughts.

THE FERTILE WORD (55:10–11)

Isaiah goes on to explain how the thoughts of the transcendent God and the ways of the immanent God come together in the work of human salvation. Using the analogy of the rain and the snow that fall from heaven, God says through His prophet that these elements come from Him and do not return to Him, yet they accomplish His purpose of creating a fertile earth. In the same way, His Word bridges the gap between His transcendent thoughts and His immanent ways. As the text says, it is His Word, from His mouth, that goes out to earth and effectively accomplishes His good pleasure, namely our salvation. Who can deny special revelation and divine inspiration after reading this passage? Isaiah's prophecy is absolutely consistent with John's prologue, "In the beginning was the Word, and the Word was with God, and the Word was God" (John 1:1), and with Paul's message to Timothy, "All Scripture is given of God, and is profitable for doctrine, for reproof, for correction, for instruction in righteousness" (2 Timothy 3:16). Or who can deny the direct connection between Isaiah's prophecy and John's proclamation of the incarnation, "The Word became flesh and dwelt among us, and we beheld His glory, the glory as of the only begotten of the Father, full of grace and truth" (John 1:14). For the foreigners who thirst for righteousness and repent of their sins, the Word of God, spoken and written, is the effective agent of their salvation.

THE EVERLASTING SIGN (55:12–13)

As always, Isaiah gives the redeemed a song to sing and a sign to remember. Returning momentarily to the children of Israel who are still in Babylonian captivity, Isaiah envisions the start of their journey on the new exodus as a time of joy rather than fear like their fathers experienced in the Exodus from Egypt and as an event when they would be led out in peace by Cyrus rather than pursued by Pharaoh. To picture the occasion, Isaiah chooses another of his favorite themes. Creation joins in the celebration of their deliverance as the mountains and hills join the singing and the trees of the field clap their hands (v. 12b). Then, as an *"everlasting sign"* of their salvation, lush cypress and myrtle trees will grow up in place of dry thorns and prickly briers (v. 13). Coming full cycle in his metaphor, green trees symbolize the newness of life nourished by the living water while brown brambles represent the deadness of life starved by sin.

Isaiah would have qualified as one of the first environmentalists. While he would not go so far as to be an environmental evangelist, he would recognize the interconnections between physical and human creation. As human sin put a curse upon earth, so human salvation will be cause for the earth to rejoice. Following that thought to its logical conclusion, Christians who are redeemed from sin should recognize that physical creation is one of our God-given resources for which we are to be faithful stewards. To pollute the environment and waste its limited resources are sins for which we will be held responsible.

With the same song of salvation and the same everlasting sign, then, foreigners will join the children of Israel in the new exodus from spiritual bondage to spiritual freedom. Together, they will come from the farthest corners of the earth to Mount Zion where they will be taught of the Lord and learn of His ways. As the servants of the Lord, they will model their lives after the Servant of the Lord and glorify His name through the works that they do. Like the lush and living cypress and myrtle trees, they will honor the name of the Lord and will be His *"everlasting sign that shall not be cut off"* (v. 13b).

NOTES

1. D. M. Kelley, *Why Conservative Churches are Growing: A Study in Sociology of Religion* (New York: Harper and Row, 1972).

CHAPTER TWENTY-SIX

The Effective Servant

Isaiah 56:1–57:27

Isaiah continues to address the implications of the Servant's completed work of redemption. Although salvation is a gift of grace that humans do not deserve and cannot earn, God still has expectations for His people after He has delivered them from sin. At the center of these expectations is the covenant between God and His people involving a mutual relationship of love demonstrated by faith and obedience. For the children of Israel, who had been schooled in the ritual and ethics of the law, the new community of faith meant a prior loyalty to the spirit of the law without neglecting the letter of the law. For the Gentiles from the far corners of the earth who would also inherit the covenant relationship, their membership in the community of faith meant the acceptance of spiritual responsibilities as well as privileges. Chapters 56–59 address these responsibilities for Jews and Gentiles who are joined together in the new covenant relationship and in the new community of faith.

What appears to be an abrupt change in literary style in chapters 56–59 has led some scholars to create a third Isaiah, or Trito-Isaiah, as the author. Still others find such variety in style that a whole school of Isaiahs is believed to be the writers. Behind these suppositions is the familiar problem of the first Isaiah, who lived in the eighth century B.C., saw God's vision for the sixth century B.C., or just before Cyrus freed the children of Israel from their bondage in Babylon and urged them to return home to Jerusalem. Without getting into the details of that debate, a case for one Isaiah can also be made on the basis of common themes, phrases, and words that pervade the book and run through these chapters. Salvation, for instance, is still the overarching theme that connects with the oracles of salvation in chapters 40–55, which are presumably written by the second or Deutero-Isaiah. Connecting phrases also lend integrity to the text. Throughout the prophecy from beginning to end, Isaiah's claim to authority is the phrase, "Thus says the Lord." Although a second and third Isaiah could adopt the phrase for their own, it would be plagiarism unless they too had encountered the Lord and received the call of the first Isaiah in chapter six. Metaphors, of which Isaiah is master, are another link between chapters 56–59 and the rest of the book of Isaiah. "Blind leaders" in chapter 56, the "highway" in chapter 57, the "watered garden" in chapter 58, and the wrath of the Lord coming as a "pent-up flood" in chapter 59 are so characteristic of Isaiah that a second or third author would have to be divinely inspired to duplicate the metaphors and communicate their meaning.

Of course, divine inspiration is the prior question that divides scholars between those who contend for a single author and those who argue for multiple authors. In either case, a choice must be made between miracles. Either God inspired one Isaiah to speak of the future as the "prophetic present" or He inspired two or more Isaiahs to speak with the mind and authority of the first Isaiah. A. S. Herbert, a scholar who accepts the theory of more than one Isaiah, nevertheless marvels at the similarity of literary style between chapters 56–69 and the earlier chapters written by the first Isaiah when he concedes, "There is much in this section which recalls the language of the eighth-century prophets."[1] The commonality of language, however, is secondary to the unity of theology in Isaiah that pervades chapters 56–59 as well as the rest of the book. From the beginning, three theological strands run through the prophet's writing: (1) The Person of God; (2) The Promise of Salvation; and (3) The Proof of Redemption in personal righteousness and social justice. The opening of chapter 56 confirms all three of these theological themes:

> Thus says the LORD: "Keep justice, and do righteousness, for My salvation is about to come, and My righteousness to be revealed.
> *Isaiah 56:1*

Holding our position for one Isaiah and a unified text then, we approach chapters 56–59 as a series of prophetic statements spelling out the implications for the new covenant and the new community of faith created by the redemptive work of the Servant of the Lord as revealed in chapters 40–55.

ESSENTIALS OF SPIRITUAL RELIGION (56:1–2)

1 Thus says the LORD:
   "Keep justice, and do righteousness,
   For My salvation is about to come,
   And My righteousness to be revealed.
2 Blessed is the man who does this,
   And the son of man
       who lays hold on it;
   Who keeps from defiling the Sabbath,
   And keeps his hand from doing any evil."

Isaiah 56:1–2

KEEPING JUSTICE (56:1a)

As we have already noted, Isaiah's continuing message is consistent in theme and tone. For both Jews and Gentiles, he preaches social justice and personal righteousness as the proof of salvation. Spiritual religion for any people in any age is still the same. Social justice and personal righteousness go hand in hand as universal virtues that God expects of His children. Throughout the ages, however, the two have become divided in the preaching and witness of the Church. In our day, for instance, liberal Christians tend to be identified with their work for social justice while conservative Christians emphasize the priority of personal righteousness. The fact that Isaiah reverses the terms from an earlier prophecy and puts *"justice"* ahead of *"righteousness"* reinforces the inseparability of the two essentials. John Wesley said, "There is no personal holiness without social holiness" and Dietrich Bonhoffer wrote, "Christianity is the most worldly of all religions." Whether justice or righteousness comes first in the listing is incidental to the fact that they are inseparable.

DOING RIGHTEOUSNESS (56:1b)

The Jewish interpretation of *righteousness* tended to divide the word into two parts. In its original meaning, righteousness meant a right relationship with the covenant of God that led to loving others as oneself and doing good in order to lead others into the same right relationship with God. Over time, the interpretation of the term narrowed into acts of doing good without the roots of a right relationship with God or the results of leading others into salvation. Christians, as well as Jews, need to recover the whole biblical interpretation of righteousness in relationship to justice as essentials of spiritual religion.

OBSERVING THE SABBATH (56:2a–b)

Further evidence of spiritual religion includes ritual and ethical expectations for both Jewish and Gentile members of the community of faith. One ritual out of the law is chosen as essential for spiritual religion. *"Blessed is the man . . . who keeps from defiling the Sabbath"* (56:2). Negative and reactionary thoughts probably flood the mind of contemporary Christians. Pushing off against the Pharisees who distorted the meaning of the Sabbath by their impossible regulations, or remembering a childhood when the restrictions of the Sabbath day destroyed the joy of living, we wonder why God raises Sabbath-keeping to the level of an essential for spiritual religion. The Old Testament gives us the answer. Like circumcision, the keeping of the Sabbath signaled the covenant relationship with God. By giving Him a day for rest and worship, we honor His name and renew our covenant relationship with Him.

If Isaiah is right, most of us who are contemporary Christians are in trouble. While we may reserve an hour or two on the Sabbath day for worship and rest, we use the other hours for our own pleasure, whether it is shopping, sports, travel, television, or home projects. God is forgotten, and the Sabbath day is desecrated. Seventh-Day Adventists are among my closest Christian friends. When I have consulted the trustees and faculty of their colleges, the sessions frequently bridge over Friday at sunset when their Sabbath begins. Although I have reacted against a restrictive background when I could not play games or watch television on Sunday, I have felt a sense of the holy when entering the Sabbath in worship with my Seventh-Day Adventist friends. Coming from their services, I find myself longing for the same sense of the holy for those of us who worship on the first day of the week.

Avoiding All Evil (56:2c)

Joining the Sabbath ritual as a spiritual essential is the ethical expectation that the person of faith *"keeps his [or her] hand from doing any evil"* (v. 2c). We come from the presence of God in Sabbath worship into a world where moral warfare is being waged. Temptations to do evil are ever-present in our daily walk. Yet, in obedience to God's command and in gratitude for His grace, we discipline ourselves against the subtle and obvious temptations to sin. Keeping the ritual of the Sabbath and avoiding the temptation to do evil are also inseparable. The Sabbath is frontline protection against sin.

An executive who traveled frequently overseas told of walking down the street in a German city when feelings of homesickness and loneliness came over him. Precisely at that moment, a beautiful woman walked up to him and asked if he needed a friend. Although she betrayed none of the hard looks and brash demeanor of a streetwalker, the executive knew the implications of her question. Momentarily, an image flashed in his mind that bridged the time gap between Germany and the United States. At home—at that very moment—he saw his family seated in church as worship began. Knowing that he could not betray them, he quickened his pace and spoke back over his shoulder to the temptress, "No, thank you."

Shock must have rippled through the Jewish community when Isaiah spoke for the Lord to say that *"foreigner[s]"* and *"eunuch[s]"* were to be given the full privileges of the faithful as a result of the Servant's redemptive work. It is one thing to imagine the gathering of all people from all nations around Mount Zion to learn of the Lord, but it is quite another to see the faces of those who are included in the relationship of the new covenant, the fellowship of the new community, and the worship of the new church. Lip service to world evangelization becomes a personal threat to the status quo and the established order.

During the days of campus protest, when student revolutionaries wore beards, long hair, and grungy clothes, I sat in a morning worship service among my clean-shaven and well-dressed, middle-class contemporaries. As we bowed in prayer for the invocation, a person walking down the center aisle caught the corner of my eye. Glancing sideways, I saw the classical picture of a hippie moving past me toward the front of the church. As the congregation looked up from prayer and saw the man moving toward the front, you could feel the fear tightening every throat. We expected the man to climb the stairs, take over the pulpit, and lash out against white, middle-class Christianity. Instead, he sat down in the first seat on the front row. He must have felt the eyes staring at the back of his head during the service, but he never made any move to react or respond. After the benediction, he did climb the steps to speak to the pastor. To satisfy my curiosity, I came up beside him to hear what he had to say. Without the slightest show of arrogance, he reached out for the pastor's hand to introduce himself as the son of the prominent Episcopalian Bishop William Pike who had just committed suicide a few days earlier. As he spoke to the pastor, he revealed his deep hurt over his father's death and his desperate need for God's help. I learned a lasting lesson from the redemptive moment that followed. If our worship and our fellowship do not make room for persons who are radically different from us, the full redemptive work of the Servant cannot be realized among us, and we are impoverished as a community because we miss the enrichment of human diversity.

INSTRUCTIONS FOR SPIRITUAL PEOPLE (56:3–8)

3 Do not let the son of the foreigner
Who has joined himself to the LORD
Speak, saying,
"The LORD has utterly separated me from His people";
Nor let the eunuch say,
"Here I am, a dry tree."
4 For thus says the LORD:
"To the eunuchs who keep My Sabbaths,
And choose what pleases Me,
And hold fast My covenant,
5 Even to them I will give in My house
And within My walls a place and a name
Better than that of sons and daughters;
I will give them an everlasting name
That shall not be cut off.
6 "Also the sons of the foreigner
Who join themselves to the LORD,
    to serve Him,
And to love the name of the LORD,
    to be His servants—

Everyone who keeps from defiling the Sabbath,
And holds fast My covenant—
7 Even them I will bring to My holy mountain,
And make them joyful in My house of prayer.
Their burnt offerings and their sacrifices
Will be accepted on My altar;
For My house shall be called a house
    of prayer for all nations."
8 The Lord GOD, who gathers the
outcasts of Israel, says,
"Yet I will gather to him
Others besides those who are gathered to him."

Isaiah 56:3–8

"Foreigners" are people who are strangers to us. We are suspicious of them unless they are willing to become like us. Even then, foreigners are always suspect because they are not pure in blood or "true blue" in their background. *"Eunuchs"* are people who are outcasts among us. In the Jewish community, they were disgraced because they were sterile and could not bear children. According to Deuteronomy 23:1, "He who is emasculated by crushing or mutilation shall not enter the congregation of the LORD." In one of the most radical commands from the Lord, Isaiah says that loyalty to the spiritual, ritual, and ethical essentials is the only requirement for participation in the full privileges of the community of faith. Eunuchs will have a home in the temple, a memorial in their honor, and a name for their recognition (56:5). Although they cannot physically bear children, they will give *"an everlasting name"* to spiritual children and will be remembered forever.

Philip's encounter with the Ethiopian eunuch on the road to Gaza is a fulfillment of that promise. As he was reading from the scroll of Isaiah while riding in his chariot, Philip jumped up beside him and asked if he understood what he read. "Tell me, please," the Ethiopian answered, "who is the prophet talking about, himself or someone else?" (Acts 8:34). When Philip explained the Scripture and told him the good news of Jesus Christ, the eunuch believed and asked to be baptized. Although his name is unknown, Ethiopia has the reputation of a Christian nation, and the "children" of the eunuch number in the millions.

A FAMILY FOR EUNUCHS (56:3–5)

Eunuchs represent all of the outcasts who will be gathered into the new community of faith. By keeping the Sabbath and holding fast to the covenant, they will be welcome in the temple, honored with a name, and remembered for the sons and daughters of faith to whom they give spiritual birth. Every generation of believers must ask itself the question, "If God welcomes outcasts into His family and His church by faith, who are the outcasts to whom we are denying the privilege?" As the Jews learned later, they lost their chosen role in God's redemptive plan because they closed their doors to those whom they feared would contaminate the purity of the family and the sanctity of the community.

A HOME FOR FOREIGNERS (56:6–8)

A special promise is also given to foreigners who serve the Lord, who love His name, worship Him, keep the Sabbath, and hold the covenant (v. 6). They will be gathered with all the faithful to Mount Zion, given joy in God's house of prayer, and blessed with the forgiveness of sins by the acceptance of their sacrifices (v. 7). In spirit and in faith, the foreigners will be the "Jews" of whom Paul wrote, "For he is not a Jew who is one outwardly, nor is that circumcision which is outward in the flesh; but he is a Jew who is one inwardly, and circumcision is that of the heart, in the Spirit, and not in the letter; whose praise is not from men but from God" (Romans 2:28–29). In one of most enlightened and radical statements, then, the Lord sees far into the future to say, *"For My house shall be called a house of prayer for all nations"* (v. 7b). No one can mistake God's intention when He announces that He will fill His house with those who are gathered out of exile and will bring them together with *"others besides those who are gathered"* (v. 8b). In rare instances across the earth, we see small clusters of believers who fulfill that promise, but by and large, we eagerly await its fulfillment.

RESPONSIBILITIES OF LEADERS (56:9–12)

> 9 All you beasts of the field,
>   come to devour,

All you beasts in the forest.
10 His watchmen are blind,
   They are all ignorant;
   They are all dumb dogs,
   They cannot bark,
   Sleeping, lying down,
      loving to slumber.
11 Yes, they are greedy dogs
   Which never have enough.
   And they are shepherds
   Who cannot understand;
   They all look to their own way,
   Every one for his own gain,
   From his own territory.
12 "Come," one says, "I will bring wine,
   And we will fill ourselves with intoxicating drink;
   Tomorrow will be as today,
   And much more abundant."

Isaiah 56:9–12

ALERT TO DANGER (56:9–10)

As we might expect, God knew that severe opposition would arise among the children of Israel from religious leaders whose position and privilege were threatened by welcoming Gentiles and outcasts into the temple and its worship. For them, Isaiah reserves his harshest words, but not unlike his earlier woes against the leaders of Judah who were drunk with wine, deceitful in sin, clever in twisting the truth, and open to bribes at the expense of the poor (5:8–25). In this case, he is even more direct in personalizing his accusation. Because Israel's prophets, who are commissioned as *"watchmen"* for the people, have become blind and dumb, he calls upon the beasts of the field to come and devour them (vv. 9–10)! Tragedy stalks any community when prophets, who are expected to be the watchmen on the walls, close their eyes to imminent danger and shut their mouths like *"dumb dogs"* when they should speak. The popular country song, "Don't Rock the Boat" is a warning to God's prophets in contemporary pulpits. Those who foresee the threats of a secular age against the Christian faith and bark the warning to complacent congregations, take the risk of a prophet's short life. But if they are faithful to

571

their calling as the Servant was to His calling, there is no alternative. What they see they must speak.

Spiritual leaders do not become blind and dumb by accident. Isaiah cites them for deliberately betraying their trust. Staying with the analogy of the dogs, he describes them as, *"sleeping, lying down, loving to slumber"* (v. 10b). In a few well-chosen words, they are lazy. Modern-day jargon would identify them as spiritual "couch potatoes," watching television, munching goodies, falling asleep, and getting fat. To see and speak the truth would disturb their lethargy and destroy their comfort zone. Security is more important than faithfulness.

ABLE TO SACRIFICE (56:11)

Isaiah's scathing indictment takes on more intense anger as he condemns leaders for having an insatiable appetite for the soft lifestyle and a greedy drive "to do their own thing" for selfish gain (v. 11). As another bit of evidence for the single-author theory of Isaiah and the unity of the book, the prophet brings back the "woe" that he pronounced against the leaders of Israel who had become "champions at mixing drinks" (5:22). Now, the false shepherds are bold to call for a drunken orgy that will dull their prophetic senses and hallucinate their vision until they believe that *"tomorrow will be as today, and much more abundant"* (v. 12).

ACCOUNTABLE FOR SIN (56:12)

Drunkenness is the only way such a fantasy can be sustained by those who are expected to be spiritual leaders. Otherwise, the reality of truth will burst upon their eyes and loosen their lips to the loss of their lazy comfort and their selfish gain. But alas, they would rather drink in a den of iniquity than pray in a house for all nations. To them, Paul's warning will be heard: "To those who are self-seeking and do not obey the truth, but obey unrighteousness—indignation and wrath" (Romans 2:8). Shepherds have a special responsibility to sacrifice themselves, to speak the truth, and to avoid evil. But in the oxymorons of Israel's leadership, selfish shepherds joined blind watchmen and dumb dogs in the contradiction of their God-given responsibility.

Consequences of Unfaithful Leaders (57:1–13)

1 The righteous perishes,
And no man takes it to heart;
Merciful men are taken away,
While no one considers
That the righteous is taken away from evil.

2 He shall enter into peace;
They shall rest in their beds,
Each one walking in his uprightness.

3 "But come here,
You sons of the sorceress,
You offspring of the adulterer
and the harlot!

4 Whom do you ridicule?
Against whom do you make a wide mouth
And stick out the tongue?
Are you not children of transgression,
Offspring of falsehood,

5 Inflaming yourselves with gods under every green tree,
Slaying the children in the valleys,
Under the clefts of the rocks?

6 Among the smooth stones of the stream
Is your portion;
They, they, are your lot!
Even to them you have poured a drink offering,
You have offered a grain offering.
Should I receive comfort in these?

7 "On a lofty and high mountain
You have set your bed;
Even there you went up
To offer sacrifice.

8 Also behind the doors and their posts
You have set up your remembrance;
For you have uncovered yourself to
those other than Me,
And have gone up to them;
You have enlarged your bed
And made a covenant with them;
You have loved their bed,
Where you saw their hand.

9 You went to the king with ointment,

> And increased your perfumes;
> You sent your messengers far off,
> And debased yourself even to Sheol.
> 10 You are wearied in the length of your way;
> Yet you did not say, 'There is no hope.'
> You have found the life of your hand;
> Therefore you were not grieved.
> 11 "And of whom have you been afraid, or feared,
> That you have lied
> And not remembered Me,
> Nor taken it to your heart?
> Is it not because I have held My peace from of old
> That you do not fear Me?
> 12 I will declare your righteousness
> And your works,
> For they will not profit you.
> 13 When you cry out,
> Let your collection of idols deliver you.
> But the wind will carry them all away,
> A breath will take them.
> But he who puts his trust in Me shall possess the land,
> And shall inherit My holy mountain."
>
> *Isaiah 57:1–13*

Isaiah is still tracing the implications of the Servant's completed work of redemption among various groups. In chapter 54, he foresaw glory for the church in Zion; in chapter 55, he invited spiritually thirsty people to drink of the living waters; in chapter 56:1–8, he opened the privileges of His chosen family to all nations; and in 56:9–12, he severely condemned Israel's unfaithful leaders for betraying their trust. Chapter 57 deals directly with the fallout of these drunken and shortsighted leaders whom he scorched with sarcasm as blind watchmen, dumb dogs, and selfish shepherds. A legitimate complaint is brought before God by righteous people who suffer most from the faithlessness of Israel's prophets and priests (57:1–2). In response, God opens court again and summons the people of Israel, who are both victims of faithless leaders and culprits of their own faithlessness as they pursue with passion the evils of idolatry and immorality under the guise of religious worship (57:3–13). God then rules in favor of contrite people whose spirits have been crushed by selfish leaders and idolatrous people. With a sharp line of division between those who are contrite in heart and those who persist in sin, God promises peace for the contrite and turmoil for the wicked (57:14–21).

PERSECUTION OF THE RIGHTEOUS (57:1–2)

One would expect universal joy and acceptance for the redemptive work of God's chosen Servant. Human perversity, however, creates a chasm between those who believe and those who reject the Servant's Word. Isaiah has already told us why some people refuse the gift of salvation. Prophets and priests in Israel refused to see, speak, and lead their people because of their own laziness, greed, and short-sightedness. Betraying their sacred trust, they made the fatal error of assuming that tomorrow would be just like today, only better. In other words, they refused to see the "new thing" that God wanted to do for them and their people. But the consequences of their sin did not remain self-contained. Because they were chosen as prophets and priests for the people, they had to oppose those who were righteous and mollify those who were wicked.

Righteous people are the first to suffer from opposition by unfaithful leaders. After hearing the drunken cry of the leaders, "Come, let me get wine! Let us drink our fill of beer! And tomorrow will be like today, or even far better" (56:12), we should not be surprised to hear the righteous complain about being persecuted. Three sad conditions mark their plight: (1) They die in loneliness and no one asks why; (2) they are imprisoned for their faith and no one understands; and (3) they are forced to flee and no one protests (v. 1). The situation is reminiscent of Pastor Niemoeller's oft-quoted statement about persecution in Nazi Germany. After being imprisoned for his faith as a Christian, he realized, "When they took away the Jews, no one spoke; when they took away the labor leaders, no one spoke; when they came to take Christians, there was no one left to speak." When spiritual leaders fail to watch, speak, and sacrifice themselves on behalf of their people, it is the faithful who suffer first.

Untimely death follows their persecution. Outwardly, at least, they find no rest from their opposition until they *rest in their beds* (v. 2). Although they may not have died by execution, the stress of physical and emotional persecution shortened their life and made them martyrs. If we put ourselves in the place of this beleaguered minority in Israel, we feel their loneliness and their confusion. Who has not asked the question, "Why do the righteous suffer?" Who among the righteous who suffer has not wondered, "Why me, Lord?" The complaint is legitimate and the confusion is understandable. God's answer to their complaint will tell us that He also understands.

INDICTMENT OF THE IDOLATERS (57:3–13)

God's concern for the righteous is evident in His abrupt command to the people of Israel whose idolatry combines with the faithlessness of their leaders to cause the faithful to be persecuted. *"But come here"* has the sound and the tone of God calling His cosmic court into emergency session. In earlier oracles, God has spoken harshly against the Jews in exile who were enamored with the idolatry of Babylon. His most severe indictment, however, is reserved for persecutors of those who put their faith in Him. Calling them *"sons of the sorceress, you offspring of the adulterer and the harlot,"* God takes the witness stand against them and charges them with the grossest of sins.

Mockery of God (57:3–4)

The first sin of people who know the truth but choose falsehood is mockery of God (vv. 3–4). To paraphrase the text, God shows His rage by asking the rhetorical question, *"Whom do you ridicule? Against whom do you make a wide mouth and stick out the tongue?"* In no uncertain terms, God lets them know that He will not tolerate their mockery. The charge is so serious that the mockers border on the unpardonable sin of flaunting the name of God and deliberately perverting the holy for evil purposes.

Child Sacrifice (57:5–7)

The second sin of the idolaters is child sacrifice (vv. 5–7). How far the chosen people have fallen! Shamelessly co-opting the bloody rites of the worshipers of Moloch, the Ammonite god adopted by the Babylonians, the children of Israel violated the sanctity of life and sacrificed their own children. Idolatry put a premium upon worshipers sacrificing the first of their sons, their harvest, and their profits. Perhaps in self-justification, they would claim that they were following the law to its logical conclusion when God commanded Israel to celebrate the Feast of Harvest with "the firstfruits of your labors which you have sown in the field" (Exodus 23:16). But God knows the evil intent of their hearts and condemns them for burning with lust in the fertility rites that were held *"under every green tree . . . in the valleys, under the clefts of the rocks"* (v. 5). Sexual gratification, not spiritual worship, motivated their idolatry. Child sacrifice, even in the name of worship, is no better than the crime of child pornography, molestation, rape, and murder. The motive of perverted sexual lust is the same.

In addition to the sacrifice of their first sons, the idolaters in Israel brought the firstfruits of their wine and grain harvests to their false gods. While relatively innocent compared with child sacrifice, giving these offerings to idols rather than Yahweh symbolized their mockery and their sneers. They were not passive idolaters. With a passion characterized as lust, they pursued every practice of the pagans and stuck out their tongues at God as they made their sacrifices.

Sexual Immorality (57:8–9)

The ultimate sin of the idolaters was practicing sexual immorality in the name of worship (v. 8). Prostitution in the name of religion is common among pagans. Whether Babylonians in the cult of Moloch, Greeks in the name of Aphrodite, or Ephesians in the temple of Diana, the practice is in clear contradiction with the moral standards of Mosaic law and the meaning of love in God's covenant with His people. Israelites could never justify bringing prostitution into their worship. So, when they did, their blatant act slapped God in the face with the mockery of His law and His covenant. Worse yet, they went behind their doors and doorposts to put up the phallic symbols of the fertility cult and to practice sexual perversion in all its forms (v. 8b). The depth of their sin is known by the fact that the *mezzuzah* was posted on the doors of the Hebrew home with the command, "The LORD our God, the LORD is one! You shall love the LORD your God with all your heart, and with all your soul, and with all your might" (Deuteronomy 6:4–5). Also, blood was smeared on the doorposts of their homes as a constant reminder of their covenant relationship with God. For a Jew to touch the door and the doorpost as a sign of obedience and love, but then go into the house and violate the law and the covenant by immoral acts of pagan worship, had to be the greatest insult to God. Adding olive oil and perfume to the orgy only sealed their fate as they sank even further in blasphemy (v. 9a).

Spiritual Despair (57:10–13)

A young woman, who had taken the route to sexual promiscuity through singles' bars, confessed that she awakened in the morning with "dirty bed sheets and ashes in her mouth." Disappointment is an advance payment on the wages of sin. The children of Israel who sacrificed their children and prostituted their worship learned this hard lesson. The symptoms of their disappointment included efforts to rid themselves of their idols by sending them far away (v. 9b), feelings of an early descent into the grave itself (v. 9c), and weariness of mind, body, and spirit (v. 10a). Yet, the grip of sin cannot be broken by human effort. After a brief interlude of abstinence, lust rises again and the sin is repeated (v. 10b).

God asks another set of rhetorical questions of the idolaters. *"Of whom have you been afraid, or feared, that you have lied and not remembered Me, nor taken it to your heart? Is it not because I have held My peace from of old that you do not fear Me?"* (v. 11). The answer to the first question is that the children of Israel fear people more than God. The answer to the second question is that God's silence has caused them to believe that He has forgotten them. But He has not. In the strongest words, God says that He will expose their hypocrisy, refuse to answer their cry, and leave their salvation in the hands of their idols (vv. 12–13). With just a puff of His breath, the idols will be blown away like chaff before the wind. But for the righteous whose complaint He has heard, God will protect them from the storm, lead them home to salvation, and give them their place in the kingdom of righteousness (v. 13b).

COMFORT FOR THE CONTRITE (57:14–21)

14 And one shall say,
    "Heap it up! Heap it up!

> Prepare the way,
> Take the stumbling block
>   out of the way of My people."
> 15 For thus says the High and Lofty One
>   Who inhabits eternity,
>   whose name is Holy:
>   "I dwell in the high and holy place,
>   With him who has
>   a contrite and humble spirit,
>   To revive the spirit of the humble,
>   And to revive the heart
>   of the contrite ones.
> 16 For I will not contend forever,
>   Nor will I always be angry;
>   For the spirit would fail before Me,
>   And the souls which I have made.
> 17 For the iniquity of his covetousness
>   I was angry and struck him;
>   I hid and was angry,
>   And he went on backsliding
>   in the way of his heart.
> 18 I have seen his ways,
>   and will heal him;
>   I will also lead him,
>   And restore comforts to him
>   And to his mourners.
> 19 "I create the fruit of the lips:
>   Peace, peace to him who is far off
>   and to him who is near,"
>   Says the LORD,
>   "And I will heal him."
> 20 But the wicked are like the troubled sea,
>   When it cannot rest,
>   Whose waters cast up mire and dirt.
> 21 "There is no peace,"
>   Says my God, "for the wicked."

Isaiah 57:14–21

After hearing the complaint of the righteous and holding court against the idolaters, God rules in favor of those who have a *"contrite and humble spirit"* (v. 15b). The meaning of contrite is not the same as repentance, although a contrite spirit is a part of repentance. In this context, a person who is contrite is one who is beaten down and crushed in spirit. We understand, then, how deeply wounded the faithful people of Israel were by the persecution of their peers. For them, God has promises of grace that include the assurance that He will clear every obstacle out of their way as they embark upon the new exodus (v. 14). Moreover, He who lives in the *"high and holy place"* will reach down to the level of the lowly, lift them up, and revive their spirits (v. 15b).

Here the great divide begins. While God will show mercy to the contrite in heart and withdraw the anger that led to exile, He will not forget their tormentors who refused to see the exile as punishment for their sins, and in fact, aggravated their sins by mocking God with their idolatry and immorality (v. 17). For the contrite in heart, He promises the full recovery of healing, guidance, comfort, praise, and peace (vv. 18–19). But for the wicked, He will leave them to the natural consequences of their sin. No description of those consequences is more apt than to picture their hearts as tumultuous as the raging, restless sea *"whose waters cast up mire and dirt"* (v. 20b). In effect, God turns them over to Rahab, the monster god of the sea, who is creator of chaos and in whom there is no peace.

Jude's picture of apostasy fits Israel's unfaithful leaders and shameless idolaters when he writes, "These dreamers defile the flesh, reject authority, and speak evil of dignitaries" (Jude 8). Also, they "speak evil of whatever they do not know; and whatever they know naturally, like brute beasts, in these things they corrupt themselves" (Jude 10). The consequences of their own sins then seal their fate. Most likely, Jude remembered Isaiah 57:20–21 when he wrote, "They are clouds without water, carried about by the winds; late autumn trees without fruit, twice dead, pulled up by the roots; raging waves of the sea, foaming up their own shame; wandering stars for whom is reserved the blackness of darkness forever" (Jude 12b–13).

NOTES

1. A. S. Herbert, *The Book of the Prophet Isaiah, Chapters 40–66*, The Cambridge Bible Commentary (Cambridge: Cambridge University Press, 1975), 136.

PART TEN

The Vision Spiritualized

Isaiah 58:1–59:21

CHAPTER TWENTY-SEVEN

The Test of Piety

Isaiah 58:1–14

Even in exile, the children of Israel continued to practice the religious traditions of their fathers. Without the temple as the holy place for their worship, they stressed the rituals that could be conducted individually and collectively without the accouterments for worship formerly provided by the temple. As proof of their piety, some held tightly to the prescribed practices, such as Sabbath observance, and added others, such as fasting. In so doing, they opened themselves up to the danger of depending upon rituals as substitutes for true piety. Consequently, they missed the meaning of the Servant's redemptive work, both for themselves and for others. Chapter 58 is addressed specifically to those who used strict adherence to the ritual of fasting as proof of their piety.

PIETY THAT SEEKS GOD (58:1–3a)

1 "Cry aloud, spare not;
    Lift up your voice like a trumpet;
    Tell My people their transgression,
    And the house of Jacob their sins.
2 Yet they seek Me daily,
    And delight to know My ways,
    As a nation that did righteousness,
    And did not forsake the ordinance
        of their God.
    They ask of Me the ordinances of justice;
    They take delight in approaching God.
3 'Why have we fasted,' they say,
        'and You have not seen?

Why have we afflicted our souls,
and You take no notice?'

Isaiah 58:1–3a

Isaiah has used a variety of commanding words to get the attention of the group of people for whom he has God's message. For the house of Jacob and the nations of the Gentiles, he called, "Listen"; for Jerusalem, he shouted "Awake"; for the barren remnant, he said, "Sing"; and for the spiritually thirsty, he cried, "Ho!" His word for the pietists who depend upon ritual is even more dramatic. God tells Isaiah, *"Cry aloud, spare not; lift up your voice like a trumpet"* (v. 1a). Some scholars envision a large assembly of Jews coming together for the day of atonement when the celebrants were to deny themselves as preparation for cleansing from sin. In the midst of the assembled company, God told Isaiah to stand and shout at the top of his voice, *"Tell My people their transgression, and the house of Jacob their sins"* (v. 1b). The shrill, trumpet-like sound would certainly startle the hearers. For one thing, they would not expect their solemn service to be interrupted by a presumptuous prophet. For another thing, they would not expect God to condemn them when they daily sought God through the discipline of their religious rituals (v. 2a). Rather than God bringing a charge against them, they felt as if they had a charge against God. *"Why have we fasted,"* they say, *"and You have not seen? Why have we afflicted our souls, and You take no notice?"* (v. 3). The motive for their ritual is revealed in their questions. Nominally, they pretend to be a righteous nation, true to the ordinances of God, and seeking His wisdom for doing justice among the people. But in truth, they use their daily ritual to draw God's attention to themselves and receive His confirmation of their piety.

Religious rituals at the national level always run the risk of becoming civil substitutes for true piety. The United States, for instance, has many residual rituals of its founding as a nation whose trust is in God. The President is sworn into office with a hand on the Bible, Congress opens each session with a prayer of invocation, and the Supreme Court is gavelled to order after the courier's call, "God bless the United States and this honrable court". Our prayer is that we will never lose these rituals that remind us of our founding principles, but at the same time, we cannot pretend that they sanctify the nation or purify its people. At best, the ritual is an open conduit through which the grace of God can flow to save the nation and redeem its people.

Ritualists in Israel made the mistake of closing off both ends of the ritual so that God could not break through to them with His righteousness, and they could not break out to others with His justice.

PIETY THAT OFFENDS GOD (58:3b–9a)

3b "In fact, in the day of your fast
  you find pleasure,
 And exploit all your laborers.
4 Indeed you fast for strife and debate,
 And to strike with the fist of wickedness.
 You will not fast as you do this day,
 To make your voice heard on high.
5 Is it a fast that I have chosen,
 A day for a man to afflict his soul?
 Is it to bow down his head like a bulrush,
 And to spread out sackcloth and ashes?
 Would you call this a fast,
 And an acceptable day to the LORD?
6 "Is this not the fast that I have chosen:
 To loose the bonds of wickedness,
 To undo the heavy burdens,
 To let the oppressed go free,
 And that you break every yoke?
7 Is it not to share your bread with the hungry,
 And that you bring to your house the poor
  who are cast out;
 When you see the naked,
  that you cover him,
 And not hide yourself from your own flesh?
8 Then your light shall break forth like the morning,
 Your healing shall spring forth speedily,
 And your righteousness shall go before you;
 The glory of the LORD shall be your rear guard.
9a Then you shall call,
  and the LORD will answer;
 You shall cry, and He will say,
  'Here I am.'

Isaiah 58:3b–9a

With the trumpet sound of the prophet's voice, God brings the pious ritualists of Israel to a moment of truth. Using the phrase *"In fact,"* He cites evidence to the contrary. Charge after charge rolls from the prophet's lips. First, on the same day that they fast, they seek their own pleasure (v. 3b). Like the revelers on Fat Tuesday in New Orleans, they gorge themselves just before Ash Wednesday of Lent when they give up something in repentance for their sins. Second, they contradict their pious act of ritual by exploiting those who work for them (v. 3b). God expects that the profession of personal righteousness will lead to social justice. To deny themselves by fasting in order to cleanse themselves from sin, while at the same time exploiting their employees, is an utter contradiction. Third, their true motive for fasting is to prove themselves holier than others (v. 4a). As fasting leads to hunger, hunger leads to irritability, and irritability leads to strife. God expects rituals in His name to be unifying experiences for His people. Any ritual that causes division in the Body is offensive to God. Fourth, contrary to the spirit of reconciliation that God intends as an outcome from spiritual discipline, the fasting of the ritualists in Israel results in the wickedness of physical violence (v. 4a). One can imagine the division between factions in the large assembly of Jews as some claim to be more spiritual than others. Quarrels lead to threats and threats lead to fist fights. Or less literally, the ritualists may be fanatics who justify forms of physical and verbal violence against those who oppose them. All in all, they profess to be pious, but in reality, they are a mean-spirited group.

No one can contest the outward show of piety by the ritualists. In their fasting they deny themselves with pain, humble themselves with bowed heads, put on sackcloth of repentance, and sit in the ashes of repentance (v. 5). Yet, God asks them, *"Is it a fast that I have chosen? . . . Would you call this a fast, and an acceptable day to the* LORD*?"* (v. 5b). Obviously, the answer is no and the reason is inferred in the words "an acceptable day to the LORD." Jesus' quotation of Isaiah 61:1, 2, as the text for His inaugural sermon in Nazareth, concluded with the statement of His purpose, "To preach the acceptable year of the Lord." The direct reference is to the Year of Jubilee, which is signaled by trumpet sound after seven sabbaths of years or forty-nine years on the Day of Atonement (Leviticus 25:8). The fiftieth year, then, is the Year of Jubilee when liberty is proclaimed "throughout all the land to all of its inhabitants" (Leviticus 25:10). As liberty is the watch cry of Jesus' ministry, it is also God's expectations for the fast that He has chosen (v. 6a).

Those who truly fast will be liberationists, not with a mixture of biblical theology and Marxian theology, but with the motive of personal righteousness that leads to social justice. The freedoms of fasting include: (a) loosing the bonds of wickedness; (b) undoing the heavy burdens; (c) letting the oppressed go free; and (d) breaking every yoke that is too heavy to bear (v. 6). Sacrificial love, not begrudging duty, is the motive for these freedoms. As a result of fasting, a person will share half of his or her bread with the hungry, open his or her house to the homeless, give the coat off his or her back to the naked, and not neglect those in his or her household while ministering to others (v. 7). Out of the same motive of love will spring intangible spiritual rewards that far exceed any public recognition of piety. God makes these promises to those who fast as He has chosen: (a) *"your light shall break forth like the morning";* (b) *"your healing shall spring forth readily";* and (c) *"your righteousness shall go before you; the glory of the LORD shall be your rear guard"* (v. 8). Coming full cycle to the question the pious asked in the beginning, the Lord says that He will answer them when they call and He will be with them when they cry (v. 9a). But even more blessings await those who fast in obedience rather than in selfishness.

PIETY THAT HONORS GOD (58:9b–12)

9b   "If you take away the yoke
      from your midst,
    The pointing of the finger,
      and speaking wickedness,
10 If you extend your soul to the hungry
    And satisfy the afflicted soul,
    Then your light shall dawn in the darkness,
    And your darkness shall be as the noonday.
11 The LORD will guide you continually,
    And satisfy your soul in drought,
    And strengthen your bones;
    You shall be like a watered garden,
    And like a spring of water,
      whose waters do not fail.

12 Those from among you
    Shall build the old waste places;
    You shall raise up the foundations
        of many generations;
    And you shall be called
        the Repairer of the Breach,
    The Restorer of Streets to Dwell In.

Isaiah 58:9b–12

"If" is the conditional word Isaiah uses to call the ritualists to repentance. *If* they break the burdensome yoke of their hypocritical fasting, stop pointing their fingers at others and accusing them of sin, and sacrifice themselves for the poor and needy, God will also give them a future with the remnant that will be freed from the darkness of exile. Led by the presence of the Lord on the new exodus, and thus assured of strength and safety for their journey, they will become builders of the New Jerusalem with the honor of being entitled *"Repairer of the Breach"* and *"Restorer of Streets to Dwell In"* (v. 12). Although God has been hard on the ritualists, He has a special word of grace for them. As forerunners of the Pharisees in Jesus' day, they need to hear His admonition as it might be paraphrased: "For you fast daily and observe all manner of ritual, and pass by justice and the love of God. These you ought to have done, without leaving the others undone" (paraphrase of Luke 11:42).

PIETY THAT PLEASES GOD (58:13–14)

13 "If you turn away your foot
        from the Sabbath,
    From doing your pleasure
        on My holy day,
    And call the Sabbath a delight,
    The holy day of the LORD honorable,
    And shall honor Him,
        not doing your own ways,
    Nor finding your own pleasure,
    Nor speaking your own words,
14 Then you shall delight yourself
        in the LORD;
    And I will cause you to ride on the
        high hills of the earth,

And feed you with the heritage of
Jacob your father,
The mouth of the LORD has spoken."

Isaiah 58:13–14

Although the issue of fasting is the case in point that Isaiah deals with in this chapter, a principle regarding rituals has been established. When Isaiah identified the essentials of true religion, he began with the spiritual virtues of justice and righteousness. These were backed by the ritual of keeping the Sabbath and the ethic of avoiding evil (56:1, 2). Quite logically, then, the principle for the ritual of fasting also applies to the ritual of the Sabbath. Reaching back to the very beginning of our study when Isaiah was outlining the themes for his prophecy, he spoke against "the New Moons, the Sabbaths, and the calling of assemblies," (1:13) which sounds ominously like the situation that he has addressed in detail just now. To honor the Sabbath and please the Lord, the same requirements hold. The children of Israel are not to use the ritual to follow their own ways, find their own pleasure, or speak their own words (v. 13b). If, on the other hand, the glory is given to God, exquisite delight will be theirs. God promises that the true, humble, and selfless keeper of the Sabbath will *"ride on the high hills of the earth"* and *"feed [on] the heritage of Jacob"* (v. 14b). The wisdom of God sees the value of religious ritual such as the Sabbath and spiritual disciplines such as fasting. Although they can be abused and divisive, they can also be the means of personal righteousness, the motive for social justice, the source of spiritual delight, and the end for the glory of God. The principle is this: *religious ritual is the means toward the spiritual ends of personal righteousness, social justice, spiritual delight, and the glory of God.* Any other purpose will evoke God's displeasure.

CHAPTER TWENTY-EIGHT

The Confession of the Community

Isaiah 59:1–21

Isaiah has a means of communication to match every situation. After Cyrus conquered Babylon, the children of Israel expected instant fulfillment of God's promise of deliverance from exile. In this oracle of salvation, Isaiah is dealing especially with the collective sin of the nation of Israel. As the chosen people of God and His Servant Nation, they assumed they could do no wrong. Necessarily, then, as they tried to explain their punishment in exile, they found multiple ways to rationalize their sin and place the blame outside themselves. Our contemporary society is playing the same game. Whether it be the faulty genes, childhood abuse, environmental circumstances, economic hardship, sexual harassment, dysfunctional families, or toxic faith, we are ingenious inventors of rationalizations to absolve our guilt and explain our sin. Collective sins of a nation or a community are no different. When we want to avoid collective guilt we find scapegoats to place the blame on and send into the wilderness.

After dealing with the implications of God's salvation for various groups among the children of Israel, Isaiah calls the whole community together to hear the Word of the Lord. Historical circumstances dictated his message. After Cyrus had conquered Babylon, the Jews expected instant fulfillment of God's promise for deliverance. When Cyrus's decree was delayed, they began to question whether God had the power or the desire to save them. Isaiah counters these false notions by putting the blame for exile directly upon the people who have sinned against God. It is not the shortness of God's arm to save them, but the separation of their sin that has put distance between them and God. Nor is it God's lack of desire to save them, but their sins that have condemned them.

Although Israel lost its national identity when it went into exile and splintered into factions, it retained a strong sense of community as God's chosen people. Memory of deliverance from bondage in the past and promise of salvation in the future served as the glue that held the community together. But its strength also became its weakness. As a community, it rebelled against God by forgetting its past and doubting its future. Under the pressure of prolonged exile these sins were aggravated. After Cyrus conquered Babylon but delayed his decree of deliverance, whatever faith Israel had mustered to believe God's promise disappeared. Using the delay as an excuse, the community shifted the blame for their bondage from themselves to God.

Isaiah's versatility as a communicator becomes evident once again when he employs a communal means to address a communal problem. A liturgical setting is created in Chapter 59 as Isaiah calls the whole community together and has different voices speaking and responding like a congregation at worship. The voices are heard through the personal pronouns.

Order of Service	Speaker	Pronoun	Text
The Call to Worship	Isaiah	"Your iniquities"	59:2
The Word of God	The Lord	"they conceive evil"	59:4
The Confession of Sin	The People	"our transgressions"	59:12
The Forgiveness of Sin	Isaiah	"His own righteousness"	59:16
The Blessing	The Lord	"My covenant"	59:21

First, Isaiah speaks as the prophet of God to the gathered community about **"your** *iniquities"* and **"your** *sins"* (59:2). Then, in confirmation and extension of the prophet's word, the voice of God Himself is heard as He says, **"They** *conceive evil and bring forth iniquity"* (59:4). Shaken and convicted, the community itself responds in unison to the stern words of God with the confession, **"Our** *transgressions"* and **"our** *sins"* (59:12). Hearing and honoring their confession, God answers through His prophet with the promise of salvation through **"His** *own righteousness"* (59:16). God then seals the prophet's word with the personalized promise and benedictory blessing of

"**My** *covenant*," "**My** *Spirit*," and "**My** *words*" (59:21). As the conclusion to this section of salvation oracles, which began with Chapter 56, we learn about the consequences of communal sin, the nature of communal confession, and the need for divine intervention in order to restore the communal covenant.

THE CONSEQUENCES OF COMMUNAL SIN (59:1–3)

1 Behold, the LORD's hand is not shortened,
   That it cannot save;
   Nor His ear heavy,
   That it cannot hear.
2 But your iniquities have separated
       you from your God;
   And your sins have hidden
       His face from you,
   So that He will not hear,
3 For your hands are defiled with blood,
   And your fingers with iniquity;
   Your lips have spoken lies,
   Your tongue has muttered perversity.

Isaiah 59:1–3

The timing of history helps us understand this salvation oracle for the children of Israel. Most likely, it came after Cyrus had conquered Babylon as God had promised, but when immediate deliverance did not come to Israel, the community lapsed back into the sin of doubting God's promise. The expectation for instant relief from social ills is not unique to our modern Alka-Seltzer™ society. Israel also expected the "plop" of Cyrus's conquest to be followed immediately by the "plop" of God's deliverance along with the miraculous "fizz" of instant relief. When Cyrus delayed his decree, their shallow faith quickly turned into deeper doubts. As a community they questioned whether the delay of their deliverance represented God's *impotence* or His *indifference*. His impotence was symbolized by a short hand that could not reach them, and His indifference by a deaf ear that could not hear them. God Himself became the scapegoat for their sins.

"When in Doubt, Blame God" is an appropriate bumper sticker for a sinning society. After exhausting other sources of blame, God becomes the target of our attack. Whether it is the Jewish holocaust in

Hitler's time or the AIDS epidemic in ours, sooner or later we can expect God to get the blame. "Why would a loving God permit this to happen?" is a familiar question that lets us breathe a sigh of relief from the reality of our own sin.

Isaiah summarily dismisses Israel's doubts about God's impotence or indifference to their suffering. Going directly to the heart of the issue, he says that it is their iniquities, not God's impotence, that have separated them from God and created the appearance that they are out of His reach (v. 2a). An old book is entitled *Our Arms Are Too Short to Box With God.* God is not impotent, we are. Isaiah also cited the sins of Israel as the reason for their contention that God had turned His face away from them creating the impression that He was indifferent to them (v. 2b). These are tactics to avoid the truth. If either the hand of God were to reach them or the face of God were to see them, they would be instantly destroyed along with their sins. Only grace and mercy, not impotence and indifference, kept the distance between God's judgment and their sins.

Impatience is justified as Isaiah advances his charge against Israel from the fact that their sin had separated them from God to the truth that their sin had fully contaminated the body politic. Four parts of the human body are identified as proof that every vestige of Israel shows sinful pollution. Highly personalized pronouns leave no doubt where the blame lies. The prophet says, "*your hands*" are defiled with the blood of innocents; "*your fingers*" are picking up the details of iniquity; "*your lips*" speak lies rather than the truth; and "*your tongue*" mutters the sounds of perversity. The allusion to fingers as well as the hand and to the tongue as well as the lips tells us how detailed and deliberate Israel had become at sinning. To use contemporary terms, they had become experts in micromanaging sin. In every part, as well as the whole, corruption had invaded the community of Israel.

THE EVOLUTION OF EVIL (59:4–8)

4 No one calls for justice,
   Nor does any plead for truth.
   They trust in empty words
     and speak lies;
   They conceive evil
     and bring forth iniquity.

5 They hatch vipers' eggs
  and weave the spider's web;
  He who eats of their eggs dies,
  And from that which is crushed
  a viper breaks out.
6 Their webs will not become garments,
  Nor will they cover themselves with their works;
  Their works are works of iniquity,
  And the act of violence is in their hands.
7 Their feet run to evil,
  And they make haste to shed innocent blood;
  Their thoughts are thoughts of iniquity;
  Wasting and destruction are in their paths.
8 The way of peace they have not known,
  And there is no justice in their ways;
  They have made themselves crooked paths;
  Whoever takes that way
  shall not know peace.

Isaiah 59:4–8

Although Isaiah spoke the Word of God when he set the record straight about Israel's sin as the reason for their punishment, the human voice is no substitute for the voice of God Himself. When God speaks, everyone listens.

In confirmation of Isaiah's rebuke of Israel for its sin, God teams with His prophet to advance his diagnosis of communal sin. As a medical specialist would track cancer cells invading the whole body, so God traces the march of sin through the social structure of Israel. Step by step, we see the making of an immoral society.

As the adage goes, "A fish rots from the head first." Thus the *loss of moral leaders* who call for justice and plead for truth is the first step in social downfall, whether in a local institution or the world community. Every generation needs to cultivate, identify, and esteem its moral leaders. Certainly, God had in mind faithful prophets of His Word, but we remember from earlier oracles that He also spoke of elders, priests, rulers, and princes among those He charged with moral responsibility. Not coincidentally, our local newspaper is carrying daily news about the state legislature going through the elaborate and costly exercise of hammering out an ethics reform bill with the hope of restoring public confidence in the integrity of our political leaders. When all is said and done, however, a free cup of coffee from a lobbyist is disallowed while massive loopholes for contributions from PAC's (Political Action Committees) still permit the building of "war chests" and influencing votes. For the state legislature and all moral leaders, whether prophets or politicians, the crucial question is, If you do not call for justice and plead for truth, who will?

When moral leaders default on their trust, *immoral leaders arise.* Society's throne of moral leadership does not remain empty for long. If leaders for justice and mercy do not occupy it, leaders for injustice, unrighteousness, and falsehood will. Worse yet, God sees those who default on their responsibility for moral leadership becoming themselves the symbols of corruption in the society. Perhaps our fears are misplaced. We worry about the adversaries against justice and truth when our concern should be for the advocates of justice and truth. Adversaries will always be present among us, but if the advocates are absent or corrupt, the moral consequences reach to every cell in the body politic. Corruption is complete when the advocates for justice and truth *"trust in empty words and speak lies; . . . conceive evil and bring forth iniquity"* (v. 4b).

Moral degeneration continues into the third stage when the corruption and perversion of moral leaders becomes a *fatal sting for the whole society.* Isaiah's metaphors of the viper's eggs and the spider's web convey unmistakable truth. Whether the viper's eggs are hatched or crushed, the viper still lives to bring moral death with its fatal sting (v. 5). Likewise, when moral leaders fall, their evil influence spins a web that entraps the whole society. Because every individual and institution in a culture is interconnected and interdependent is some way, there is no escape from the web of immorality that these leaders spin. Putting the two metaphors together, God describes a society that is morally paralyzed and utterly helpless against the sting of evil that will bring its death. History proves the point. Civilizations die from moral corruption, not military attack. The viper's sting and the spider's web are symbols of truth that a civilization or a society will ignore at the price of death.

Once the symptoms of death are spread throughout the body politic, *the populace becomes part of moral perversion.* God cites the symptoms of communal sin: (a) works are substituted for righteousness (v. 6a); (b) violence outweighs justice (v. 6b); (c) evil is actively pursued (v. 7a);

(d) oppression is done easily and taken lightly (v. 7b); (e) iniquitous thoughts stimulate their planning (v. 7b); and (f) the shalom of peace among people is lost (v. 8). These are all symptoms of a morally bankrupt society.

Social degeneration bottoms out in the final stage when *"crooked paths"* of oppression and falsehood replace the straight paths of justice and truth (v. 8). Sociologists talk about the *moral mazeways* of society by which individuals find their way through an ethical no-man's land to the knowledge of right and wrong. The term *mazeways* is used because contemporary moral issues are seldom black and white or simple and direct. Every moral decision we make has implications for other issues and trade-offs or consequences. A pro-life stance, for instance, is not limited to abortion, but involves the full range of personal issues from contraception to euthanasia and not without the social issues of capital punishment and military action. A society that has lost its way will leave its people wandering in a moral mazeway that has no boundaries and no end. A perverse society is even worse because it will lead its people through the mazeway of crooked paths to a false end where right and wrong are reversed.

We are not far from those crooked paths in our taste for entertainment. A youth minister who substituted for the senior pastor on a radio broadcast brought me up short with conviction when he said, "Today we laugh at the sins for which Jesus died." He referred specifically to the television, movies, and video tapes we watch. When yesterday's R rating is today's PG rating with a parade of sins condemned by the Word of God, he spoke hard truth. If the moral standard for our entertainment contradicts biblical truth, we are either dupes of crooked paths or sinners of false ends. When a society laughs at the sins for which Jesus died, moral bankruptcy has bottomed out in the perversion of truth.

THE COMMUNAL CONFESSION (59:9–15a)

9 Therefore justice is far from us,
   Nor does righteousness overtake us;
   We look for light,
      but there is darkness!
   For brightness,
      but we walk in blackness!

10 We grope for the wall like the blind,
     And we grope as if we had no eyes;
     We stumble at noonday as at twilight;
     We are as dead men in desolate places.
11 We all growl like bears,
     And moan sadly like doves;
     We look for justice, but there is none;
     For salvation, but it is far from us.
12 For our transgressions are multiplied before You,
     And our sins testify against us;
     For our transgressions are with us,
     And as for our iniquities,
        we know them:
13 In transgressing and lying
        against the Lord,
     And departing from our God,
     Speaking oppression and revolt,
     Conceiving and uttering from the heart
        words of falsehood.
14 Justice is turned back,
     And righteousness stands afar off;
     For truth is fallen in the street,
     And equity cannot enter.
15a So truth fails,
     And he who departs from evil makes
        himself a prey.

Isaiah 59:9–15a

God's shock treatment jolted Israel. When His truth struck home, they realized how their initial rebellion had not only caused their exile but had corrupted their culture. As a people, then, they no longer blamed their fathers or their God for their punishment. Taking the full weight of guilt and shame upon themselves, they confessed that their sins had separated them from God's justice and righteousness (v. 9a), plunged them into darkness (v. 9b), made them grope and stumble in the search for truth (v. 10a), left them as good as dead (v. 10b), and caused them to be as angry as bears and as mournful as doves (v. 11a). In contemporary terms, they had dead-ended in social injustice and spiritual despair (v. 11b).

The people continued their confession with the acknowledgement that God is right. Their transgressions had separated them from God, caused their punishment, and haunted every moment of their existence (v. 12). Then, being harder on themselves than either God or His prophet, the people admitted that their sin had undermined the moral foundations of their community. Justice, righteousness, truth, and equity were all victims of their sin. The breakdown was so complete that anyone who advocated truth had no hearers, and anyone who rejected evil was persecuted (v. 15). To confess that they stoned the prophets and persecuted the righteous is the level of honesty to which a morally perverse society must come before God. Anything less falls short of full confession.

THE INTERVENTION OF GOD (59:15b–20)

15b Then the LORD saw it,
    and it displeased Him
    That there was no justice.
16 He saw that there was no man,
    And wondered that there was no intercessor;
    Therefore His own arm brought
      salvation for Him;
    And His own righteousness,
      it sustained Him.
17 For He put on righteousness as a breastplate,
    And a helmet of salvation on His head;
    He put on the garments of vengeance for clothing,
    And was clad with zeal as a cloak.
18 According to their deeds,
    accordingly He will repay,
    Fury to His adversaries,
    Recompense to His enemies;
    The coastlands He will fully repay.
19 So shall they fear
    The name of the LORD from the west,
    And His glory from the rising of the sun;
    When the enemy comes in like a flood,
    The Spirit of the LORD will lift up a
    standard against him.
20 "The Redeemer will come to Zion,
    And to those who turn from
      transgression in Jacob,"
    Says the LORD.

Isaiah 59:15b–20

Israel's corruption had become pervasive and perverse. Like a fly trapped in a spider's web, the helpless community could only await the viper's fatal sting. But with the honest confession of their condition, God responds with radical action equal to their hopeless plight. Surveying the scene, even God finds it hard to believe that no one is left to contend for justice or intercede for the community. Shades of Sodom! When Abraham could not find ten righteous men remaining in the totally corrupted city, God sent two angels in the form of men to evacuate Lot and his family before the fire fell (Genesis 19). Israel deserved the same fate because God could find no one who called for justice, who pled for truth or interceded for the community (v. 16a). Only God's grace could make the difference. Rather than destroy the corrupted community of Israel, God dons the armor of war and prepares to do battle on behalf of His people (v. 17). Commenting on this passage, John F. A. Sawyer calls God "The Reluctant Warrior" because He would prefer to save His people as "The Suffering Servant." In Israel's case, however, total corruption required forceful action. Without divine intervention, the community could not be saved.

The key to understanding God's decisive act is found in the pronouns used by the prophet, "**His** *own arm brought salvation for Him*" and "**His** *own righteousness, it sustained Him*" (v. 16). He will show Israel that His arm is not short or lacking power, but only through the means of His righteousness and toward the end of their salvation. And He will be decisive. Along with the breastplate of righteousness and the helmet of salvation, He will also clothe Himself in the garments of *"vengeance"*—better interpreted as vindication—and *"zeal"* (v. 17b). Paul the Apostle used similar figures in Ephesians 6:14–17. The breastplate of righteousness and the helmet of salvation are the same, but in Isaiah the garments of vindication and zeal replace the shield of faith, the sword of the Spirit, and the equipment of peace. Israel's circumstances are unique because there is no one left in the community to do battle for truth. God must intervene with the power and precision of a warrior—but not in violation of His own character. His zealous action to vindicate the truth will be taken within the character of His righteousness and the goal of His salvation.

A sobering lesson underlies God's decision to intervene forcibly on behalf of Israel's corrupt community. A society can become so corrupt and perverse that renewal or revival cannot save it. Divine intervention may be the only alternative. But how do we know when a society reaches that point? Isaiah gives us the answer. When there is no moral leader—prophet, priest, elder, ruler, prince, or even common person—to call for justice or intercede for the people, God must become the Reluctant Warrior. With this truth, we should take new hope for our society and our civilization. Despite the invasion of evil forces into our communities, the voice of truth is still heard, and the prayer of intercession is on the rise. We cannot imagine a society so corrupt that no one speaks for God or prays for God, but it is possible. To avoid this happening in our society, we must adopt the confession of Israel acknowledging the totality of our sin and the inability to save ourselves. Whether as the Suffering Servant or the Reluctant Warrior, God will intervene on our behalf.

If God must go to war to save His people, His adversaries will feel His fury, and His enemies will know His justice. As ironic as it may seem, whenever God intervenes in human affairs, His action is grace to some and judgment to others. For those who trust in Him, His grace is known, but for those who defy Him, His fury is felt (v. 18). In either case, God intervenes for only one purpose: to glorify His name throughout the earth from the beginning to the end of every waking day of human existence (v. 19). Great hope follows God's intervention. In the oft-quoted promise that applies to individuals and institutions, communities and civilizations, we know that when it seems as if the enemies of God will sweep over us like a flood, God will don His armor, raise His standard, and do battle for us (v. 19b). And He will win. As He promised redemption to Zion as a community and to all people who turn from their transgressions to Him, so He gives us the same assurance. When we confess that we are caught in the web of our own sins and helplessly await the viper's fatal sting, God will go to war and save us—because He says so (v. 20).

THE BENEDICTION OF BLESSING (59:21)

21 "As for Me," says the LORD, "this is My
covenant with them: My Spirit who is upon you, and
My words which I have put in your mouth, shall not
depart from your mouth, nor from the mouth of your
descendants, nor from the mouth of your
descendants' descendants," says the LORD, "from this
time and forevermore."

Isaiah 59:21

No one can ever say that God is not true to His Word. Even His most radical action of divine intervention in a totally corrupt society has the single aim of restoring His covenant relationship with His people. When the voice of God follows the prophet's word of truth once again, He says, *"As for Me."* Three personal pronouns reveal the love that motivates every action of God. *"My covenant"* speaks of His relationship with us; *"My Spirit"* promises His presence within us; and *"My words"* assures His truth for us.

God has made these promises to His people before. But now He puts His own character on the line when He promises that never again will the community of faith lack an advocate who calls for justice and pleads for truth. As sure as His promise to Noah that He would never send a flood upon the whole earth again and to the children of Israel that they would never go into exile again, God makes the vow to His people that His Word will remain in their mouths and be spoken by them to all generations. The fear of a society so corrupt and so perverse that no one can be found to speak for God is dispelled. In the twentieth century, the Soviet Union and Red China stand as witnesses to this covenant. After forty or more years under dictators who tried every measure of persecution to eliminate Christianity from their culture, untold thousands of believers sprang forth in witness to Christ at the first sign of freedom. God's Word is good. Gag rules on Christian witness, boycotts on Bibles, suppression of religious freedom, and persecution of Christians stimulate rather than stifle the faith. For those who doubt the validity of God's covenant, the presence of His Spirit, and the indestructibility of His Word, the burden of proof is on them.

PART ELEVEN

The Vision Celebrated

Isaiah 60–66

CHAPTER TWENTY-NINE

The Songs of Zion

Isaiah 60–62

It is time to sing. Throughout the Book of Isaiah, jubilant songs of praise have followed the prophet's promising words of deliverance from the punishment of sin. In chapter 59, the effects of Israel's sin bottomed out when the people confessed the total contamination of their culture and their abject inability to save themselves. Only the intervention of God's redeeming grace could make a difference. And God did intervene. With the full power of His own mighty arm, He brought redemption to Zion and reaffirmed His everlasting covenant with His people. Naturally then, it is time to sing, not just an intermittent chorus as in the earlier pattern of Isaiah, but a trilogy of songs that give glory to God for His redeeming grace. Chapter 60 is The Song of the City, in which the prophet sings of the glory of the New Jerusalem; chapter 61 is The Song of the Servant, in which the Messiah sings of the joy that will come with the New Covenant; and chapter 62 is The Song of the Church, in which God sings of the love that gives Zion its new name. A rising crescendo of praise awaits us as we sing with the prophet.

THE SONG OF THE CITY (60:1–22)

1 Arise, shine;
 For your light has come!
 And the glory of the LORD
  is risen upon you.
2 For behold, the darkness shall cover the earth,
 And deep darkness the people;
 But the LORD will arise over you,
 And His glory will be seen upon you.

3 The Gentiles shall come to your light,
  And kings to the brightness of your rising.
4 "Lift up your eyes all around and see:
  They all gather together,
      they come to you;
  Your sons shall come from afar,
  And your daughters shall be nursed at your side.
5 Then you shall see and become radiant,
  And your heart shall swell with joy;
  Because the abundance of the sea shall
      be turned to you,
  The wealth of the Gentiles shall come to you.
6 The multitude of camels shall cover your land,
  The dromedaries of Midian
      and Ephah;
  All those from Sheba shall come;
  They shall bring gold and incense,
  And they shall proclaim the praises of the LORD.
7 All the flocks of Kedar shall be
      gathered together to you,
  The rams of Nebaioth shall minister to you;
  They shall ascend with acceptance on My altar,
  And I will glorify the house of My glory.
8 "Who are these who fly like a cloud,
  And like doves to their roosts?
9 Surely the coastlands shall wait for Me;
  And the ships of Tarshish will come first,
  To bring your sons from afar,
  Their silver and their gold with them,
  To the name of the LORD your God,
  And to the Holy One of Israel,
  Because He has glorified you.
10 "The sons of foreigners shall build up your walls,
  And their kings shall minister to you;
  For in My wrath I struck you,
  But in My favor I have had mercy on you.
11 Therefore your gates shall be open continually;
  They shall not be shut day or night,
  That men may bring to you the wealth of the Gentiles,
  And their kings in procession.
12 For the nation and kingdom
      which will not serve you shall perish,

And those nations shall be utterly ruined.

13 "The glory of Lebanon
    shall come to you,
The cypress, the pine,
    and the box tree together,
To beautify the place of My sanctuary;
And I will make the place of My feet glorious.

14 Also the sons of those who afflicted you
Shall come bowing to you,
And all those who despised you
    shall fall prostrate at the soles of your feet;
And they shall call you
    The City of the LORD,
Zion of the Holy One of Israel.

15 "Whereas you have been forsaken and hated,
So that no one went through you,
I will make you an eternal excellence,
A joy of many generations.

16 You shall drink dry the milk of the Gentiles,
And shall milk the breast of kings;
You shall know that I, the LORD,
    am your Savior
And your Redeemer,
    the Mighty One of Jacob.

17 "Instead of bronze I will bring gold,
Instead of iron I will bring silver,
Instead of wood, bronze,
And instead of stones, iron.
I will also make your officers peace,
And your magistrates righteousness.

18 Violence shall no longer be heard
    in your land,
Neither wasting nor destruction
    within your borders;
But you shall call your walls Salvation,
And your gates Praise.

19 "The sun shall no longer be your light by day,
Nor for brightness shall the moon give light to you;
But the LORD will be to you an everlasting light,
And your God your glory.

20 Your sun shall no longer go down,
Nor shall your moon withdraw itself;

For the LORD will be your everlasting light,
And the days of your mourning shall be ended.
21 Also your people shall all be righteous;
They shall inherit the land forever,
The branch of My planting,
The work of My hands,
That I may be glorified.
22 A little one shall become a thousand,
And a small one a strong nation.
I, the LORD, will hasten it in its time."

Isaiah 60:1–22

The glory of God is beyond human comprehension. Light, brighter than the light of the sun, is as close as we can come to describing the shining glory of God's redeeming presence. In this first song of the trilogy, Isaiah does his best to communicate the sunburst of God's glory upon Jerusalem, a city that is still in ruins and desolation. He asks that the imagination of his hearers be stretched to its limits as he gives them a song to sing. The coming of the Redeemer to Israel will be like a dazzling dawn (vv. 1–3) in which they will see Jerusalem turned from rags to riches (vv. 4–9), become the center of *"eternal excellence"* for the nations of the world (vv. 10–18), and bask in the glory of God's everlasting light (vv. 19–22).

A key to understanding the truth of this chapter is to remember that Isaiah did not separate the material world from the spiritual world in his theology as the Greeks did in their philosophy centuries later. So when Isaiah speaks of the city of Jerusalem he is also talking about the spiritual Body of the Church, and when he refers to the material restoration of the New Jerusalem he is also foreseeing the spiritual restoration of the Church identified as Zion. To force the text into a historical setting and demand evidence of prophetic fulfillment on a human time schedule is to miss the spiritual and theological meaning of Isaiah's prophecy. For instance, when the children of Israel returned from exile to the ruined city of Jerusalem, the restoration of its walls (60:10 and 18) began with financial assistance from Darius I, King of Persia, but controversy bogged down the project for almost one hundred years until Nehemiah rallied the people to complete the work. Although Isaiah's prophecy is confirmed by history wherever the two converge, we must keep in mind that these songs of salvation are primarily spiritual and theological poetry, not historical prose. From this perspective, we will see not only the richness and beauty of the text but we will foresee God's promise for the coming of His Messiah and the future of His Church.

THE DAZZLING DAWN (60:1–3)

Isaiah's song of salvation opens with a refrain that might be sung after each of the stanzas to follow. With the double imperative *"arise, shine"* the prophet invokes the power of God to bring the people of Israel from their prostrate position in the dust of sin to the dignity of standing with the self-esteem of the redeemed. By the same redemptive power, they will personally glow with the *Shekinah* of His presence as a reflection of their righteousness.

The Creative Light (60:1)

Not surprisingly, God's glory is likened to the light of the sun. As the sun is the source of light in the physical universe, so God is the source of light in the spiritual universe. No moon is a source of light in itself. It shines only as it reflects the sun. So it is with Zion, as symbolized by the New Jerusalem. No light is self-generating. Only as the light of God rises over the city and within the hearts of its people will the New Jerusalem reflect the glory of His redeeming presence. But without the light of His presence, all is darkness.

Added meaning is given to the analogy of the light, as representative of the glory of God, with the special meaning of the phrases, *"And the glory of the LORD is risen upon you"* (v. 1b) and *"the LORD will rise over you"* (v. 2b). Witnesses to a dawn in the Middle East report that the sun does not gradually arise to bring the daylight. Rather, the sun bursts upon the horizon to turn deep darkness into dazzling splendor. The glory of God's redemption is also like a sunburst. Sin's deep darkness is instantly turned into the radiance of redemption.

The Redeeming Light (60:2)

Isaiah's analogy of light in this chapter fills in the details of his earlier prophecy "The people who walked in darkness have seen a great light; those who dwelt in the land of the shadow of death, upon them a light has shined" (9:2). The analogy of light, as representative of the glory of God, also links back in the history of Israel to the exile in Egypt when God sent a plague of darkness over the land—a darkness so deep that its gloom could be felt, and people could not see each other. "But all the children of Israel had light in their dwellings" (Exodus 10:21–23). In still another contrast between the light and darkness, John says of Christ, "In Him was life, and the life was the light of men. And the light shines in the darkness, and the darkness did not comprehend it" (John 1:4, 5). Against the darkest of darkness, then, the light of the glory of God is even more radiant and brilliant.

The Attractive Light (60:3)

Light attracts—especially a bright light that shines in the darkness. While driving downtown at night, one of our children spotted the beam of a searchlight piercing the darkness overhead and turning against the black sky. Our curiosity got the best of us. Weaving through the city streets with the beam in view, we did not stop until we came to the source of the light. Although the huge search light signaled only the opening of a new car wash, we commended the owner for a creative approach to advertising. A bright light on a dark night will always get our attention. According to Isaiah, Gentiles and kings will be drawn to the light of the glory of God that will shine in the New Jerusalem. Gentiles will come to the light that frees them from sin, and kings will come with the recognition that their glory fades against the brightness of His shining (v. 3b).

THE SPLENDOR OF RICHES (60:4–9)

Jerusalem suffered economic impoverishment as well as spiritual darkness because of its sin. The population had been decimated by siege and exile. Commerce had ground to a halt because the city lay in ruins. Treasuries of the city had been sacked by its Babylonian conquerors, and the gold and silver of its Holy Temple had been stripped for tribute to its enemies. Even the modest pride the dwellers once had in their flocks of sheep had been lost and never recovered. But with the rising of the light of the glory of God upon the city, its rags will turn to riches. With a magnetic draw, sons and daughters of Israel will begin to come home (v. 5a), entrepreneurial Gentiles will invest in the city (v. 5b), camel caravans again will make Jerusalem an intersection for world trade (v. 6a), gold and silver will arrive from the once-hostile land of Sheba (v. 6b), and flocks of sheep, with a plentiful number of rams, will be driven from distant lands to fill the hillsides and provide choice animals for religious sacrifice (v. 7a). By the drawing power of His light, God Himself says, *"And I will glorify the house of My glory"* (v. 7b).

Isaiah paints an unforgettable picture of the nations being drawn to the radiant light of God's glory in Jerusalem when he envisions the magnificent ships of Tarshish flying like white clouds across the sea to bring home the new children of faith and the wealth of nations to Jerusalem (v. 8–9). Having sailed on Puget Sound in Washington State, I have also enjoyed watching the sailboats in the annual regatta to Victoria, British Columbia. No more spectacular sight can fill the eye than to see a hundred white and billowing sails accented against the blue waters, bright sun, and snowcapped mountains in the distance. Although Isaiah was landlocked in the dry land of Judah, he must have seen a similar sight through the eyes of the Spirit. Imagine hundreds of tall ships of Tarshish, the queen of the sea, flying across the waters like white clouds and winging their way like soaring doves as they bring home the children of faith and the wealth of nations for the restoration of Jerusalem. No wonder Isaiah writes that they come *"to the name of the LORD your God, and to the Holy One of Israel, because He has glorified you"* (v. 9b). In all His good works, His name is glorified, but perhaps most of all, when His children come home and His city is restored.

THE RADIANCE OF RECONCILIATION (60:10–14)

Make no mistake. The light of the glory of God did not arise upon Jerusalem so that its people could bask with self-indulgence in its splendor. As always, the glory of God's presence is given for the purpose of glorifying Him through service to others. In the case of Jerusalem, foreigners had destroyed its walls, kings had subdued its people, violence had become commonplace, the temple had been destroyed, Israel had the reputation of a "worm," and the city had become isolated from commerce and communication in the ancient world. Physical restoration of the city was not enough. Spiritual reconciliation with their neighbors, their enemies, and their despisers confronted the citizens of Jerusalem as their greater challenge.

Controversy and misunderstanding are part and parcel of human relationships. Anytime a significant issue arises in a family, a church, or a community, there will be differing opinions and volatile reactions. The test of faith in a family, church, or community is not the absence of conflict but the evidence of reconciliation. Even now, I am dealing with a situation in which two national Christian organizations are vying for millions of dollars left in a will that was changed just before the donor's death so that one organization lost a large portion of its share. Ugly accusations and costly legal fees are ahead for these Christians if the case is taken to court. When someone suggested reconciliation through the Christian Legal Society, I immediately said yes. Even though it might mean a decision that costs us money, the reputation of Christians as a reconciling community is far more important than the dollars.

Evidence of reconciliation between the citizens of Jerusalem and their neighbors, enemies, and despisers is a reflection of the radiance of God's glory upon the city. Foreigners who were once suspicious now help build the walls, and kings who once oppressed the people now minister to them. Consequently, the fear of violence gives way to the freedom of peace. In a most significant symbol, the gates of the city are left open day and night because reconciliation works.

A modern example of this beautiful truth comes from Los Angeles, California, where the management and union of a large newspaper locked horns in hostile words and violent reprisal. The front door to the newspaper was locked and all employees had to pass through tight security at the back door. When the issue forced the resignation of the president and the election of a new chief executive, his first decision was to open the front door and dismiss the guards. Symbolically, he sent the signal that his administration would be open to negotiation and free from fear. When the union got the signal, both sides sat down at the negotiating table and worked out an agreement that is a model of management-labor relations. Like the opening of Jerusalem's gates, the opening of the front door symbolized the meaning of reconciliation.

Another symbol of reconciliation is given in Isaiah's words that the *"glory"* of Lebanon's rich hardwoods would be brought to Jerusalem to beautify the sanctuary of the Lord and form the floors upon which His feet would walk (v. 13). Our memory takes us back to 40:16 when craftsmen of Babylon carefully selected the most exquisite hardwoods of Lebanon to make idols. Later, in 41:19, God used the planting of the same hardwoods of Lebanon as a symbol to herald the new exodus and assure His people of their sustenance during the long march home. Now, a great reversal takes place. The same woods that had been used to make idols will beautify the walls and glorify the floors of God's sanctuary. Reconciliation is not limited to human relationships. When the hardwoods of Lebanon beautify His sanctuary, reconciliation between the natural environment and spiritual realm is complete. Natural creation, which groans with us under the burden of sin, also waits in eager expectation for the sons of God to be revealed (Romans 8:19).

As the outcome of human and natural reconciliation, enemies and archenemies of Israel will bow in worship before God and acknowledge that the New Jerusalem is *"the City of the* LORD, *Zion of the Holy One of Israel"* (v. 14). But again, it is God who is glorified, not the city.

THE CENTER OF EXCELLENCE (60:15–18)

Striking contrast will follow the light of God's glory upon Jerusalem. As another consequence of its physical devastation and spiritual impoverishment, the city had lost its self-esteem. Forsaken, hated, and avoided, Jerusalem had the social standing of a "worm" in the mind of the world. No more. When the dazzling light of God's glory shines upon the city, He promises, *"I will make you an eternal excellence, a joy of many generations"* (v. 15).

Excellence is an overworked word and an underachieved goal in contemporary society. We know what Plato meant when he wrote in *The Republic*, "Excellence is rare." Almost everyone strives for excellence, but few achieve it. Yet, as John Gardner states "Unless our philosophers and our plumbers are excellent, neither our philosophies nor our pipes will hold water." Although Gardner inspired my generation to seek excellence, he saw it as a bootstrap operation of self-discipline and human integrity. At best, human excellence is temporary and partial.

The eternal excellence that God promises for the New Jerusalem is another reflection of the light of His glory. The forsaken, hated, and avoided city has no resources for excellence in itself. Only the knowledge that *"I, the* LORD, *am your Savior, and your Redeemer, the Mighty One of Jacob"* (v. 16b) can transform a "worm" into a place of eternal excellence and a "joy of many generations." We realize how radical the change will have to be when God invokes the power of His four names—LORD, *Savior, Redeemer, Mighty One of Jacob*—to enact the transformation. And the process will be more evolutionary than revolutionary. Expressive of the process, God says that He will upgrade the city from good to excellent by advancing its qualities from bronze to gold, iron to silver, wood to bronze, and stones to iron (v. 17). But again, material objects are used to represent spiritual virtues. Throughout Isaiah's prophecies, he has spoken of the twin virtues of personal righteousness and social justice as the qualities of life that reflect the presence of God. In the New Jerusalem, the *"peace"* and *"righteousness"* of rulers and elders will set the tone for the city (v. 17b) so that violence, waste, and destruction will not be known within its borders. According to custom, the rebuilt walls and gates of the city will be given names that are more than memorials of the past or ideals for the future. Walls called *"Salvation"* and gates named *"Praise"* will be, in fact, the qualities that give the New Jerusalem its *"eternal excellence"* (v. 18b).

PROMISE OF THE NEW ORDER (60:19–22)

With the rising and shining of the light of the glory of God, the New Order has arrived. Six promises of the New Order bring the Song of the City to a grand ending. First, the people of Zion are promised that the Lord will be their *"everlasting light"* (v. 19a). Primordial light from the sun or reflective light from the moon, both of which rise and wane, will no longer be necessary. The glory of God will be their source of everlasting light that will not wane and the dazzling light that they will personally reflect as they glorify God. Second, with the rising of the "everlasting light" the *"days of . . . mourning shall be ended"* (v. 20b). Revelation 21:4 echoes this promise in the comforting words, "And God will wipe every tear from their eyes; there shall be no more death, nor sorrow nor crying, and there shall be no more pain for the former things have passed away."

Third, righteousness will reign in the hearts of the people (v. 21a). Spirituality will be a matter of being created by divine redemption and human faith. Isaiah's preaching of truth will no longer seem futile. His prophecy will be vindicated. Fourth, as a direct result of righteousness, the people of Zion will claim their rightful inheritance to the land promised to them. In the patriarchal society, the inheritance of land symbolized the legitimacy of the birthright. Because of sin, the children of Israel had forfeited their birthright. But, with faith as the qualifier and righteousness as the quality for relationship in the New Order of Zion, the birthright is restored and the land is given as proof of their inheritance. Fifth, closely related to the inheritance of the land is restoration as the *"branch"* of God's own planting. God's disappointment with the vineyard that He had planted and nurtured is no more (5:1–7). Righteousness will replace rebellion and God will be glorified through the life and the work of His people. Sixth, a company of people known as *"little"* and *"small"* will become large and strong among the nations of the earth. The "worm" has turned. No longer will Zion be a woman who is forsaken, hated, and despised. Dame Zion will be attractive, loved, and honored because she reflects the glory of God in her character and glorifies God in her conduct.

When will these promises of the New Order take place? In God's good timing. Some of His promises will take place immediately; others will await His good pleasure. Yet, as we shift our thoughts from the physical restoration of Jerusalem to the spiritual potential of Zion, or God's Church, we realize that all of these promises are ours. Our light has come in Jesus Christ, and the glory of the Lord has arisen upon us. After E. Stanley Jones fell to a crippling stroke, he chose "The Divine Yes" as the one sermon by which he wanted to be remembered. His text came from Moffat's translation of 2 Corinthians 1:20, "For all the promises of God in Him are 'yes' and in Him 'amen,' to the glory of God through us." In the Song of the City, God gave us His "Divine Yes" in the promises for the New Order. Our "yes" will claim those promises.

The Song of the Servant (61:1–11)

1 "The Spirit of the Lord GOD
   is upon Me,

Because the LORD has anointed Me
To preach good tidings to the poor;
He has sent Me to heal the brokenhearted,
To proclaim liberty to the captives,
And the opening of the prison to those
　　who are bound;
2 To proclaim the acceptable year
　　of the LORD,
And the day of vengeance of our God;
To comfort all who mourn,
3 To console those who mourn in Zion,
To give them beauty for ashes,
The oil of joy for mourning,
The garment of praise for the spirit of heaviness;
That they may be called trees of righteousness,
The planting of the LORD,
　　that He may be glorified."
4 And they shall rebuild the old ruins,
They shall raise up the former desolations,
And they shall repair the ruined cities,
The desolations of many generations.
5 Strangers shall stand
　　and feed your flocks,
And the sons of the foreigner
Shall be your plowmen
　　and your vinedressers.
6 But you shall be named
　　the Priests of the LORD,
Men shall call you
　　the Servants of our God.
You shall eat the riches of the Gentiles,
And in their glory you shall boast.
7 Instead of your shame
　　you shall have double honor,
And instead of confusion
　　they shall rejoice in their portion.
Therefore in their land
　　they shall possess double;
Everlasting joy shall be theirs.
8 "For I, the LORD, love justice;
I hate robbery for burnt offerings;
I will direct their work in truth,

And will make with them an
    everlasting covenant.
9 Their descendants shall be known
    among the Gentiles,
And their offspring among the people.
All who see them
    shall acknowledge them,
That they are the posterity
    whom the LORD has blessed."
10 I will greatly rejoice in the LORD,
My soul shall be joyful in my God;
For He has clothed me
    with the garments of salvation,
He has covered me
    with the robe of righteousness,
As a bridegroom decks himself
    with ornaments,
And as a bride adorns herself
    with her jewels.
11 For as the earth brings forth its bud,
As the garden causes the things that
    are sown in it to spring forth,
So the Lord GOD will cause
    righteousness and praise to spring forth before all
    the nations.

Isaiah 61:1–11

Four poems earlier, Isaiah introduced us to the One whom God called "My Servant." Each of the poems advanced our understanding of the Servant from His initial calling to His redemptive suffering. None of the earlier poems, however, specified His Servant role as definitively as chapter 61. This Song of the Servant, then, might well be read as the fifth of the servant poems because it is needed to help us understand the role of the Servant and especially, the outcomes of His ministry.

Joy is the keynote that gives the Song of the Servant its melody. Isaiah speaks of the *"oil of joy"* (v. 3), *"everlasting joy"* (v. 7), and the *"joyful"* soul (v. 10). By definition, joy is an inner quality of life that depends upon a right relationship with God, but at the same time, is independent of external circumstances. We understand the biblical meaning of joy as we study this Song of the Servant. The Song begins with the Servant defining His redemptive task in the context of the Year of Jubilee, which brings joy to those who are forgiven and freed (vv. 1–2). Their joy is expressed in four freedoms: (1) freedom to live (v. 3); freedom to serve (vv. 4–7); (3) freedom to act (vv. 8–9); and (4) freedom to celebrate (vv. 10–11).

THE TASK OF JOY (61:1–2)

By prophetic declaration, the Servant of the Lord sees the vision, states the mission, and sets the tone for His redemptive ministry. No job description has ever been more detailed or demanding. The fact that Jesus quoted this passage for the announcement of His public ministry (Luke 4:17–19) confirms the connection between Isaiah's prophecy and Christ's fulfillment. Those who contend that this passage applies only to the Servant Nation of Israel, and not to the Servant Person of Jesus Christ, are hard-pressed to carry their case. Even if they agree that Jesus became the personification of the Servant Nation of Israel when He took this text to announce His own ministry, more than a symbol is intended. Whether it is Isaiah quoting the Servant in his prophecy or Jesus accepting the role of the Servant, the connection is too direct and the tasks are too specific to be symbolic. In fact, in my book on Christian leadership entitled *Power to Follow, Grace to Lead*, I contend that these opening verses of the Song of the Servant give us a model for vision, mission, and tone of leadership for all generations. Note how the text can be analyzed according to requirements for writing a task description that is a model for others to follow:

His Mandate:	"The Spirit of the Lord GOD is upon Me"
His Motivation:	"The LORD has anointed Me:
His Method:	"to preach"
His Message:	"good tidings"
His Market:	"the poor . . . brokenhearted . . . captives . . . those who are bound"
His Measure:	"preach good tidings to the poor . . . heal the broken-hearted, to proclaim liberty to the captives, and the opening of the prison to those who are bound"
His Mood:	"to proclaim the acceptable year of the LORD and the day of vengeance of our God"

618

No leader, spiritual or secular, has ever accepted and announced such a detailed and demanding task. Every expectation is made public so that the Servant can be held accountable for His performance in every area of His ministry. One of the tests of Jesus' integrity is to ask, "Did He do what He said He would do and achieve what He set out to achieve?" All of the evidence of the Gospels supports the accountability report that He gave to His Father in John 17:4; "I have glorified You on the earth. I have finished the work which You have given Me to do." The effectiveness of Jesus' performance is a model for all leaders.

It is one thing to be effective in the work that we are called to do and quite another thing to create and communicate joy as a product of our performance. When Jesus quoted Isaiah 61:1 and 2, he concluded his reading of the passage with the words, "To preach the acceptable year of the LORD" (Luke 4:19). It is wrong to assume that He wanted to avoid the thought of the Lord's *"vengeance"* or setting wrongs right as a part of His ministry because on other occasions He did not shy away from that fact. Some scholars suggest that He read enough to bring the whole passage to the minds of His well-schooled listeners. Perhaps He also wanted to set the tone of joy as the keynote for His ministry. The *"acceptable year of the LORD"* refers to the Year of Jubilee or the Year of Liberty (Leviticus 25:10). With this reference, Jesus set the tone for His ministry. *"Liberty,"* which is synonymous with freedom and symbolic of salvation, is His goal, and with liberty comes *"joy,"* which is the tone of His ministry. We know that Jesus found joy in His work despite conflict, disappointment, and suffering. In John 17:13 He asks the Father that His disciples might have "My joy fulfilled in themselves." Jesus prayed that He would communicate the joy He found in His work to His disciples so that they, in turn, might communicate it to others. The remaining stanzas of the Song of the Servant, in Isaiah 61, tell how joy is communicated through the forgiveness and freedom of the Year of Jubilee.

FREEDOM TO LIVE (61:3)

Israel still cowered in fear under the shadow of death. All of the symptoms of a funeral hung over them—the symbol of ashes, the sound of mourning, and the spirit of heaviness (v. 3a). Their self-esteem had bottomed out. Not only did they suffer the indignity of being considered a "worm" by other nations, but they had come to believe it themselves. First and foremost, then, Israel needed freedom from its fears and restoration to the joy of living.

Self-esteem is not a quality of life that can be artificially created by external achievements of fame or fortune. Howard Hughes, a genius for making airplanes, movies, and money, became a recluse cowering in the dark with his own fears. Kiss-and-tell biographies of famous people, whom we admire for their self-confidence, expose the insecurities of their personal lives and private moments. Even their dreams reveal their insecurity. Psychiatrists tell us that the most common dream of highly successful people is the fear of falling from a cliff or a high building. Inwardly, they know that the higher they rise, the farther they can fall. Outwardly, they are citadels of self-esteem, but inwardly, they are "nurseries of hidden fears," as C. S. Lewis described himself before his conversion.

Understandably, then, the redemptive work of the Servant begins with inner transformation. Isaiah gives us a comparative picture of a person who is prepared for a funeral and one who is dressed for a wedding. The symbol of ashes, the sound of mourning, and the spirit of heaviness are appropriate for a funeral. Israel suffered these symptoms because the people had given up and considered themselves as good as dead. The *"good tidings"* preached by the Servant will change all of that. Isaiah returns to his favorite image of Dame Zion to illustrate his point. Imagine a woman, dressed for a funeral, who receives the message that an error has been made. The announcement of death should have been an invitation to a wedding. Immediately, she washes the ashes from her face, puts on her makeup, and crowns her head with a garland of flowers. Ugly ashes of death have given way to the beautiful crown of life. Something also happens to the sounds she makes. Sympathetic moans are fitting for a funeral, but joyous humming and excited chatter precede a wedding. Isaiah likens this change to Dame Zion putting on perfumed body oil that gives off the delicate sense of inner joy. Then, instead of the rough and torn sackcloth that expresses the heaviness of soul in mourning, Dame Zion puts on an exquisite wedding dress as the *"garment of praise"* to symbolize the emergence of a transformed character. She is now the beautiful bride dressed for her wedding, not the sad mourner heading for her own funeral.

As an ordained clergyman who has married many couples, I have seen this description in Isaiah come to life before my eyes. No sight is more beautiful than the fresh glow of joy on the face of a bride coming down the aisle toward the wedding altar. There is no such thing as an ugly bride. Beneath the garland of lace on their head and the garment of silk on their body, their eyes, cheeks, and lips radiate the inner joy of their highest moment. If any moment in human events expresses the spiritual meaning of being a "new creature," it is when a bride comes down the aisle to meet the one she loves. With this contrasting picture between the mourner and the bride, we understand how radical a transformation is promised for Israel and for us through the work of the Servant.

Isaiah does not hesitate to mix his metaphors, probably to accentuate his point. As further proof of the change of character, he describes the people of Israel as *"trees of righteousness"* (v. 3b). In several instances, the prophet has referred to trees in the forest of Lebanon. Especially, we remember that the trees of Lebanon will joyously herald the march of the children of Israel as they return home from exile (14:8), and they will provide the finest wood in the world to beautify the floors in the restored Temple where the Spirit of God will walk (60:13). Now, they symbolize the beauty of a redeemed people and reveal the secret of their joy. Inner righteousness is the source of their beauty and the reason for their self-esteem. But again, righteousness not of their own making. *"Trees of righteousness"* are *"the planting of the LORD that He may be glorified"* (v. 3c). True self-esteem is characterized by three fundamental facts: (1) our joy in life is the result of being redeemed by God from the inside out; (2) our beauty of character is the evidence of God's righteousness in us; and (3) our glory is to have God glorified in us.

FREEDOM TO SERVE (61:4–7)

When we are free to live, we are free to serve. People who lack the self-esteem that results from a right relationship with God tend to be self-centered in their motivation and interest. They cannot take the risk of giving themselves away for the sake of others. Quite to the contrary, the centripetal force of self-interest is subject to increasing intensity. A person who is internally insecure will act out of self-interest only to find that insecurity is increased so that the acts of self-interest must continue to escalate in intensity. A vicious cycle is created in which radical self-interest is aggravated rather than satisfied. Equity theory in psychology is based upon the assumption that self-interest motivates all human behavior. Even acts of charity are explained by the motivation that we give only as we get.

Isaiah defies the law of self-interest by foreseeing the freedom to serve as the natural corollary of the freedom to live. Acting out of the self-esteem of righteousness, Israel can become known as the *"Priests of the LORD"* and the *"Servants of our God"* (v. 6). Neither priests nor servants act out of self-interest. In gratitude for the grace given to them by the redeeming work of the Servant, they become servants themselves and a channel of grace for others. Servanthood is never easy. Their job description calls for them to *"rebuild the old ruins,"* *"raise up the former desolations,"* and *"repair the ruined cities"* (v. 4).

Another astounding truth confronts us. As the Servant gives Himself to transform Israel from a mourner in ashes to a bride of beauty, a servant of the Servant will also work with rejects. Jesus set the example. He transformed a tax collector into a disciple, a prostitute into a saint, a skeptic into an apostle, a madman into a family man, and a thief into a friend. As a lesson of Scripture, we know that we are not fully forgiven until we forgive others. By the same lesson, we can say that we are not fully served until we serve others. More specifically, we will seek to serve those who represent the ruins caused by personal and social sin. To be true to our servant role, we must ask, "Where are the ruins that need to be rebuilt and the desolate places that need new life?" Needless to say, if we intentionally asked that question and followed through as servants of the Servant, our priorities as institutions and individuals would be radically altered. But once self-interest is given up, double honor for God's name and a double portion of God's blessing would give us *"everlasting joy"*—the greatest reward of all.

Another task for the redeemed Israel is to be priests and servants for the Gentiles, identified again as strangers and foreigners (vv. 5 and 6b). In return for their physical labor of helping to rebuild the city, shepherding the flocks, and dressing the vineyards, Israel is to teach them God's work, lead them in God's way, and offer sacrifices for their sins. The division of labor is neither discriminatory nor demeaning for the Gentiles. In Acts 6, a fast-growing church required the apostles to give full time to preaching, teaching, and prayer. Consequently, under the guidance of God's Spirit, seven deacons were chosen to wait on tables and assure fair distribution of food among the believers. Such a division of labor in the tasks of the church is not popular today. Lines have become blurred between clergy and laity in the name of participatory democracy and lay ministry. Certainly, a corrective for absolute clerical authority and exploited pastoral privilege is needed to restore vision and vitality for the church. At the same time, over-correction can deny the call of God upon persons who are exclusively given to preaching, teaching, and prayer. Rather than succumbing to the secular trend against authority, a biblical division of labor, defined horizontally by function rather than vertically by position, would make the church more effective.

Isaiah, in keeping with his Hebrew theology, does not draw a dividing line between physical and spiritual labor for servants of the Servant. For Israel to rebuild the walls and city of Jerusalem is a physical and spiritual task that is symbolic of the servant's role. Nor would the prophet draw a dividing line between rebuilding justice in social structures and redeeming individual persons. The sequence is clear. Righteousness precedes servanthood, but the servant's task may be personal or social. Similar to Jesus' analogy of salt and light, servants of the Servant will work as "salt" for a just society and as "light" for a righteous people.

How does this apply to the Church today? First, *the primary task of the Church is to be the servant who serves others.* Someone once identified the Church as the only human institution whose sole purpose is to serve others. If so, the self-serving church is a contradiction in terms. From time to time, the Church should put itself to the test, "Are we serving ourselves or serving others?" Second, and as companion to its primary task, *the servant church exists to produce servants.* Jesus infers this task in the Great Commission when He called the twelve to "Go therefore and make disciples of all the nations" (Matthew 28:19). A disciple is more than a convert of evangelistic effort. He or she is one who follows the example of the Church by self-sacrificing service for others. If the Great Commission were taken seriously, church statistics would be revised to go beyond head counts of attendance, membership, converts, and baptisms. The most revealing statistic would come out of the question, "How many disciples in the church are actively serving others?"

Third, *the church is to be the rebuilder of ruins.* As Jesus worked with "rejects," so the church must work with "ruins." Sin gives destruction, desolation, and death a natural momentum in human society, whether in social structures or human relationships. Social institutions, for instance, that began for the express purpose of serving unmet human needs, drift toward the sin of perpetuating the organization. Marriages, under the pressure of a secular society bent toward self-interest, individual rights, and personal happiness, are drawn toward conflict, abuse, and divorce. Rebuilding social structures and human relationships is a special task of the servant church in this generation.

Fourth, as an extension of its servanthood, *the servant church is to be the priest for strangers and foreigners.* Usually, we think of the priestly role of the church as focused upon its own membership. But again, we are reminded that the primary purpose of the church is to serve others, meaning strangers and foreigners. Strangers are those people whom we do not like, and foreigners are those who are not like us. In either case, they are a threat to us. A priest, however, is a person who is called to self-sacrificing service to those who are not liked and to those who do not like us. Examples abound in modern society. Strangers are those among us from whom we feel alienated because of social differences such as education, economics, political party, or denominational affiliation. To the rich, for instance, the poor are strangers. Foreigners are those from whom we are alienated by ethnic differences such as race, language, ancestry, religion, or culture. To white Anglo-Saxons, for instance, yellow-skinned Asians are foreigners. When Kristi Yamaguchi won the Gold Medal for the United States in the 1992 Olympics, she failed to win the lucrative advertising contracts normally assured for an Olympic winner because the general public did not accept her as a full-fledged American.

How can we become priests for strangers and foreigners? Certainly not with condescending evangelistic techniques or demands for conformity to the customs of the evangelical subculture. No barriers of interpersonal strangeness or cultural foreignness should ever stop the free flow of the gospel. Moreover, like a paramedic giving mouth-to-mouth resuscitation to a victim of a heart attack without asking whether or not the person has a contagious disease, a priest does not calculate the risk of ministering to strangers and foreigners. It is too bad that the church has become positioned as homophobic in the controversy over gay rights and the AIDS epidemic. Without forfeiting its prophetic position that homosexuality is a sin, the church could have served as a priest to AIDS victims by taking the lead in opening clinics, providing counseling, and showing care for their physical, interpersonal, and spiritual needs at the risk of contagion. When Jesus violated the taboos of His culture by reaching out and touching the leper, He showed us the way to be "Priests of the LORD" and "Servants of our God."

FREEDOM TO ACT (61:8–9)

Personal righteousness, according to Isaiah, is always expressed in social justice. By direct connection, then, the people who are called "trees of righteousness" are also those in whom the Lord puts His love for justice (v. 8a) and directs "their work in truth" (v. 8b). God's truth is the guidance system for social justice. If the guidance system goes awry, human efforts at social justice become evil. *Time* magazine for March 15, 1993, entitled its lead editorial, "In the Name of God" as a commentary on religious fanatics who justify violence and terror as holy acts. Two sentences in the editorial speak the hard truth, "Faith, the sweetest refuge and consolation, may harden, by perverse miracle, into a sword—or anyway into a club or a torch or an assault rifle. Religious hatreds tend to merciless and absolute." Terrorists who bombed the World Trade Center and cultists who held off the police at Waco, Texas were the subject of the editorial. Yet, in the same week that the editorial was published, a protester at an abortion clinic in Pensacola, Florida gunned down a doctor who performed abortions. In response to the killing, some pro-life leaders denounced that violence, others used the occasion to call abortionists "killers," and still others inferred that violence is the next step in protest if blockades are ruled illegal.

Something is seriously wrong. Truth cannot be the guidance system for violent action, even if the name of God is invoked and the love of justice is proclaimed. The legacy of such violent action in the name of social justice will never meet the standards set by the Lord in

Isaiah. Righteous servants who act for social justice will be: (1) representative of His *"everlasting covenant"*— a redemptive relationship (v. 8c); (2) known by their descendants among the Gentiles (v. 9a); and (3) acknowledged as *"the posterity whom the LORD has blessed"* (v. 9b). As the guidance system to direct our work for social justice, truth keeps us on balance by our relationship with God, our gift to the future, our evidence of His blessing, and our results that give Him the glory. Protesters who resort to physical violence in the name of God fail the guidance test. Freedom to act for social justice as the servants of the Servant works within Spirit-guided boundaries.

FREEDOM TO CELEBRATE (61:10–11)

Not everyone can celebrate. In their doubt and despair, the children of Israel had sunk into mourning with its symbol of ashes and its spirit of heaviness. Consequently, their social gatherings and religious feasts were more like a funeral than a wedding. Through the ministry of the Servant, however, all was changed. According to Isaiah, the children of Israel will celebrate a wedding rather than commiserate at a funeral. Rather than being represented by the symbol of a withered reed (42:3), they will be like the fresh green shoot that springs up overnight in a fertile garden.

Cocktail parties confound me. In my official duties as a university president, I have appeared at predinner receptions where cocktails are served. In the spirit of celebration, the participants raise a toast and clink their glasses, but after a drink or two the conversation degenerates into small talk and inane utterings. Never have I left a cocktail reception with a joyous sense of celebration.

Worship services that are graced by the presence of the Holy Spirit are just the opposite. With clear heads and open hearts, the worshipers come together to celebrate their freedom in Christ, to praise God for His grace, and to give Him the glory for His marvelous works. As I have said so many times after worshiping with our students in the Asbury Seminary chapel, "I could fly home without wings."

Isaiah expands upon the preparation for a wedding, the most joyous of human events, to communicate what it means for the Church to celebrate its freedom. Earlier in the chapter, we saw the bride prepare for her wedding by putting on the garland of beauty, the oil of joy, and the garment of praise. Now, we see both the bride and the bridegroom clothed in the garments of salvation and the robe of righteousness as symbols of their purity of heart (v. 10b). Although Israel had sinned against God and sullied its character, the Servant's redemptive work forgives their sin and cleanses their soul. Righteousness, not rebellion, is the quality of their character. Adorning the wedding garment are ornaments and jewels that accent their beauty. Perhaps like the stars in the crown of the redeemed, the jewels symbolize their self-giving love as servants for others.

God desires the same spirit of celebration in His Church. Clothed as His bride in the garments of righteousness, adorned with the jewels of selfless servanthood, and radiant with the glow of His glory, God envisions the witness of *"righteousness and praise to spring forth before all the nations"* (v. 11b).

THE SONG OF THE CHURCH (62:1–12)

1 For Zion's sake I will not hold My peace,
  And for Jerusalem's sake I will not rest,
  Until her righteousness goes forth
      as brightness,
  And her salvation as a lamp that burns.
2 The Gentiles shall see your
      righteousness,
  And all kings your glory.
  You shall be called by a new name,
  Which the mouth of the LORD will name.
3 You shall also be a crown of glory
  In the hand of the LORD,
  And a royal diadem
  In the hand of your God.
4 You shall no longer be termed
      Forsaken,
  Nor shall your land any more be termed Desolate;
  But you shall be called Hephzibah,
      and your land Beulah;
  For the LORD delights in you,
  And your land shall be married.
5 For as a young man marries a virgin,
  So shall your sons marry you;
  And as the bridegroom rejoices over the bride,

So shall your God rejoice over you.
6 I have set watchmen on your walls,
    O Jerusalem,
Who shall never hold their peace
    day or night.
You who make mention of the LORD,
    do not keep silent,
7 And give Him no rest till He establishes
And till He makes Jerusalem
    a praise in the earth.
8 The LORD has sworn by His right hand
And by the arm of His strength:
"Surely I will no longer give your grain
To be food for your enemies;
And the sons of the foreigner
    shall not drink your new wine,
For which you have labored.
9 But those who have gathered it
    shall eat it,
And praise the LORD;
Those who have brought it together shall drink it in
    My holy courts."
10 Go through,
Go through the gates!
Prepare the way for the people;
Build up,
Build up the highway!
Take out the stones,
Lift up a banner for the peoples!
11 Indeed the LORD has proclaimed
To the end of the world:
"Say to the daughter of Zion,
'Surely your salvation is coming;
Behold, His reward is with Him,
And His work before Him.'"
12 And they shall call them
    The Holy People,
The Redeemed of the LORD;
And you shall be called Sought Out,
A City Not Forsaken.

Isaiah 62:1–12

God's promise of comfort for His exiled people (ch. 40) culminates in the Song of the Church (ch. 62). Every theme of hope is repeated and confirmed in the verses of the song. Beginning with the promise that salvation will come upon Jerusalem with the brightness of light piercing the darkness (62:1), promise after promise is repeated until Zion is known as *"the Holy People,"* and *"the Redeemed of the LORD"* so that every nation on earth seeks after them (62:12). With each promise of a glorious future is also the assurance that Israel will never again be like a widowed nation forsaken and desolate (v. 4), shamed before the world (v. 7), subject to foreign domination (v. 8), or despised as unknown and unnamed among the kingdoms of the earth (v. 12).

The historical setting to which this prophecy speaks is uncertain. One alternative is to place the song in the time when the children of Israel returned to Jerusalem and found the city in ruins, the citizens demoralized, and the conditions of poverty and shame still prevailing. The high hopes of faith that motivated them to leave Babylon were now dashed by impatience upon the rocks of God's unfilled promises. The Song of the Servant (ch. 61) only deepened their despair. To sing a song of joyous freedom is a hollow sound against the reality of their plight.

Another alternative for the historical setting is to imagine the children of Israel coming up to the gates of Jerusalem and getting their first glimpse of the ruined city. Physically, emotionally, and spiritually, they were exhausted by the arduous seven-hundred-mile trek from Babylon. Rather than the sight of the ruined city, they needed a spurt of new faith for the last short leg of their journey—a spurt that could only come from a fresh view of God's glorious vision for the future of the city of Jerusalem and the people of Zion. The double imperative *"Go through, Go through the gates"* (v. 10) lends credence to this alternative, although the command may be interpreted to go *out* through the gates as servants to the world or to go *in* through the gates by constructing a ramp over the ruins so that they can claim God's promise for them.

Whichever historical setting is chosen, each shares a common fact. The children of Israel are demoralized and impatient because God's promises are not immediately fulfilled. A fresh vision of the glorious future for Zion is needed.

Who is the singer of the song? Scholars are divided on the answer. Some hear the prophet Isaiah singing, as best he can, the Word of the Lord that he has heard. Others hear the Lord singing His own song, which Isaiah records. In either case, we know that the church is given this song as the Word of the Lord. *"Indeed the* LORD *has proclaimed to the end of the world"* (v. 11a) is a declaration that is repeated twenty-nine times in the book of Isaiah. Therefore, it is consistent with the text to study Isaiah 62 as God's response to the intercessory prayer of the prophet on behalf of a demoralized people. If so, the Song of the Church is more than a repetition of past promises. God is letting His people know that He holds Himself accountable for the promises He has made. From this perspective, Zion will find new hope for the future, not just because God clears their vision once again but because He backs up the vision by holding Himself accountable for His own Word (vv. 1–5), His own prophet's words (vv. 6–7), His own oath (vv. 8–9), His own command (v. 10), and His own purpose for the world (vv. 11–12).

GOD'S ACCOUNTABILITY FOR HIS WORD (62:1–5)

Anyone who has engaged in intercessory prayer will find special meaning in God's response to the plight of His people and the prayer of His prophet. Although the words of Isaiah's prayer are not recorded, we can almost hear him pleading for his people with the fervor of a righteous man (James 5:16) and the importunity of the desperate widow (Matthew 15:21–28). Prophets of God, whether in Isaiah's day or in our time, carry a dual role and responsibility. They are called to speak God's Word and to intercede for God's people. Earlier chapters in Isaiah emphasized the prophet's oracles of judgment and salvation. Now, we learn that a life of intercessory prayer on behalf of his people undergirded the stern warnings of the judgment and the visionary promises of salvation for his people.

Long before James wrote the words in his Epistle, God's response to Isaiah's intercession confirms the truth "The effective, fervent prayer of a righteous man avails much" (James 5:16). God not only repeats His promise of restoring Zion and Jerusalem to splendor, but He seals the promise with the declaration of His own Word, *"For*

Zion's sake, I will not hold My peace, and for Jerusalem's sake I will not rest, until her righteousness goes forth as brightness, and her salvation as a lamp that burns" (v. 1). Intercessory prayer, which knows no peace or rest until the prayer is answered, conveys emotions as well as petitions to God. In turn, God responds to the prayer of intercession by saying that He too will not be at peace or rest until the Word of His promise is fulfilled. From the depth of His own troubled soul, then, He gives His past promises the superlative touch. Zion and Jerusalem will be a light so bright that it will pierce through the blackest of darkness (v. 1b); their orphan nation will be given a name that kings will honor (v. 2b); Israel's fear of being like a widow forsaken and desolate will be quelled by a royal wedding (vv. 3–4); their poverty will be relieved by the richest of dowries (v. 4b); and God Himself will rejoice over them like a bridegroom rejoices over his bride (v. 5).

At the center of God's response is the declaration of His Word, *"You shall no longer be termed Forsaken, nor shall your land any more be termed Desolate"* (v. 4a). Dame Zion has experienced the disgrace of being a woman who is unmarried and undesirable. She is named Forsaken and Desolate. But God has plans for her. Instead of Forsaken, she will be named Hephzibah, which means *"The LORD delights in you,"* and instead of Desolate, she will be named Beulah, which means *"your land shall be married."* Throughout the Scriptures, God gives new names to those who gain new status as recipients of His promise. Israelites with a sense of history would know the special meaning of their new names. God changed Abram's name to Abraham as "father of the nations" (Genesis 17:5) and Sarai's name to Sarah meaning "mother of the nations" (Genesis 17:15). Jacob received the name Israel as "the one who struggled with God and overcame Him" (Genesis 32.28). God honored Gideon with the new name Jerubbaal to identify him as the one who "broke down Baal's altar" (Judges 6:32), and God showed His favor for David and Bathsheba's son of their sin when He sent Nathan to give Solomon the name Jedidiah or "loved by the LORD" (2 Samuel 12:25). To be included in the select company of those whom God had given a new name, would leave no doubt that He would not only marry Israel but would rejoice over her like a young man who marries a virgin (v. 5). Accountable to His Word, the new names would assure Dame Zion that she would never again be Forsaken and Desolate.

GOD'S ACCOUNTABILITY FOR HIS PROPHETS (62:6–7)

Leaders of people soon learn the fundamental principle that they can delegate their authority, but not their responsibility, to others. God follows this principle as a comfort for His church. When He called prophets to serve figuratively as "watchmen on the walls of Jerusalem" to warn of enemy attacks and internal decay, God not only gave them authority to speak but took the risk that their presence and their prophecies would be ever before Him as a reminder of the promises He had made. As assurance for Israel, God says that He never expects His watchmen or prophets to hold their peace, keep their silence, or take a rest until He fulfills His purpose for Jerusalem (v. 6b and 7a). Isaiah's picturesque image of God's accountability to His own prophets extends beyond the *"watchmen on [the] walls"* to an official recorder in a royal court who takes minutes of proceedings as the king makes pronouncements, policies, and promises to his subjects. In later sessions of the royal court, the king's recorder or secretary refers to the minutes of past meetings, constantly reminds the king of what he has said, and thus holds the king accountable for his words. By God's choice, His prophets function in the same way. Although they are subject to Him, He holds Himself accountable to them as an ever-present check on His integrity and an ever-visible reminder of His responsibility.

God also accepts responsibility for the end result that He has promised His people through the word of His prophets. The final goal on which He is to be judged is to make *"Jerusalem a praise in the earth"* (v. 7b). Accountable to His own prophets, He does not expect them to hold their peace, keep their silence, or take a rest until the avowed end is achieved. In a way that we can understand, God is willing to let His prophets be His critics and keep Him honest.

GOD'S ACCOUNTABILITY FOR HIS OATH (62:8–9)

It is one thing to make a promise and quite another thing to swear that the promise will be fulfilled. Politicians are quick to make promises during a campaign, but they would be equally quick to avoid an oath that would make or break their credibility after assuming office. God's action is even more rare because He does not need to swear by His name or His power. Throughout Isaiah, it is enough for Him to say that "*I the LORD of Hosts, the Holy One of Israel*" will do it. Yet with compassion for His demoralized people, God is willing to go beyond His sovereignty to take an oath on the power of His right hand and the strength of His arm (v. 8a). With good reason. Evidently the children of Israel still suffered from the burden of paying taxes and giving tribute to foreign powers. As meager as their earnings might be, Persian tax collectors still extracted heavy duties on their products of food and wine (v. 8b). The burden would be extra heavy because God had promised them complete freedom from foreign domination and even a reversal in which the nations would pay tribute to Jerusalem. No wonder they were demoralized. To say nothing about receiving tribute from foreign powers, they still felt the sting of exile each time they were forced to pay Persian taxes on the staples of food and wine.

God does not chide or punish Israel for a lack of faith. Understanding their dilemma, He takes the step of swearing by His power and strength. " . . .*Those who have gathered [in food] shall eat it, and praise the LORD; those who have brought it together shall drink it in My holy courts*" (v. 9). God has sworn for public record. If He violates His oath, He can never again claim to speak with credibility and confidence as "The LORD of Hosts" and "The Holy One of Israel."

GOD'S ACCOUNTABILITY FOR HIS COMMAND (62:10)

Imperative after imperative rings out as the Lord commands His people to move off dead center and get into action. God is all-wise. He knows that the best therapy for a demoralized people is to get their attention off themselves and embark on a constructive venture. Whether the command to "*go through the gates*" means to build a ramp over the ruins into the entrance of the city or to leave the city and build a highway for the gathering of the nations, the effect is the same. Israel will be taking a healing step toward the fulfillment of God's purpose and having a hand in its own destiny.

Physical therapy is a common technique of clinical psychologists for emotionally-disturbed people who aggravate their symptoms by hours of introspection and inactivity. To set them at work painting a picture, weaving a rug, molding clay, or pounding nails draws their focus to an external object rather than themselves. In some cases, creative physical activity may be the major therapy they need.

Nevertheless, God takes a risk with His action-oriented commands. If the people go through the gates of the city, prepare the way, build up the highway, take out the stones, and lift up a banner, God must do His part to bring the nations to Zion from the far corners of the earth. Nothing is more demoralizing to a people than to follow a charismatic leader to the dead-end of empty promises. Rallied by hope, they sink back into deeper despair when the rug of hope is jerked out from under them once again. So God makes Himself accountable for His own command. If the children of Israel move into action, He too will back up His words with action.

CHAPTER THIRTY

The Glorious Finale

Isaiah 63–66

While the songs of chapters 60–62 began with the announcement of the Year of Jubilee, the final prophecies of Isaiah in chapters 63–66 begin with the Day of Vengeance. To the reader who comes from the glorious Song of the Church (ch. 62) to the gory Day of the Lord's Vengeance (ch. 63), Isaiah may appear to be guilty of wild mood swings between salvation and judgment. True, the prophet foresees the escalation of conflict between good and evil as he projects forward to end-time prophecies. But we remember a consistent truth throughout the book of Isaiah in which the prophet makes salvation and judgment two sides of the same coin. When God intervenes in human history to bring salvation to His people, His action invariably strikes judgment upon sin. Paul wrote to the Romans "Where sin abounded, grace abounded much more" (Romans 5:20). As sin and grace are inseparable, so too are judgment and salvation. So, when the Servant comes with the good tidings of the Year of Jubilee, He also comes with the judgment of the Day of Vengeance when righteousness is vindicated and evil is destroyed. As strange as it seems, the presence of the Holy God gives comfort to the faithful while striking mortal fear into the heart of the sinner.

The final chapters of Isaiah need to be read with these truths in mind. First, as the prophet's vision reaches toward the end time, the conflict between good and evil escalates so that God's actions are more pronounced in both arenas. Second, although the judgment of God against sin in the last days may seem extreme, His acts of grace are even more frequent, abundant, and full of mercy. Third, a maturity of theological understanding is required to hold the prophetic paradox in balance. In the first thirty-nine chapters of Isaiah, oracles of judgment dominated the prophecy. Beginning with chapter 40, then, Isaiah's major theme shifts toward oracles of salvation without losing the reality of judgment, but with greater emphasis upon hope. Now, in the grand finale of his prophecy, the themes of judgment and salvation in the end time become point and counterpoint in the escalating drama.

Our human minds find it difficult to grasp such diverse truths, particularly when they are as futuristic and extreme as God's warlike acts of vengeance upon His enemies (ch. 63) or as idealistic as the creation of the New Heaven and the New Earth (ch. 66). As Isaiah taught us in the beginning of his prophecy, the best way to understand these events is to fix our focus upon the character of God. When we do, we realize that Isaiah remains consistent throughout all of his prophecies. The Creator of all is at one and the same time "the LORD of Hosts" with all power over human history, "the Holy One of Israel" who cannot condone sin, "the Redeemer" who sends His Servant with good news, and "the Father" of all mercies who will not give up on His rebellious children. The integrity of God's character is the essence of Isaiah's message throughout the prophecy and especially in the closing chapters when Isaiah uses end-time (eschatological) events to summarize his message and leave prophetic truth as his legacy for all generations.

THE DAY OF VENGEANCE (63:1–6)

1 Who is this who comes from Edom,
   With dyed garments from Bozrah,
   This One who is glorious
       in His apparel,
   Traveling in the greatness
       of His strength?—
   "I who speak in righteousness,
       mighty to save."
2 Why is Your apparel red,
   And Your garments like one who
       treads in the winepress?
3 "I have trodden the winepress alone,
   And from the peoples no one was with Me.
   For I have trodden them in My anger,
   And trample them in My fury;
   Their blood is sprinkled upon My garments,
   And I have stained all My robes.

4 For the day of vengeance is in My heart,
  And the year of My redeemed has come.
5 I looked, but there was no one to help,
  And I wondered
  That there was no one to uphold;
  Therefore My own arm brought salvation for Me;
  And My own fury, it sustained Me.
6 I have trodden down the peoples
    in My anger,
  Made them drunk in My fury,
  And brought down their strength
    to the earth."

Isaiah 63:1–6

Isaiah's genius for imagery is unexcelled in epic poetry when he creates the picture of the watchman challenging a battle-worn but victorious warrior who approaches the city gates. By bringing the watchman into the scene, the prophet pulls the thread connecting the glory of Zion's Year of Redemption in chapter 62 with the violence of God's Day of Vengeance against His enemies in chapter 63:1–6. Here is a prime example of our prophetic paradox. The same God who comes to fulfill all of His promises for the Church of Zion also comes, at one and the same time, to vindicate Himself and His people against the forces of evil. Righteousness, like the Word of God, is a double-edged sword. Whenever God wields the sword of righteousness in the world, He cuts a swath between the forces of good and evil and between friends and enemies. We should not be surprised then to find Isaiah's account of the Day of Vengeance immediately following the prophet's description of the Year of Redemption.

THE CHALLENGE OF THE WATCHMAN (63:1–2)

Without a doubt, the Warrior who hears the watchman's challenge is the Lord Himself. He answers the watchman's double challenge, *"Who is this who comes from Edom with dyed garments from Bozrah?"* and *"Why is Your apparel red?"*

Edom, a name that means red, identifies the ancestors of Esau, The Red (Genesis 36:1, 8, and 9). Although blood relatives of Israel, the Edomites never lost their hatred for the favored sons of Esau's brother Jacob. Over a period of time, their hostility earned them the reputation as representing evil within the larger family of Abraham's ancestors (Psalm 137:7). Bozrah, Edom's greatest city, adds symbolic meaning to the text as a name derived from "winepress." Taken together, Edom and Bozrah represent the treading of the winepress with the red blood of warfare.

In response to the watchman's challenge, the Warrior identifies Himself as *"I who speak in righteousness, mighty to save"* (v. 1c). Once again God makes Himself accountable for His actions. In chapter 62, He held Himself accountable for the fulfillment of His promises of salvation; in chapter 63, He accepts full responsibility for His punishment of evil. So, when He answers, "I who speak in righteousness, mighty to save" (v. 1c), He puts His warring action into the perspective of a righteous war. Scholars debate the question, "When is war justified?" The Just War theory sets moral guidelines of a just cause, just means, and a just end as the basis for going to war. God's justification for a *righteous war* advances the theory from moral to spiritual reasons. In His response to the watchman, God sets two criteria for His warring action: (1) the means of warfare must be righteous; and (2) the end of warfare must be salvation. This twofold test is preventive against militant religious actions that result in greater evil than the moral wrong they are trying to correct.

More often than not, in militant religious action the means becomes an end in itself. When pressed into a corner, religious militants go to war for the sake of war or they foment revolution for the sake of revolution. If asked whether or not they have considered whether the end of their conflict will bring salvation, they go on the defensive behind the position that the warfare is justified for its own sake. The righteous-means test eliminates any tactic that requires excessive force, and the saving-end test requires a redemptive outcome. Who can meet this twofold test? By and large, the answer is God alone. Only in the rarest of circumstances can physical force in the name of God be justified. Even then, as long as the human mind and motivation is involved, the means of righteousness and the end of salvation cannot be assured.

THE CAUSE OF THE WARRIOR (63:3–6)

A second challenge goes out to the Warrior who approaches the city gate. *"Why is your apparel red, and your garments like One who treads in the winepress?"* (v. 2). Despite the watchman's recognition of the Warrior's appearance of splendor and strength, the blood-splattered garments tell the story of a vicious and gory battle, likened to the Warrior treading out the winepress all alone. Sawyer has appropriately entitled this section "The Grapes of Wrath" because victory has come at the price of a costly and exhausting struggle. He also notes that this epic passage inspired the verse in "The Battle Hymn of The Republic."[1]

> Mine eyes have seen the glory
> of the coming of the Lord;
> He hath trampled out the vintage
> where the grapes of wrath are stored.

No glee attends the Warrior's triumph. He had to fight alone (v. 5), with great fury (v. 6a), and at high personal cost (v. 6b). His righteous character left Him no alternative. Both the Day of Vengeance and the Year of Redemption are in His heart (v. 4).

PRAYER OF INTERCESSION (63:7–64:12)

7 I will mention the lovingkindnesses of the LORD
  and the praises of the LORD,
   According to all that the LORD has bestowed on us,
   And the great goodness toward the house of Israel,
   Which He has bestowed on them
      according to His mercies,
   According to the multitude of His lovingkindnesses.
8 For He said,
      "Surely they are My people,
   Children who will not lie."
   So He became their Savior.
9 In all their affliction He was afflicted,
   And the Angel of His Presence
      saved them;
   In His love and in His pity
      He redeemed them;
   And He bore them and carried them
   All the days of old.
10 But they rebelled and grieved
      His Holy Spirit;

So He turned Himself against them as an enemy,
And He fought against them.
11 Then he remembered the days of old,
Moses and his people, saying:
"Where is He who brought them up out of the sea
With the shepherd of His flock?
Where is He who put His Holy Spirit within them,
12 Who led them by the right hand of Moses,
With His glorious arm,
Dividing the water before them
To make for Himself
an everlasting name,
13 Who led them through the deep,
As a horse in the wilderness,
That they might not stumble?"
14 As a beast goes down into the valley,
And the Spirit of the LORD causes him to rest,
So You lead Your people,
To make Yourself a glorious name.
15 Look down from heaven,
And see from Your habitation,
holy and glorious.
Where are Your zeal
and Your strength,
The yearning of Your heart
and Your mercies toward me?
Are they restrained?
16 Doubtless You are our Father,
Though Abraham was ignorant of us,
And Israel does not acknowledge us.
You, O LORD, are our Father;
Our Redeemer from Everlasting
is Your name.
17 O LORD, why have You made us stray from Your ways,
And hardened our heart from Your fear?
Return for Your servants' sake,
The tribes of Your inheritance.
18 Your holy people have possessed it but a little while;
Our adversaries have trodden down Your sanctuary.
19 We have become like those of old,
over whom You never ruled,
Those who were never called

by Your name.

1 Oh, that You would rend the heavens!
  That You would come down!
  That the mountains might shake
    at Your presence—

2 As fire burns brushwood,
  As fire causes water to boil—
  To make Your name known
    to Your adversaries,
  That the nations may tremble
    at Your presence!

3 When You did awesome things for which
    we did not look,
  You came down,
  The mountains shook at Your presence.

4 For since the beginning of the world
  Men have not heard
    nor perceived by the ear,
  Nor has the eye seen any God besides You,
  Who acts for the one who waits for Him.

5 You meet him who rejoices and does righteousness,
  Who remembers You in Your ways.
  You are indeed angry,
    for we have sinned—
  In these ways we continue;
  And we need to be saved.

6 But we are all like an unclean thing,
  And all our righteousnesses are like filthy rags;
  We all fade as a leaf,
  And our iniquities, like the wind,
  Have taken us away.

7 And there is no one who calls
    on Your name,
  Who stirs himself up to take hold
    of You;
  For You have hidden Your face
    from us,
  And have consumed us
    because of our iniquities.

8 But now, O LORD,
  You are our Father;
  We are the clay, and You our potter;

> And all we are the work of Your hand.
> 9 Do not be furious, O LORD,
> Nor remember iniquity forever;
> Indeed, please look—we all are Your people!
> 10 Your holy cities are a wilderness,
> Zion is a wilderness,
> Jerusalem a desolation.
> 11 Our holy and beautiful temple,
> Where our fathers praised You,
> Is burned up with fire;
> And all our pleasant things are laid waste.
> 12 Will You restrain Yourself
> because of these things, O LORD?
> Will You hold Your peace,
> and afflict us very severely?
>
> *Isaiah 63:7–64:12*

Isaiah recognizes that no one with sin in his or her heart can escape the Lord's Day of Vengeance. Repentance through prayer is the only hope. So, for himself and his people, he records his prayer of intercession as a model for us. Isaiah's prayer will have a familiar ring of text and tone. In many ways it parallels The Lord's Prayer as given to us by Jesus Christ. To each of these models of prayer, we come with the yearning of the disciples, "Lord, teach us to pray" (Luke 11:1).

MEMORIES OF MERCY (63:7–14)

In the Lord's Prayer, direct acknowledgment is given to the fatherhood, holiness, power, will, and love of God as the petitioner comes into His presence. Isaiah comes before Him in the same way but with the memories of His mercy in the life and history of Israel. The prophetic paradox is never more pronounced than in the key words that draw the contrast between the Day of Vengeance in chapter 63:1–6 and the memories of mercy in chapter 63:7–14. "Greatness," "strength," "anger," and "fury" characterize God the Warrior, treading the winepress alone against His enemies during the Day of Vengeance. But when Isaiah intercedes to the same God on behalf of his people during the time of prayer, the key words change to *"lovingkindnesses," "praises," "goodness," "mercies," "love,"* and *"pity."* As with us, the prophet knows that we have no recourse against the holiness of God, which exposes sin and brings death to the sinner. At best, our appeal must be to the mercy of God without claim upon our own rights or merit.

Isaiah's prayer sounds as if God needs a history lesson to remind Him of His love. In truth, the memories of mercy are necessary for Isaiah and his people, not for God. When sinful people come face to face with the Holy God, mercy is the only plea. Like a condemned criminal bowing beneath the executioner's sword, life or death depends upon a last-minute appeal for mercy, not justice. And, as Thomas Carlyle once said, "Attendance at your own hanging wonderfully clears the mind." With impeccable clarity, Isaiah recalls: (1) God's own words claiming Israel as *"My people"* (v. 8a); (2) His role as their Savior (v. 8b); (3) His affliction when they were afflicted (v. 9a); (4) His deliverance of them from the Angel of Death in Egypt (v. 9b); and (5) His unfailing presence that carried them in their wanderings in the wilderness (v. 9c).

An honest and realistic memory of God's mercy is not complete without the remembrance of human sin. Isaiah cannot forget how Israel flaunted the lovingkindness of God through haughty rebellion that grieved the Holy Spirit (v. 10). By aligning themselves with sin, the children of Israel made the choice to become the enemies of God. Those who question the justice of God in his vengeance against sin forget the fact that He endowed His human creation with free will. The choice to become an enemy of God belongs to us. Humbly, we remember that God's choice is to continue to nourish and care for His children like the caretaker tends a beloved vineyard (ch. 5).

With an ingenious move, Isaiah reminds God that He, too, has done memory work. When God remembered (v. 11) how He chose Israel as His children for the special purpose of being His servant nation for fulfilling His redemptive purpose in the world, He exercised His mercy, rather than His wrath, to deliver them from Egypt, lead them through the wilderness, and bring them to rest in the Promised Land (vv. 12–13). Isaiah then reminds God that He showed His mercy for His own *"glorious name,"* not for any inherited privilege or earned status of a sinful people (v. 14). Memories of mercy, then, become Isaiah's confession of faith in the God who will again save His sinful people.

PENANCE FOR SIN (63:15–19)

In Isaiah's memory work, all of the motivation for mercy came from God. As for the children of Israel, they stubbornly continued to rebel against Him. God acted on their behalf solely because of His love for His own children and for the glory of His name. Now, Isaiah shows us another side of the character of God that is even more appealing. As the key word in Isaiah's confession of faith is *mercy*, so the central thought in his penance for sin is *Father*. Anticipating the relationship of all believers to God through the death of Christ and the work of the Holy Spirit, Isaiah might well have cried, "Abba, Father" (Romans 8:15). Instead, he says, *"Doubtless You are our Father"* and *"You, O LORD, are our Father"* (vv. 16a and b).

Isaiah understands the special nature of love that bonds a father to a child. Within the confidence of that love, he knows that he can come like a prodigal with his prayer of repentance and be heard. So, he prays, *"Where are Your zeal and Your strength, the yearning of Your heart and Your mercies toward me? Are they restrained?"* (v. 15). To this tug on the Father's love, the prophet adds the question that appeals to the honor of the family name, *"O LORD, why have You made us stray from Your ways, and hardened our heart from Your fear?"* (v. 17a) By inference, at least, Isaiah plays upon the prophetic paradox that holds in tension divine sovereignty and human freedom. The Fatherhood of God is the way to resolve the paradox. For the sake of His own chosen servants (v. 17b), the tribes of His inheritance (v. 17c), and the Holy People (v. 18), Isaiah calls upon God to return to Israel (v. 17b), restore His relationships with them (v. 19a), and rename them as His own (v. 19b). The prophet knows the father heart of God so well that he comes boldly to the throne of grace to intercede for his people.

APPEAL FOR HELP (64:1–7)

Isaiah's boldness takes a leap from the Father's love to the Sovereign's power when he appeals to God for a dramatic show of strength on behalf of his people. *"Oh that You would rend the heavens!"* is a call for miraculous help in which supernatural power breaks through to the natural world. In effect, he dares to call for the same power and zeal that God the Warrior used to destroy His adversaries to be exercised for the salvation of His people (v. 5b). Against the righteousness of the power, however, Isaiah confesses their sin as *"an unclean thing,"* *"filthy rags,"* a fading leaf, and iniquity-driven *"wind"* (v. 6).

Isaiah's choice of the word *we* is a significant insight into the prophet's role. Intercessory prayer is prayed in the third person by the intercessor. Of course, we may intercede for others using the second person *he, she,* or *them,* but when the prayer is for the confession of sins, none of us can stand before the Holy God without acknowledging that we share in the unclean nature, unrighteous deeds, fading mortality, and imperfect motives of all humanity. In fact, the more like God we become, the more humble we are in His presence. Isaiah, like Christ, is so intimately identified with his people that he takes their sins as his burden. In him, we see the true intercessor. Although he had experienced personal cleansing at the time of his commissioning as a prophet, Isaiah still feels inadequate to call upon the Lord's name or to contend with the Holy God (v. 7a). Instead, he confesses that because of their sin God is justified in hiding His face from them and consuming them with His righteous anger.

REQUEST FOR FORGIVENESS (64:8–12)

Given the power of God and the sins of the people, Isaiah has no alternative but to throw himself on the mercy of the court and ask forgiveness. Like a defense attorney in a final plea to the jury, he acknowledges God as all-powerful, all-loving, and all-wise in relationship to His creation (v. 8). But, on the same basis, he implores God to look and see what has happened to His Chosen People, His Holy City, and His Sacred Temple (vv. 9a–11a). Having pulled out every emotional and rational stop, Isaiah can leave God only with the questions, *"Will You restrain Yourself because of these things, O LORD,"* and *"Will You hold Your peace and afflict us very severely?"* (v. 12). Isaiah knows his God so well that he can count upon an affirmative response. After all, what creator can fail his creation, and what father can deny his children? Intercessors such as Isaiah have good reason to believe that God the Creator and God the Father will answer their prayer for forgiveness.

THE TRUE NEW AGE (65:1–16)

1 "I was sought by those who did not ask for Me;
  I was found by those who did not seek Me.
  I said, 'Here I am, here I am,'

To a nation that was not called
    by My name.
2 I have stretched out My hands
    all day long to a rebellious people,
  Who walk in a way that is not good,
  According to their own thoughts;
3 A people who provoke Me to anger
    continually to My face;
  Who sacrifice in gardens,
  And burn incense on altars of brick;
4 Who sit among the graves,
  And spend the night in the tombs;
  Who eat swine's flesh,
  And the broth of abominable things
    is in their vessels;
5 Who say, 'Keep to yourself,
  Do not come near me,
  For I am holier than you!'
  These are smoke in My nostrils,
  A fire that burns all the day.
6 "Behold, it is written before Me:
  I will not keep silence, but will repay—
  Even repay into their bosom—
7 Your iniquities and the iniquities
    of your fathers together,"
  Says the LORD,
  "Who have burned incense on the mountains
  And blasphemed Me on the hills;
  Therefore I will measure their former
    work into their bosom."
8 Thus says the LORD:
  "As the new wine is found in the cluster,
  And one says, 'Do not destroy it,
  For a blessing is in it,'
  So will I do for My servants' sake,
  That I may not destroy them all.
9 I will bring forth descendants from Jacob,
  And from Judah an heir of My mountains;
  My elect shall inherit it,
  And My servants shall dwell there.
10 Sharon shall be a fold of flocks,
  And the Valley of Achor a place for herds to lie down,

For My people who have sought Me.
11 "But you are those who forsake the LORD,
Who forget My holy mountain,
Who prepare a table for Gad,
And who furnish a drink offering for Meni.
12 Therefore I will number you for the sword,
And you shall all bow down to the slaughter;
Because, when I called,
   you did not answer;
When I spoke, you did not hear,
But did evil before My eyes,
And chose that in which I do not delight."
13 Therefore thus says the Lord GOD:
"Behold, My servants shall eat,
But you shall be hungry;
Behold, My servants shall drink,
But you shall be thirsty;
Behold, My servants shall rejoice,
But you shall be ashamed;
14 Behold, My servants shall sing
   for joy of heart,
But you shall cry for sorrow of heart,
And wail for grief of spirit.
15 You shall leave your name as a curse
   to My chosen;
For the Lord GOD will slay you,
And call His servants by another name;
16 So that he who blesses himself
   in the earth
Shall bless himself in the God of truth;
And he who swears in the earth
Shall swear by the God of truth;
Because the former troubles are forgotten,
And because they are hidden
   from My eyes.

Isaiah 65:1–16

THE WAITING GOD (65:1)

God's character is the touchstone for His response to Isaiah's intercessory prayer. Whereas Isaiah had prayed to Him as the Warrior invoking His anger against the forces of evil in the Day of Vengeance, God answers with the tenderness of His love. *"Here I am, here I am"* is a double declaration that gives His words extra strength and meaning, not unlike Jesus saying, "Verily, Verily" when He wants to call attention to profound truth. In this case, the profound truth is that God has never moved from His position. He is ready and waiting for His people to return to Him. Even more, He has never stopped stretching out His hands as the welcome gesture of a father beckoning a prodigal child home (v. 2a).

THE ULTIMATE IDOLATRY (65:2–7)

Against this picture of gracious love, the rebellion of the children of Israel is hard to believe. Flaunting their free will in God's face (v. 3a), they practiced every idolatrous ritual of a pagan people, rituals that God had specifically condemned—sacrificing to nature in the gardens, burning incense on altars of bricks, worshiping the dead, eating prohibited pork, and boiling meat in milk (vv. 3 and 4). Most of all, they denied God's character and claimed to be holier than He (v. 5). For the God who savors the sweet-smelling incense from the holy altar in heaven, the supreme insult is to smell the stench of pagan sacrifices offered by His own children as a pretense of holiness (v. 5b). Those who contend that God discriminates in favor of His people lose their argument at this point. To be consistent with His character, the Holy God must vindicate Himself by setting things right where there is iniquity, idolatry, and blasphemy (v. 7).

SWEET AND SOUR GRAPES (65:8–10)

Returning to the oft-used analogy of the vineyard, Isaiah sees God's righteousness dividing the house of Israel between sweet and sour grapes (v. 8a). Although the cluster of grapes representing the house of Israel is predominately sour, there are a few grapes out of which the new wine of the future can be made. For them, the blessing of God will be as pronounced as His consuming curse upon the sour grapes. God calls this remnant *"My servants"* and indicates that they are the buffer against a show of His wrath that would destroy the whole bunch (v. 8b). In this small cluster of His servants, sorted out as those who have sought after Him, is the hope of Israel. They will have the descendants promised to Abraham; they will inherit the land of their fathers; and they will prosper with herds and flocks (vv. 9–10).

SLAUGHTER OF THE GUILTY (65:11–12)

The line is now drawn between the loyal remnant of God's servants and the apostate Jews who forsake the Lord, forget His Holiness, and deny the birthright of their name as the Holy People and the Redeemed of the Lord to take on the pagan names of *"Gad"* or fortune and *"Meni"* or destiny (v. 11). When faith falters, superstition invariably rises. For those who once knew saving faith and turned aside, cults become a special attraction. In our family history is the memory of one of the most sensitive and spiritual Christian women we have known. When she forsook her faith, however, she became an equally strong witness for the cult of Scientology. In my last conversation with her she had so steeped herself in Scientology and steeled herself against Christianity that our longtime friendship stalemated in silence.

For the apostate Jews in Israel, God forecasts slaughter by the sword. Even then, He puts their destruction in the future, perhaps with one last hope that they will hear His call, see His outstretched arms, and come home (v. 12b).

DIVISION OF THE HOUSE (65:13–16)

A clear line of demarcation separates servants from the apostates in the house of Israel. Servants are those who have heard His call and sought Him out; apostates are those who have shut their ears and turned to idols. In a rapid-fire series of statements introduced by the call, *"Behold,"* the blessings of God's servants and the curses of Israel's apostates are listed. God's servants will eat, drink, rejoice, and sing while apostate Jews will be hungry, thirsty, ashamed, and sorrowful (vv. 13 and 14a). Their legacy to the future will also reflect their relationship to God. Apostates will leave a name that is a curse against God's chosen people while servants will be given *"another"* or new name in honor of the blessing from the hand of God (v. 15 and 16). Their name may be the Holy People, the Redeemed of the Lord, or just Amen, the affirmation of God's blessing.

THE NEW CREATION (65:17–25)

17 "For behold, I create new heavens
      and a new earth;
    And the former shall not be
      remembered or come to mind.
18 But be glad and rejoice forever in what I create;
    For behold, I create Jerusalem
      as a rejoicing,
    And her people a joy.
19 I will rejoice in Jerusalem,
    And joy in My people;
    The voice of weeping shall no longer be heard in her,
    Nor the voice of crying.
20 "No more shall an infant from there live
      but a few days,
    Nor an old man who has not fulfilled his days;
    For the child shall die one hundred years old,
    But the sinner being one hundred years old
      shall be accursed.
21 They shall build houses
      and inhabit them;
    They shall plant vineyards
      and eat their fruit.
22 They shall not build
      and another inhabit;
    They shall not plant and another eat;
    For as the days of a tree,
      so shall be the days of My people,
    And My elect shall long enjoy the
      work of their hands.
23 They shall not labor in vain,
    Nor bring forth children for trouble;
    For they shall be the descendants of
      the blessed of the LORD,
    And their offspring with them.
24 "It shall come to pass
    That before they call, I will answer;
    And while they are still speaking,
      I will hear.
25 The wolf and the lamb
      shall feed together,

The lion shall eat straw like the ox,
And dust shall be the serpent's food.
They shall not hurt nor destroy in all
    My holy mountain,"
Says the LORD.

Isaiah 65:17–25

Of all the half-truths perpetrated by the New Age Movement, none is a greater falsehood than the name itself. The *new age* is a time that can come to pass only by the power and grace of God. Without Him, the idea of a new age is just another fantasy concocted in finite minds out of a theological hodge-podge of assumptions about human goodness, evolutionary theory, and Eastern reincarnation. As with all utopian dreams built out of the figments of human imagination, the New Age Movement will disappear like the foam washed up on the seashore from the surging ocean. Isaiah's vision of the true New Age, however, will not die. As the culmination of God's redemptive plan for His creation, its reality is a continuation of His promises. If one of His promises had failed, we would have reason to doubt Isaiah's vision of the coming New Order and the true New Age. But with the assurance that not one of God's promises has ever failed, we can foresee the reality of Isaiah's vision through eyes of faith. Sound reason, then, backs up Isaiah's farsighted view of the future. Following the same line of logical reasoning with which the prophet assured Israel of its deliverance, Isaiah would remind us that the same omnipotent God who created the universe has the power to recreate what He had already made. Without apology, then, we reclaim the full biblical truth from the half-truth of contemporary cultists and name Isaiah's final vision, "The True New Age."

A NEW HEAVEN AND EARTH (65:17)

With the new name of His servants as the springboard, God shows Israel how He will embark upon a New Creation as spectacular as His first creative days. Beginning with the physical environment of the heavens and the earth, which groan under the weight of sin, He will do the new thing with such glorious splendor that the memories of the old heavens and the old earth will fade into forgetfulness. Anyone who has witnessed a Western sunset, an Eastern coastline, the

Northern tundra, or a Southern garden, can hardly imagine the beauty of a new earth that would make us forget our present world. Or, for those astronauts who have looked back from space at our "Big, Blue Marble," and could not find words to describe its beauty, we wonder how the new heavens can be more spectacular. Yet, that is God's promise for His New Age. As the environment for His people, God will recreate His heavens and His earth with a beauty unsurpassed.

A New City and People (65:18–25)

Jerusalem and her people will also be recreated (v. 18). Little is said about the physical restoration of the New Jerusalem. Perhaps it has already been written in the earlier prophecy of chapter 60. More important now is the new life that God will create for its citizens, who are offspring of God's faithful servants. Eden without sin is recreated with these benefits for its inhabitants: (1) there will be no tears or weeping; (2) the life span will be a hundred years or more; (3) private property will be owned, built upon, lived in, and farmed without taxes or servitude; (4) labor will be productive; (5) families will be joyful; (5) God's presence will assure instant, two-way and responsive communication; (6) the symbol of *shalom* or peace shall prevail in the New Age; and (7) even the "Law of the Jungle" among animals will be transformed into a covenant of reconciliation and peace (vv. 19–25).

A desire for Utopia is a natural impulse of our humanity. No generation passes without some charismatic leader setting up a Shangri-la, an Atlantis, a Sunny Brook farm, or a Walden II with the dream of recreating paradise. Shakertown, a religious community built with utopian expectations, continues to exist as a tourist site a few miles from our home in Kentucky. The history is fascinating, the culture is unique, and the creativity of the Shakers is amazing. But while awaiting the coming of the Lord in their idealistic community, the Shakers prohibited procreation. Consequently, when the Lord delayed His coming, the community died out and the few survivors will soon be gone. As beautiful as Shakertown may be, its stone houses, picturesque fields, and well-known furniture serve as silent reminders that God alone can recreate heaven on earth.

Isaiah's idealistic vision of God's New Age does not stand alone. Every quality of life prophesied by the prophet is repeated and reaffirmed

in the book of Revelation. To discount Isaiah's vision is to deny the
Revelation and to deny the Revelation is to limit the redemptive purpose
of God. Far better to be on the side of God's servants who hear His
call, receive His grace, and believe His promise, than to lapse into the
skepticism that opens the door to superstition, idolatry, and apostasy.

THE NEW TEMPLE (66:1–6)

1 Thus says the LORD:
"Heaven is My throne,
And earth is My footstool.
Where is the house that you
    will build Me?
And where is the place of My rest?
2 For all those things My hand has made,
And all those things exist,"
Says the LORD.
"But on this one will I look:
On him who is poor
    and of a contrite spirit,
And who trembles at My word.
3 "He who kills a bull is as if he slays a man;
He who sacrifices a lamb,
    as if he breaks a dog's neck;
He who offers a grain offering,
    as if he offers swine's blood;
He who burns incense,
    as if he blesses an idol.
Just as they have chosen
    their own ways,
And their soul delights
    in their abominations,
4 So will I choose their delusions,
And bring their fears on them;
Because, when I called,
    no one answered,
When I spoke they did not hear;
But they did evil before My eyes,
And chose that in which I do not delight."
5 Hear the word of the LORD,
You who tremble at His word:

"Your brethren who hated you,
Who cast you out for My name's sake, said,
'Let the LORD be glorified,
That we may see your joy,'
But they shall be ashamed."
6 The sound of noise from the city!
A voice from the temple!
The voice of the LORD,
Who fully repays His enemies!

Isaiah 66:1–6

THE PLACE OF HIS PRESENCE (66:1)

Another facet of God's character becomes the touchstone for the final chapter of Isaiah. As Creator of the heaven and the earth, both old and new, all of the physical universe is God's throne and footstool. Likewise, the temple, which is built and rebuilt with human hands, comes under His domain as a physical symbol of His glory and a place of His presence. But first and foremost, God is a Spirit, not a physical creature. Logically, then, He sees the physical universe as a showcase for His glory and the physical temple as a means to spiritual worship. If the spiritual purpose of the universe is subjugated to glorifying the creation and not the Creator, or if the spiritual purpose of the temple is lost in the worship of artifacts and architecture, the physical world has become an idol in itself.

THE PLACE FOR OUR SPIRIT (66:2)

In God's New Age, therefore, the place of God's presence and the center of worship will not be in a physical temple but in the spirit of the human heart. The thought of a New Temple is as revolutionary as the creation of a New Heaven and a New Earth. Humans are symbol-making creatures. When American pioneers settled the Western frontier, they immediately built their homes, schools, and churches as physical symbols of their spirit of community. We, too, need physical symbols with spiritual meaning. When the hippies rejected all of the symbols of the establishment during the 1960s and 1970s, they quickly created a new set of symbols for themselves. The inverted *Y* of the peace symbol became as much a badge of their culture as the cross represents Christianity. Physical symbols, whether secular or sacred, are intended to convey intangible truths, moral values, and spiritual meaning. A stylized fish on the back of an automobile, for instance, tells us that a Christian is driving the car. Whenever I see the sign, I find myself watching the driver and expecting courtesy at stop lights and legal speeds through residential areas.

Israel had fallen into the trap of elevating the temple and its rituals of worship into substitutes for spiritual religion. As the corrective of God's New Age, the New Temple and the place of God's presence will be in the heart of the person who is *"poor"* or humble before God, *"contrite"* or honest in spirit, and who *"trembles"* with reverential fear at the Word of the Lord (v. 2). Jesus fulfilled this prophecy when He dared to challenge the Pharisees who used the symbol of the Temple to protect their own spiritual corruption. Certainly, a part of the case against Jesus included His bold declaration to the Samaritan woman, "But the hour is coming, and now is, when the true worshipers will worship the Father in spirit and truth; for the Father is seeking such to worship Him. God is a Spirit and those who worship Him must worship in spirit and truth" (John 4:23–24).

THE PLACE FOR OUR WORSHIP (66:3–4)

Without a humble heart and a contrite spirit, and without trembling at the Word of the Lord, our worship cannot be pleasing to God. As a substitute for spiritual worship in the Temple, the Israelites performed four illegal sacrifices: (1) killing a bull as if slaying a man; (2) sacrificing a lamb as if breaking a dog's neck; (3) offering grain as if offering swine's blood; and (4) burning incense as if blessing an idol (v. 3a). Evidently, these were the rituals of apostate Jews who pursued their own selfish motives and took glee in blasphemous abominations (v. 3). For them, God will let their own delusions and fears become the punishment for their sins. Superstition is grounded in fears that if released in full force are sufficient to destroy a person (v. 4).

THE PLACE OF OUR TREMBLING (66:5–6)

Just the opposite will come to the humble hearts and contrite spirits who tremble at the Word of God. They will be vindicated when the apostate Jews are shamed by the joy of God's true servants (v. 5b).

Again, we hold this truth in a prophetic paradox. Presumably, the same pattern of worship and ritual can bring glory and joy to some, but judgment and shame to others. A humble heart, contrite spirit, and a trembling mind before the truth makes all the difference.

THE NEW JERUSALEM (66:7–17)

7 "Before she travailed, she gave birth;
   Before her pain came,
   She delivered a male child.
8 Who has heard such a thing?
   Who has seen such things?
   Shall the earth be made to give birth
      in one day?
   Or shall a nation be born at once?
   For as soon as Zion travailed,
   She gave birth to her children.
9 Shall I bring to the time of birth, and not cause
      delivery?" says the LORD.
   "Shall I who cause delivery shut up the womb?
      says your God.
10 "Rejoice with Jerusalem,
   And be glad with her,
      all you who love her;
   Rejoice for joy with her,
      all you who mourn for her;
11 That you may feed and be satisfied
   With the consolation of her bosom,
   That you may drink deeply and
      be delighted
   With the abundance of her glory."
12 For thus says the LORD:
   "Behold, I will extend peace to her like a river,
   And the glory of the Gentiles
      like a flowing stream.
   Then you shall feed;
   On her sides shall you be carried,
   And be dandled on her knees.
13 As one whom his mother comforts,
   So I will comfort you;
   And you shall be comforted in Jerusalem."

14 When you see this,
>   your heart shall rejoice,
> And your bones shall flourish like grass;
> The hand of the LORD shall be known
>   to His servants,
> And His indignation to His enemies.
15 For behold, the LORD will come with fire
> And with His chariots,
>   like a whirlwind,
> To render His anger with fury,
> And His rebuke with flames of fire.
16 For by fire and by His sword
> The LORD will judge all flesh;
> And the slain of the LORD
>   shall be many.
17 "Those who sanctify themselves
>   and purify themselves,
> To go to the gardens
> After an idol in the midst,
> Eating swine's flesh and the
>   abomination and the mouse,
> Shall be consumed together,"
>   says the LORD.

Isaiah 66:7–17

REBIRTH OF THE CITY (66:7–11)

Jerusalem, the Holy City, needs the same recreative touch of God as His Holy Temple does. Father love shifts to mother love when God speaks about His beloved city. Those who claim that the Word of God is sexist fail to read this prophecy. Isaiah had no trouble envisioning the special qualities of father love or mother love in the Person of God. Neither *he* nor *she* is inconsistent with the Scriptures. At the same time, it is unfair to force the issue by rewriting Scripture in nonsexist language. Isaiah's God is "He" with all of the virtues of "She." In today's controversy over inclusive language, Isaiah would be baffled. His position is strong because he can speak of father love or mother love with equal ease. Most likely, he would scold us for stressing a minor point when the greater truth of God's Word is the purpose of his writing.

MATURITY OF THE CITY (66:12–17)

Mother love for Jerusalem will bring the long-suffering city to rebirth, according to Isaiah (v. 7). As a mother who has carried a child for nine months, it is absurd to think that God will not bring the City to delivery. *"Shall I bring to the time of birth, and not cause delivery?"* or *"Shall I who cause delivery shut up the womb?"* says your God (v. 9). Furthermore, God says that it is time to rejoice because mother love will also nourish the infant at her breast until he or she is fully satisfied (v. 11a).

Mother love continues for Jerusalem as the child grows through the stages of being carried on the mother's hip, jiggled on her knees, and comforted during the storm and stress of youth (vv. 12 and 13). Jerusalem can count on rebirth from the womb, nourishment as a suckling baby, care during childhood, and comfort during youth. The city that has struggled through a painful pregnancy will actually grow up to fulfill the purpose that God intended—to be the light of the world for the Word of God and the gathering place for all nations (v. 18). But, at the same time, Jerusalem will be the center of the *"whirlwind"* of God's fury against His enemies, within and without (vv. 15–17).

THE NEW ZION (66:18–24)

18 "For I know their works and their thoughts. It shall be that I will gather all nations and tongues; and they shall come and see My glory.

19 "I will set a sign among them; and those among them who escape I will send to the nations: to Tarshish and Pul and Lud, who draw the bow, and Tubal and Javan, to the coastlands afar off who have not heard My fame nor seen My glory. And they shall declare My glory among the Gentiles.

20 "Then they shall bring all your brethren for an offering to the LORD out of all nations, on horses and in chariots and in litters, on mules and on camels, to My holy mountain Jerusalem," says the LORD, "as the children of Israel bring an offering in a clean vessel into the house of the LORD.

21 "And I will also take some of them for priests and Levites," says the LORD.

22 "For as the new heavens
   and the new earth
   Which I will make shall remain before
   Me," says the LORD,
   "So shall your descendants
   and your name remain.
23 And it shall come to pass
   That from one New Moon to another,
   And from one Sabbath to another,
   All flesh shall come to worship before
   Me," says the LORD.
24 "And they shall go forth and look
   Upon the corpses of the men
   Who have transgressed against Me.
   For their worm does not die,
   And their fire is not quenched.
   They shall be an abhorrence to all flesh."

Isaiah 66:18–24

THE FULLNESS OF SALVATION (66:18–23)

Isaiah's end-time prophecy culminates in his image of the New Zion that arises out of the remnant and fulfills the role of Israel as God's servant nation. Most of the characteristics of the New Zion have been prophesied earlier, but when taken together as Isaiah's last word, the impact is more powerful than ever. The Church of the New Zion will be *global in scope* as God gathers all nations (v. 18), *cross-cultural in nature* as all tongues comes together (v. 18), *evangelistic in mission* as the remnant is dispersed to proclaim God's glory among the Gentiles (v. 19), *holy in character* as the people offer themselves as clean vessels in the House of the Lord (v. 20), *inclusive in leadership* as the Lord chooses priests and Levites among the Gentiles (v. 21), *eternal in time* as the Name of the Lord is perpetuated from generation to generation (vv. 22 and 23), and *righteous in judgment* as it witnesses the everlasting punishment of transgressors who reject God's love and defy His Word (v. 24).

THE FULLNESS OF JUDGMENT (66:24)

Isaiah leaves us suspended in the tension of the prophetic paradox.

After raising our expectations for the mission and ministry of the New Zion, he concludes with the most vivid picture of a burning, literal hell where the *"worm does not die"* and the *"fire is not quenched"* (v. 24b). The scene is so disturbing that scholars consider the final verse tacked on to the text, and Jewish congregations find it so negative that they bring Isaiah to a close on the affirmation of the Lord, *"All flesh shall come to worship before Me"* (v. 23b). However, neither the nature of the text nor the reality of human nature will let us off so easily. Although the primary mission of the Church of the New Zion is world redemption, Isaiah never wavered from the truth that God's presence divided servants and apostates, true worshipers from idolaters, saints from sinners, and the faithful from the rebellious. To end on the grace note of world redemption would have made the prophecy come out right in our human terms, but realism tells us that sin is rebellion against God's love, not vice versa. If so, Isaiah had to be true to God's vision as he saw it. Not even the New Zion will be free of sinful opposition, and as long as humans continue to exist with freedom of will, sinful rebellion against God and His Church will remain a live option. Understandably, then, as the New Zion shall remain forever before the Lord (v. 22), it will be witness to both eternal life and eternal death. The prophetic paradox is resolved when we realize that Isaiah's final word is the assurance of God's presence to redeem the world at the risk of human rebellion exercised by free will. After all, knowing Isaiah as we now do, we believe he would never end his prophecy on a whimper.

NOTES

1. J. F. A. Sawyer, *Prophecy and the Prophets of the Old Testament: Isaiah, Volume 2* (Oxford: Oxford University Press, n.d.), 178.

Epilogue

Isaiah leaves us with irrefutable evidence of his gift for communicating the vision of God. When he accepted the prophetic call, he put his vow "Here am I, send me" at the bottom of a blank page and let God fill in the details. Little did he know about the future. Only a genuine love for his rebellious people and an unswerving commitment to trust God motivated him to begin a journey of faith that took him into the courts of kings, onto the streets of the city, and up to the watchtower high on the walls where he proclaimed the Word of God without fear or favoritism. Other prophets accepted the same call and spoke with the same boldness. Isaiah, however, stands apart as the greatest of the Old Testament prophets because he broke new ground by prophesying far beyond his time, maintaining into the future the integrity of his message, and withstanding generations of scholarly controversy over his authorship.

Our study of Isaiah confirms his uniqueness. We can never forget the *consistency* of his prophetic themes, the *continuity* of his vision through time, the *clarity* of his communicative style, the realistic *balance* of his message, and the *strategic view* of an exciting future. As a master communicator, Isaiah spoke and wrote under the mantra: "Tell them what you are to say, say it, and then tell them what you have said." No one can fault Isaiah for disobeying this dictum. Whether in his theology, Christology, or his eschatology, he never forsakes the major themes that he set in the opening chapters of his book. His theology of the character of God, for instance, can be traced with unbroken consistency from the beginning to the end of the prophecy. At one and the same time, God is The Lord of Hosts, The Holy One of Israel, The I Am, Yahweh, The First and The Last; He is also the father or mother of nourishing love. Out of God's character, then, come the prophetic themes of righteousness, justice, punishment, promise, vengeance, and grace, but always with the ultimate goal of salvation for all humankind.

The Christology of Isaiah is an extension of these same themes in the personhood of God's chosen Servant, the Messiah. His birth rises out of the seed of Jesse, His name Immanuel signifies His deity, His character is without violence or deceit, His Word is a double-edged sword of truth, His message is Good News, His ministry is suffering, and His sole purpose is to be The Light of the World for the salvation of all nations and all people.

Isaiah's eschatology carries these same prophetic themes into the end time. The final Day of the Lord is both a day of vegeance and redemption, revealing at one and the same time the wrath of God the Warrior and the grace of God the Redeemer. Then, Isaiah is witness to the fulfillment of his prophecy when righteousness and justice reign on earth, and the glory of God is seen in the time of peace, prosperity, reconciliation, and celebration, when the faithful from every corner of the earth gather on Mount Zion to sing the praises of the Lord. With one more leap of faith, Isaiah foresees the distant creation of a new heaven, a new earth, a new Jerusalem, and a new Zion where sorrow, death, and darkness are wiped away by the everlasting light of God's glorious presence, but the wicked are condemned to everlasting fire by God's holy character.

Based upon these interlocking themes, The Book of Isaiah can be likened to a seamless web of visionary truth that serves as its own internal witness to divine inspiration, prophetic integrity, and single authorship. As one final case in point, Isaiah's choice of the word for the rebellious children of Israel who will come under God's judgment in Isaiah 1:2 is the same word that he uses in the last verse of his prophecy to describe the rebels against God who will be condemned to the everlasting fire of hell (66:24). Like bookends on the text, Isaiah warns all those rebel against God, whether Jews or Gentiles, that His righteousness will prevail. Isaiah may have been a visionary, but he was also a realist whose integrity of character matched the integrity of his message.

The *clarity* of Isaiah's style of communication is another unforgettable result of our study. Every literary stop is pulled in the resounding poetry of Isaiah's prophecy. Whether alliteration, hyperbole, metaphor, chiasmus, personification, simile, or onomatopoeia, the poetic style of Isaiah is a study in itself. For us, however, his masterful deployment of symbols has given us markers of meaning like signposts along the way. Among these symbols, we especially remember God's beloved vineyard with its sweet and sour grapes (5:1–7); "streams in the desert" with their life-giving water (32:2); fire in the "furnace of affliction" (48:10); the trees of Lebanon clapping their hands as they exalt in Israel's deliverance from exile (14:8 and 33:9); the wedding of Dame Zion as a virgin bride restored from adultery by the New Covenant (62:4); the "garments of praise" and the "robe of righteousness" to signify her new status (61:3); the birth of her children who will include the Gentiles (49:20–21); and, of course, the "Light of Life" that is the hope of the world (13:11). The ability to draw analogies is a mark of high intelligence by which the complex becomes simple, clear, and meaningful. It is also a gift of the creative mind through which a new perspective or paradigm changes the way we look at the world. We can argue that the ability to use symbols and draw analogies is a special gift of divine inspiration. Isaiah's gift for symbolism is exceeded only by Jesus Christ who also communicated through the images of family, marriage, and children and the analogies of water, wind, grass, trees, seeds, birds, and vineyards. For those who want to cultivate the art of effective communication, Isaiah and Jesus are the ideal teachers.

Isaiah's *passion* to communicate the Word of God is another distinctive characteristic of His ministry for us to emulate. Capturing the urgency of God's Word, he often began with the cry "Behold" to get the attention of his hearers. And who can ever forget the picture of him walking naked through the public square for three and one-half years to illustrate the warning of exile. Although we do not know what kind of temperament he had when God called him to the prophetic ministry, we do know that he demonstrated the adage of Woodrow Wilson after the staid university president disciplined himself in the craft of public speaking to sway and move a mass audience. Wilson said, "Passion is the pith of eloquence." Centuries earlier, Pericles, the renowned Greek orator, made the same discovery. Pericles said, "When I speak, people say 'How well he speaks'; but when Demosthenes speaks, the people say, 'Let us march!'"

Isaiah's passion to speak the Word of God put him in the company of Demosthenes. After reading his impassioned pleas to Israel to leave their exile in Babylon and start the journey of the New Exodus back to Jerusalem, we want to say with them, "Let us march!"

Isaiah's *impartiality* in communicating the Word of God is still another virtue of note. Although his overarching theme is salvation, he does not shrink from the reality of God's judgment upon sin. His account of God the warrior, for instance, does not spare the gory details of the blood-drenched garment that had been stained when He trod the winepress alone against the forces of evil (63:1–6). Standing by itself, the account seems contradictory to the fatherly love that Isaiah appeals to in the intercessory prayer that follows almost immediately after his account of The Day of Vengeance (64:8–12). One of the internal proofs for the inspiration of Scripture, however, is the fact that no one is spared the truth. David's sins of adultery, deception, and murder are reported without gloss even though the King is a man "after God's own heart" and the seed through whom the Messiah will come. Isaiah adds to the line of proof by his brutal honesty about judgment upon the Israel he loves and of which he was a part. Perhaps the best example comes from the opening and closing verses of his prophecy. After introducing himself as "Isaiah, the son of Amoz, who saw the vision of God" (1:1), he sets the dominant theme for the whole book when he describes God's nourising love for his beloved children of Israel despite their haughty and persistent rebellion against Him (1:2). The story of Isaiah is the account of God's judgment specifically upon the rebellious children of Judah and Jerusalem, and generally upon all people and nations who rebel against Him. Even though the purpose of His righteous judgment is redemptive, the truth remains.

In the final verse of the prophecy, the same word for "rebel" is used to describe all of those who will be punished with "everlasting fire." Rather than stopping short of the final verse of our reading of Isaiah, as some Jewish congregations do, or concluding that judgment, not salvation, is God's ultimate purpose, we should read the final words as another evidence of Isaiah closing the loop on the hard truth that God asked him to speak. As he began with the comparison of God's love leading to salvation and human rebellion leading to judgment, so he closes with the same word of truth. Freedom of will is the intervening factor that God will not violate and the factor that makes rebellion possible. Consistent with the prophetic paradox in which eternal truth is always found, Isaiah's idealistic vision of God's New Creation for His servants must be balanced by the realistic vision of everlasting fire for those who exercise the freedom of will to rebel against God and bring upon themselves His righteous judgment.

All of Isaiah's gifts as a communicator culminate in his role as a *strategist* who sees God's future. Recruiting announcements for executive leaders in Christian organizations regularly cross my desk. Almost without exception, "visionary leadership" is the first requirement for the job. In truth, however, visionary leaders are rare. Some can see clearly ahead through the narrow tunnel of their expertise in management, finance, personnel, or public relations, but the "bigger picture" remains a blur. Others project the future by incrementally adding or multiplying current facts and circumstances. Their concern is with the question *how* should we move into the future rather than *what* should the future be. The latter question requires the ability to take a serendipitous leap along the timeline of history and foresee the big picture of a new and exciting future.

Isaiah qualifies as a visionary leader with strategic foresight. In current leadership language, his prophecy of the future is a paradigm shift of greatest magnitude. The new paradigm that Isaiah foresees is not just a patched-up remake of the old order. Rather, he envisions God once again exercising the power of His creative energy to produce an age in which all things are new. "Behold, I will make all things new" (42:9) is a promise activated to create a New Zion that is *global* in scope, *inclusive* of all people, *spiritual* in worship, *holy* in character, *just* in governance, *peaceful* in relationship, *joyful* in spirit, and *glorious* in witness. Pivotal to this new order of creation is the redemptive ministry of God's New Servant, none other than Jesus Christ, who personifies the New Covenant with Israel and all nations. Although the New Order is yet to be realized, Isaiah answered the question, "What should the future be?" from the vantage point of God's redemptive purpose.

Once Isaiah saw God's vision for the future, he never looked back. The progression of his prophecy from the current events of his lifetime, to the new exodus from Babylonian exile, followed by the coming of the Messiah and the redemption of all nations gives us our marching orders. Sounding again the double imperative for Israel and the redeemed of all generations to come, Isaiah urges us to leave the comfort and the splendor of our Jerusalems to become His servants in the world.

> Depart! Depart! Go out from there,
> Touch no unclean thing;
> Go out from the midst of her,
> Be clean,
> You who bear the vessels of the LORD.
>
> For you shall not go out with haste,
> Nor go by flight;
> For the LORD will go before you,
> And the God of Israel will be your rear guard.

Isaiah 52:11–12

NOTES

1. John F. A. Sawyer, *Prophecy and the Prophets of the Old Testament: Isaiah, Volume* 2. (Oxford: Oxford University Press).

Bibliography

Alexander, J. A. *Commentary on the Prophecies of Isaiah.* New York: Scribner's, 1846.

Allis, O. T. *The Unity of Isaiah: A Study in Prophecy.* Philadelphia: Presbyterian and Reformed, 1950.

Barnes, A. *Notes on Isaiah.* Volume 1. Grand Rapids: Baker, 1980.

Boutflower, C. *The Book of Isaiah Chapters I–XXXIX in Light of the Assyrian Monuments.* London: SPCK, 1930.

Cambridge Ancient History, The. Volume 3. Cambridge: Cambridge University Press, 1929.

Clements, R. E. *Isaiah 1–39.* New Century Bible Commentary. London: Marshall, Morgan & Scott; Grand Rapids, Eerdmans, 1980.

Delitzsch, F. *Biblical Commentary on the Prophecies of Isaiah.* Volume 1. Edinburgh: T. & T. Clark, 1874–1875.

Eissfeldt, O. *The Old Testament, An Introduction.* Tr. P. Ackroyd. New York: Harper & Row, 1965.

Engnell, I. *The Call of Isaiah: An Exegetical and Comparative Study. UUA 4.* Uppsala: Lundequistska, 1949.

Gardiner, A. *Egypt of the Pharaohs: An Introduction.* Oxford: Clarendon Press, 1961.

Gray, G. B. *A Critical and Exegetical Commentary on the Book of Isaiah, I–XXXIX.* Edinburgh: T. & T. Clark, 1912.

Harrison, R. K. *Introduction to the Old Testament.* Grand Rapids: Eerdmans, 1969.

————. *Old Testament Times.* Grand Rapids: Eerdmans, 1970.

Heschel, A. J. *The Prophets.* New York: Harper, 1962.

Jennings, F. C. *Studies in Isaiah.* Neptune, New Jersey: Loizeaux, 1935.

Kaiser, O. *Isaiah 1–12: A Commentary.* Old Testament Library. 2nd ed. Tr. J. Bowden. Philadelphia: Westminster, 1983.

Kaufmann, Y. *The Babylonian Captivity and Deutero-Isaiah.* Tr. C. W. Efroymson. New York: Union of American Hebrew Congregations, 1970.

Kennett, R. H. *The Composition of the Book of Isaiah in the Light of History and Archaeology.* London: Published for the British Academy by H. Frowde, 1910.

Kissane, E. J. *The Book of Isaiah*. Volume 1. Rev. ed. Dublin: Browne & Nolan, Ltd., 1960.

Koch, K. *The Prophets*. Volume 1. Philadelphia: Fortress Press, 1984.

Leupold, H. C. *Exposition of Isaiah*. 2 vols. Grand Rapids: Baker, 1963–1971.

Margalioth, R. *The Indivisible Isaiah: Evidence for the Single Authorship of the Prophetic Book*. New York: Yeshiva University, 1964.

Oswalt, J. *The Book of Isaiah, Chapters 1–39*. The New International Commentary on the Old Testament. Grand Rapids: Eerdmans, 1986.

Saggs, H. W. F. *The Greatness That Was Babylon*. London: Sidgwick & Jackson, 1962.

Scott, R. B. Y. "Introduction and Exegesis of the Book of Isaiah, Chapters 1–39," *The Interpreters Bible*. Volume 3:149–381. V. ed. G. Buttrick, et al. Nashville: Abingdon, 1956.

Seitz, C. R., ed. *Reading and Preaching the Book of Isaiah*. Philadelphia: Fortress Press, 1988.

Skinner, J. *The Book of the Prophet Isaiah*. Volume 1. Rev. ed. Cambridge: Cambridge University Press, 1925.

Smith, G. A. *The Book of Isaiah*. Volume 1. Rev. ed. Expositor's Bible. London: Hadden and Stoughton, 1927.

VanGemeren, W. A. *Interpreting the Prophetic Word*. Grand Rapids: Academie Books, 1990.

Ward, J. M. *Amos and Isaiah: Prophets of the Word of God*. Nashville: Abingdon, 1969.

Watts, J. D. W. *Isaiah 1–33*. Volume 24. Word Biblical Commentary. Waco, Texas: Word Books, 1985.

Young, E. J. *The Book of Isaiah*. Volume 1 and 2. Grand Rapids: Eerdmans, 1964–1972.

———. *Who Wrote Isaiah?* Grand Rapids: Eerdmans, 1958.